Religion and Politics
in Saudi Arabia

A project of the Michigan State University
Muslim Studies Program

RELIGION AND

POLITICS IN

SAUDI ARABIA

Wahhabism and the State

EDITED BY
Mohammed Ayoob
Hasan Kosebalaban

LYNNE
RIENNER
PUBLISHERS

BOULDER
LONDON

Published in the United States of America in 2009 by
Lynne Rienner Publishers, Inc.
1800 30th Street, Boulder, Colorado 80301
www.rienner.com

and in the United Kingdom by
Lynne Rienner Publishers, Inc.
3 Henrietta Street, Covent Garden, London WC2E 8LU

Library of Congress Cataloging-in-Publication Data
Religion and politics in Saudi Arabia : Wahhabism and the State / edited by
    Mohammed Ayoob and Hasan Kosebalaban.
        p. cm.
Includes bibliographical references and index.
    ISBN 978-1-58826-637-8 (hardcover : alk. paper)
    1. Islam and state—Saudi Arabia. 2. Islam and politics—Saudi Arabia.
3. Wahhabiyya—Saudi Arabia. I. Ayoob, Mohammed, 1942–   II. Kosebalaban,
Hasan.
BP63.S33R45 2009
297.8'14—dc22

                                                        2008025410

British Cataloguing in Publication Data
A Cataloguing in Publication record for this book
is available from the British Library.

Printed and bound in the United States of America

   ⟳   Printed on 30% postconsumer recycled paper

        The paper used in this publication meets the requirements
   ∞   of the American National Standard for Permanence of
        Paper for Printed Library Materials Z39.48-1992.

   5 4 3 2 1

Contents

Part 3 Saudi-US Relations

Part 4 Conclusion

Preface

The idea for this volume germinated in the immediate aftermath of the terror attacks of September 11, 2001, when the religio-political ideology of Wahhabism was identified by many commentators as being chiefly responsible for the tragedy. Saudi Arabia, the font of Wahhabism and also home to fifteen of the nineteen suicide attackers, immediately came into focus as the ideological producer of terror—which appeared paradoxical in the context of the strong strategic and economic relations that the United States had had with the Saudi kingdom for more than half a century.

It also became clear that understanding Wahhabism, in both its political and religious dimensions, was important for the future of US relations with the Muslim world in general and the Middle East in particular. The Muslim Studies Program at Michigan State University therefore decided to organize its first project on the theme "Understanding Wahhabism." We invited several leading scholars and analysts of Wahhabism, Saudi Arabia, and US-Saudi relations to participate in the project, and one of the end results is this book. We are very grateful to the participants for working diligently to give final shape to their contributions for publication.

We are also grateful to a number of other people for making the project possible. President Lou Anna Simon of Michigan State University has been a great supporter of the Muslim Studies Program and its predecessor, the Muslim Studies Initiative. Others at MSU who aided the endeavor in various ways include Provost Kim Wilcox; Dean Jeff Riedinger of International Studies and Programs; Dean Sherman Garnett of James Madison College; Dean Marietta Baba of the College of Social Sciences; Professor Richard Zinman, executive director of the Le Frak Foum; and Professor Norman Graham, director of European and Eurasian Studies. This volume would not have been published without their generous assistance.

—Mohammed Ayoob
Hasan Kosebalaban

1

Introduction:
Unraveling the Myths

Mohammed Ayoob and Hasan Kosebalaban

The political and academic discourse that emerged in the West in the aftermath of the terrorist attacks of September 11, 2001, linked the attackers' motivations to what has come to be known as Islamic "fundamentalism," and more particularly to a subcategory of this phenomenon called "Wahhabism" that has its roots in Saudi Arabia, the country from where the majority of the terrorists emanated. This discourse assumed that Islamic radicalism, as manifested in the Al-Qaida network and related groups that targeted the United States and its allies, was the product in large part of presumed Wahhabi teachings that mandated incessant hostility if not warfare by believing Muslims against all nonbelievers. Wahhabism was often portrayed in this discourse as an abstract ideology divorced from history and context. The transnational jihadist organization Al-Qaida was similarly portrayed in an ahistorical and acontextual form as an offshoot of a universal militant ideology that crossed the boundaries of time and space.

Furthermore, this discourse posited a direct relationship between Wahhabism and Al-Qaida unmediated by contextual variables. Much of such analysis ignored the fact that Al-Qaida was primarily a product of US- and Saudi-sponsored insurgency in Afghanistan against Soviet occupation, which spawned transnational jihadism by facilitating the ingathering of Islamist militants from around the world in Afghanistan and the bordering areas in Pakistan. It also ignored the fact that it was the Gulf War (1990–1991) and the accompanying US military presence on Saudi soil, aimed at protecting the kingdom from Saddam Hussein and at evicting Iraqi forces from Kuwait, that turned transnational jihadists led by Osama bin Laden against the United States. It further neglected the variable that the collapse of the Afghan state, caused by internecine warfare among insurgent groups following the Soviet withdrawal and the emergence of the Taliban with the support of Pakistan,

1

a US ally, led to Al-Qaida creating a state within the Afghan state and making it the base for its international operations. Finally, it overlooked the general disenchantment within the Muslim world with US policy toward the Middle East, especially Washington's unquestioning support for Israeli policies that radicalized segments of Muslim opinion and prompted a small minority among the radicals to take violent action against US interests both within and outside the United States.

Wahhabism may have formed a part of this volatile mix, but it was neither the sole nor even the primary determinant of terror attacks on the United States by transnational jihadists. Analyses reflecting the dominant discourse that equates Wahhabism with transnational jihadism, therefore, tend to be misleading by identifying a particular ideology as the root cause of a major problem while excluding the political, economic, and psychological contexts in which Islamist militancy has emerged in the Middle East and elsewhere. Furthermore, they represent a shallow understanding of the doctrine of Wahhabism itself by interpreting it as an ahistorical and acontextual phenomenon that can be transplanted from one locale to another in divergent circumstances with relative ease.

Given the dominance of this discourse in the media and much of academia, it appeared imperative that scholars familiar with the Wahhabi religio-political ideology, the history of state formation in the Arabian Peninsula, the internal political dynamics of Saudi Arabia, and the kingdom's relations with the West—especially the United States—come together to unravel the myths that have led to equating Wahhabism with Islamic fundamentalism and terrorism. This volume is the outcome of this endeavor.

It is conceived in part to situate Wahhabism concretely in time and place so that one may understand its contemporary impact in a more intellectually rigorous manner. The book tries to accomplish this task in various ways. It attempts to do so first by situating this religio-political doctrine in the specific milieu of the Arabian Peninsula, where it emerged. The goal here is make clear the fact that Wahhabism is no mere abstraction, but has a specific history tied to a time and place. It was in eighteenth-century Najd, in the heart of the Arabian Peninsula, that Muhammad ibn Abd al-Wahhab's alliance with the al-Saud led to the formation of the Saudi state, which in its third incarnation came to encompass most of the peninsula and became known as Saudi Arabia. The relationship between Wahhabism as a doctrine of religious reform and renewal, and its political dimension as the ideological vehicle of state formation in the Arabian Peninsula from the eighteenth century onward, is therefore very intimate. Consequently, it is a profoundly statist ideology that commands unreserved allegiance to the ruler and cannot be understood in isolation from the process of state formation in what is now Saudi Arabia. Its transnationalization is a very recent phenomenon that has in many ways stood its basic assumptions on their head. Several of the chapters in this volume contextualize Wahhabism by addressing from different perspectives the close relationship between its theology cum ideology and the formation and legitimation of the Saudi state.

The second objective of the volume is to analyze Wahhabism within the Saudi context as a dynamic ideology that has been interpreted differently by different actors to suit their own purposes. Wahhabism is no monolith and has evolved and fractured over time as a result of its interaction with wider social, economic, and political conditions in the kingdom as well as with political and ideological trends in the broader Middle East. This is clear from the fact that while Wahhabism has traditionally acted as the main vehicle for regime legitimation in Saudi Arabia, some of its contemporary manifestations are intensely anti–status quo and have seriously threatened not only the legitimacy but also the very existence of the Saudi regime.

The siege of the Grand Mosque in Mecca in November 1979 by a group of radical Wahhabis, many of them students at the Islamic University at Medina, was the most dramatic manifestation of the ideology's anti–status quo potential. Coming as it did on the heels of the Iranian Revolution next door, this event demonstrated clearly the revolutionary potential of Wahhabism and how it could be put to good use by disgruntled elements within Saudi Arabia and in other parts of the Muslim world. Much of the opposition to the Saudi regime today, both violent and nonviolent, owes its ideological origins to the revolutionary interpretations of Wahhabi teachings by the leaders of the 1979 siege and their intellectual and theological sympathizers.

However, such opposition is also highly contextual and to a substantial extent the product of ideological hybridization. This hybridization is itself the result of Wahhabism's encounter with radical modern Islamist ideologies, such as those of Egyptian thinker and activist Sayyid Qutb, who was executed by President Gamal Abdul Nasser in 1966 for his anti-regime activities. Many of his followers fled Egypt and were given refuge in Saudi Arabia in large part because of the Saudi establishment's antipathy to Nasser's Arab nationalist rhetoric and to policies that were contradictory to Saudi interests. Several of Qutb's disciples, including his brother Muhammad Qutb, became teachers at Saudi seminaries and universities and disseminated his revolutionary ideas to their disciples. The neo-Wahhabi challenge to the Saudi regime evolved out of the mixture of Qutbist political radicalism with Saudi social conservatism and religious orthodoxy. This variant of Wahhabism, now a mortal enemy of the House of Saud, emerged out of the interaction between Wahhabi doctrine and a modern political ideology. The traditional Wahhabi religious establishment, which is allied to the Saudi regime, has also transmuted as a result of its own encounter with modernity, in the form of a Saudi state and an oil-based rentier economy that have come to dominate the political and economic life of the Arabian Peninsula. The Wahhabi religious establishment has legitimized policies of the modern Saudi state, regarding the economy and security spheres, that would have been anathema to Wahhabi theologians a couple of generations ago.

The third objective of the volume is to situate Saudi Arabia's strategic and economic links with the United States in the context of the traditional Wahhabi suspicion of contact with non-Muslim polities and societies, a wariness born out of the desire to maintain the "purity" of Islamic society as practiced in the kingdom. Consequently, the Wahhabi ideology, which is a very important component of the Saudi legitimacy formula, has had great potential to act as a major brake on Saudi Arabia's economic and security engagement with the West in general and the United States in particular. However, the regime has demonstrated a great degree of deftness at balancing its ideological underpinnings with its pragmatic security and economic interests. It has been able to do so by a strict separation of the cultural and social spheres from the political, security, and economic arenas. The former are largely overseen by the Wahhabi religious establishment and made to conform to Wahhabi orthodoxy. The latter are the preserve of the House of Saud, with minimal interference from the religious establishment. In other words, the regime has provided the Wahhabi establishment with the sop of cultural and social control domestically in exchange for the latter giving up its opposition to the government's economic policies and security alliances.

This division of labor engineered by the Saudi rulers has allowed the Saudi regime to juggle the Wahhabi orthodoxy and its corollary, the maintenance of cultural insularity and social conservatism, with its strategic dependence upon the United States and, due to the kingdom's role as a major energy exporter, its very close economic relationship with Western industrialized states. The Saudi regime was able to balance these contradictory concerns quite well until 1979, keeping the religious establishment satisfied, the citizenry largely apolitical, and security and economic matters securely in the hands of the ruling house. However, the seizure of the Grand Mosque that year seriously challenged the status quo. It forced the regime to make further concessions to the Wahhabi establishment in the social and cultural spheres in order to buy time for things to settle down. This accommodation worked until 1990, when the Iraqi invasion of Kuwait brought significant numbers of US troops into the kingdom, thus upsetting the balance and setting off the chain of events that culminated in the terrorist attacks on New York and Washington, D.C., on September 11, 2001.

The terrorist attacks, in which fifteen of the nineteen terrorists involved allegedly came from Saudi Arabia, created a major backlash within the United States against Saudi Arabia and Wahhabism, which was perceived as the ideological wellspring for the attack. It brought Saudi Arabia's domestic policies, including its school curriculum, under close scrutiny in the United States and, for the first time, the kingdom's social and cultural practices, including the status of women, became a public concern in Washington. Until that time, Saudi Arabia, as a close strategic ally in the Middle East and a major energy producer and supplier, had been by and large immune from criticism in the United States. The backlash that followed September 11 was thus a dramatic break from the more or less pleasant relationship that had prevailed in the past. Given this apparent shift in the nature of US-Saudi relations following September 11, this volume attempts to analyze the impact of the terrorist attacks as well as that of Wahhabi orthodoxy on this crucial relationship, bringing together both the ideological and the pragmatic variables that have a bearing on it.

Much of the existing scholarly literature on Wahhabism is overly technical, covering isolated aspects of the subject in detail while assuming that the reader has adequate background knowledge to put such analysis in perspective. The popular literature on Wahhabism is overly journalistic, treating the subject matter in a sensational way and without adequate historical depth. Typically, such books on Wahhabism are also one-sided, in that they reflect the particular viewpoints of their authors. The present volume is an attempt to provide a forum for scholarly yet accessible discussion of Wahhabism and Saudi Arabia by bringing together distinct perspectives of leading scholars and analysts who study and write on the issue.

The contributors to this volume represent a great diversity of views. Explanations provided by some of the chapter authors run contrary to those provided by others. Some emphasize the element of religious reform, integral to Wahhabism, as part of an overall effort for reform and renewal in the Muslim world in the eighteenth and nineteenth centuries, while others concentrate on more specific conditions in the Arabian Peninsula as the primary explanatory variables for the emergence of the Wahhabi movement in that particular locale. On the whole, the volume aims to provide a balanced perspective on the phenomenon in order to help the reader locate the current situation within a solid historical and political context.

The volume is organized into four parts. Part 1 explores the rise of Wahhabism as a movement for religious reform and renewal, situating it in the overall context of reform movements in the Muslim world in the eighteenth and nineteenth centuries, as well as in the context of the specific political, social, and economic conditions in the Najd region of central Arabia, where the movement emerged and took root.

In Chapter 2, Natana DeLong-Bas bases her explanations of the rise of Wahhabism on original Wahhabi texts, especially the writings of Muhammad ibn Abd al-Wahhab. Her central thesis is that ibn Abd al-Wahhab was not as close-minded and rigid as he is often made out to have been. She argues that he was actually quite a tolerant figure for his times and, contrary to common belief, desisted from issuing the edict of *shirk* (associating others with God) against Muslims who did not agree with his strict interpretations of religion. She sees this strand of tolerance in contemporary

Wahhabi thinking as well, and makes an argument that the conventional wisdom that equates Wahhabism with inflexible literalism and fundamentalism is incorrect. Her argument has major contemporary implications, suggesting that Wahhabi ideology could not have been principally responsible for driving the September 11 terrorists to do what they did.

In Chapter 3, Khalid al-Dakhil underplays the religious nature of the Wahhabi movement and emphasizes its political dimension instead. He locates it in the context of the socioeconomic transformations in the Arabian Peninsula, particularly the urban settlement accompanied by detribalization that took place in central Arabia beginning in the sixteenth century. He argues that this in turn facilitated and legitimized the further centralization of political authority and thus enhanced the state-making project in Najd under the aegis of the House of Saud. Al-Dakhil's contribution is also significant in that he represents a generation of Saudi-born social scientists who are now more than ever ready to examine their own country's history through the lenses of critical thinking. It thus provides an insider's view of the relationship between Wahhabism and state formation in Arabia, which is very different from the conventional wisdom espoused by many scholars, Saudi and non-Saudi alike.

In Chapter 4, David Commins discusses the history of the interaction between the Wahhabi religious movement and the ebb and flow of Saudi military and political power. He also examines the early reactions to Muhammad ibn Abd al-Wahhab's religious ideas by scholars within the Arabian Peninsula, including the denunciation of those ideas by Muhammad's own brother, Sulayman ibn Abd al-Wahhab, and analyzes contemporary interactions between the Wahhabi doctrine and radical Islamism. Commins provides interesting comparisons between the early scholarly responses to Wahhabism, when it was a dynamic doctrine of political opposition at the end of the eighteenth century, and Wahhabism's own reaction to the new radical Islamism, which has become a doctrine of the Saudi political establishment in the twentieth and twenty-first centuries.

Part 2 of the volume begins by concentrating on the process of state making and the expansion of Saudi power, first in Najd and then in other parts of the peninsula, most especially Hijaz, the cradle of Islam, where the religion's holiest sites are located. John Habib and William Ochsenwald analyze strategies adopted by Abd al-Aziz ibn Abd al-Rahman al-Saud, known in the West as ibn Saud, in the creation of the Kingdom of Saudi Arabia and the tensions they generated with his loyal, but at the same time most fundamentalist, supporters, known as the Ikhwan. In Chapter 5, Habib concentrates on ibn Saud's attempt to domesticate the radicals while keeping the Wahhabi religious establishment on his side, thus highlighting the fact that, in the final analysis, the Wahhabi religious establishment accepted its subsidiary role vis-à-vis the state. In Chapter 6, Ochsenwald relates the story of the expansion of the Saudi state into Hijaz and its incorporation, not without some pain, of the Islamic holy sites of Mecca and Medina. The themes addressed in both chapters have contemporary resonance in terms of the current tensions between radical Wahhabis and the House of Saud, reminiscent of ibn Saud's struggle with the Ikhwan, and of the subterranean Hijazi dissatisfaction with Saudi-Najdi political dominance over the Saudi political system.

Gwenn Okruhlik and Toby Jones address the central tensions within the Saudi kingdom today. In Chapter 7, Okruhlik concentrates on the contradiction between the exclusive definition of Saudi identity in Wahhabi and Najdi terms, and an inclusive definition of citizenship that incorporates all the people of the kingdom, including the Shias and the Hijazis. The latter, she argues, is essential for the creation of a modern Saudi state that can count upon the loyalty of most if not all of its citizens. In Chapter 8, Jones highlights the tension between two contrary trends that have emanated from within Wahhabism: the politically docile stance of the Wahhabi establishment, based on its acceptance of the primacy of Saudi temporal power, and the purist and oppositional tendency, in its various forms, demonstrated by the *sahwa* (literally "awakening"), a term used to refer to younger ulama, among others, who are critical of the Saudi regime. This has pitted "Wahhabism from below" against "Wahhabism from above," with the former challenging the legitimacy both of the House of Saud and of the religious establishment. These two chapters together lay bare the contradictions within the Saudi polity and point toward what may be impending systemic crises within the kingdom.

Part 3 of the volume addresses the impact of Wahhabism on Saudi foreign policy, specifically how it has affected the critical relationship between Saudi Arabia and the United States. In Chapter 9, Thomas Lippman determines that US-Saudi relations have by and large evolved autonomously of Wahhabi influences and have been based on raison d'état and more particularly on the calculations of regime survival by the House of Saud. In Chapter 10, Gregory Gause highlights, among other things, the fact that the Wahhabi establishment has almost always done the Saudis' bidding when it comes to security and political issues, including such controversial decisions as the deployment of US forces in the kingdom in the 1990s. He argues that, consequently, it appears that Wahhabism in its official form has had little or no impact on the Saudi regime's close relationship with the United States, despite certain Wahhabi injunctions regarding the impermissibility of dealing with non-Muslim powers. While these conclusions may have held true so far, recent events make one wonder whether the course of US-Saudi relations will continue to be as smooth as it has been in the past if either evolutionary or revolutionary changes take place within the Saudi system that radically shift the balance of social power domestically.

In Part 4, John Voll provides an overall assessment of the place of Muhammad ibn Abd al-Wahhab's ideas in the movements for reform and renewal in the Muslim world beginning from the eighteenth century, and of the long-term impact of the Wahhabi tradition on this process. He distinguishes between two genres of writings about Wahhabism, one that tends to be grounded in history and context, and one that defines the movement in a "mythic" manner, either extolling its virtues or, more commonly in Western writings, portraying it as a negative and reactionary ideology. While Voll traces the history of this second genre to colonial times, when the term "Wahhabi" was used to denigrate and delegitimize resistance to European domination of Muslim lands, it has achieved contemporary resonance since the 1990s, particularly in the wake of September 11, 2001. The term "Wahhabi" has now taken on a generic meaning and is applied to all sorts of Muslim groups and movements that are viewed negatively in the West for one reason or another. These include not only Al-Qaida, which is virulently opposed to Wahhabi institutions and leadership, but also the transnational missionary movement Tablighi Jamaat and the transnational political movement Hizb al-Tahrir, both of which have been condemned by the Wahhabi establishment. Voll's chapter brings together historical facts and contemporary concerns about Wahhabism to demonstrate the fuzzy nature of much of recent writings about this religio-political ideology. It demonstrates forcefully why a volume such as this is essential to counter the lack of informed debate and discussion about Wahhabism, Saudi Arabia, and US-Saudi relations.

Overall, the volume brings out elements of continuity and change in the narratives of Wahhabism and the Saudi state. It also lays bare tensions, both actual and potential, within the kingdom, as well as in the realm of Saudi relations with the United States. Both sets of tensions seem to be coming to a head as "Wahhabism from below" challenges "Wahhabism from above" and as the strategic importance of Saudi energy reserves becomes ever more obvious. With Wahhabism, the legitimating ideology of the Saudi regime, failing to provide a mechanism for regime change, escalating tensions are likely to lead to political instability that will have an impact far beyond the borders of Saudi Arabia.

If this conclusion is correct, then US policymakers need to seriously reassess their commitment to the House of Saud. If the Saudi regime falls or even becomes unstable, most of Washington's calculations regarding the oil-rich Gulf region will be thrown into disarray and scenarios of the past might be replayed, such as the events that followed the overthrow of the Shah of Iran in 1979 by what came to be called an "Islamic" revolution. This is but one of many issues the volume raises, directly or indirectly, that need serious consideration.

PART 1

Wahhabism: Religious Movement and Political Ideology

2

Wahhabism and the Question of Religious Tolerance

Natana J. DeLong-Bas

Since September 11, 2001, interest in the phenomenon popularly referred to as "Wahhabism" has markedly increased. Analysts and experts from various fields have used the term broadly to refer to any movement that claims Islam as a source of inspiration for combating existing governments, secular ideologies, other religions, and other Muslims, particularly Shias and Sufis, who have purportedly failed to adhere to a ritually strict and conservative interpretation of Islam that has no tolerance for deviation from its vision of the "straight path." Although many of these concerns are legitimate with respect to questions of religious and political freedom, not all of the movements currently gathered under the umbrella of Wahhabism are necessarily religious in orientation or derive their religious inspiration from Wahhabism.[1]

Because the term "Wahhabism" itself is so politically charged and widely used, it is important to return to the original sources of the movement to determine whether Wahhabism as founded was inherently violent, extremist, and intolerant and whether changes in Wahhabi thought and practice have occurred over time. The most important concluding question is whether Wahhabism contains within itself the seeds for reform.

▧ Defining Wahhabism and Its Major Themes

Properly defined, Wahhabism was a revival and reform movement founded in central Arabia in the mid-eighteenth century by scholar and jurist Muhammad ibn Abd al-Wahhab. Although ibn Abd al-Wahhab himself did not seek to found an overtly political movement, the political implications of his movement calling for belief in God's unity *(tawhid)* and the unity of the Muslim

11

community, the umma, quickly became clear to local leaders who sought to unite fragmented tribes.[2]

The importance of this central doctrine of the unity and uniqueness of God was apparent in the term used by ibn Abd al-Wahhab to refer to his followers—*muwahhidin* (literally, those following *tawhid*).[3] The term "Wahhabi" appears to have been coined by ibn Abd al-Wahhab's Ottoman opponents to suggest that the movement fell outside of mainstream Islam and was focused upon ibn Abd al-Wahhab as a leader, rather than on God.[4]

In ibn Abd al-Wahhab's writings, *tawhid* stands in a dialectical relationship with *shirk* (the association of anyone or anything with God) in the sense that one cannot exist without the other and that every action a human being undertakes reflects either one or the other, whether overtly or covertly. Because of the importance of thinking through both the intent and the result of one's actions, ibn Abd al-Wahhab dedicated many of his legal and theological writings to an exploration of the dynamics of *tawhid* and *shirk*, with the express goal of eliminating *shirk* from Muslim thought and practice. The critical issues were the methodology by which *shirk* was defined and the proposed means by which *shirk* was to be eliminated.

Although, in the twenty-first century, it is generally assumed that such elimination can only occur through the use of violence, this was not the vision outlined by ibn Abd al-Wahhab. Ibn Abd al-Wahhab posited the combined use of *dawa* (calling people to proper observance of Islam) and education as the appropriate method for eliminating *shirk*. This construct was intended to be both nonviolent and process-oriented in the sense of taking place over time, rather than instantaneously; it was not intended to be mistaken for a call to jihad as holy war or to engage in forced conversions under the penalty of death if one refused to convert.[5] Ibn Abd al-Wahhab made it very clear that the desired conversion was one that came from the heart, rather than out of the fear of death.[6]

On *Kuffar, Mushrikun,* and *Dhimmis*

The prominence of the themes of *tawhid* and *shirk* in the writings of ibn Abd al-Wahhab and subsequent Wahhabi scholars led to accusations that Wahhabism was founded as a *takfiri* ideology (the practice of declaring any Muslim not in agreement with Wahhabi teachings to be a *kafir,* or infidel, who is subject to jihad as holy war). The historical record reflects the implementation of this approach by some Wahhabis, although certainly not all, particularly in the realms of mosque preaching and textbook instruction in contemporary Saudi Arabia.[7] Because of the widespread concerns about and implications of *takfiri* ideology today, it is particularly important to examine how these issues are addressed in ibn Abd al-Wahhab's own writings prior to examining contemporary interpretations of and challenges to this ideology.

Ibn Abd al-Wahhab did not use the terms *kafir* (infidel or unbeliever) or *mushrik* (associationist) to refer to an individual who disagreed with his teachings. These terms were reserved for individuals who had committed specific actions. Furthermore, these terms were not used interchangeably.

A *kafir* was defined as someone who had studied Islam, proclaimed the declaration of faith *(shahada)*, and then either engaged in downright idolatry or publicly rejected the previously accepted faith. A *mushrik* was defined as someone who committed an action that violated God's *tawhid,* such as using good luck charms or praying to saints for intercession with God. The critical difference between a *kafir* and a *mushrik* was the question of deliberate intent. Ibn Abd al-Wahhab recognized *kafir* status as the result of a deliberate act of the will occurring after an individual received proper instruction in the faith, whereas a *mushrik* had not necessarily received proper instruction and therefore could not necessarily be held responsible for deliberately violating God's *tawhid.* In other words, a *kafir* was someone who acted deliberately against knowledge already obtained, whereas a *mushrik* might act out of ignorance and could not reasonably be held responsible.[8]

Despite this important difference, ibn Abd al-Wahhab prescribed the same approach to dealing with both cases: calling the person back to the faith and providing education to demonstrate why a particular action was incorrect. Only if the person persisted in committing the wrong action to the point of denying Muslims the right to practice their own faith was the death penalty as punishment to be considered. Ibn Abd al-Wahhab made it clear that the assignment of the death penalty could apply only to an individual, not to a community or other group.[9] In other words, the determining factor was whether the *kafir* or *mushrik* blocked other Muslims from practicing their faith. Furthermore, the declaration of a jihad as holy war against a group or community was not an appropriate response.

In dealing with communities of alternative religious persuasion, ibn Abd al-Wahhab preferred the option of establishing a truce or armistice relationship *(hadanah),* citing the legal principle of *maslahah* (public interest) in support. He argued for *hadanah* as prescribed by both the Quran and Sunna (example of the Prophet Muhammad):

> It is permitted according to the saying of the Most High: [withdrawal is from God and His Messenger; Quran 9:1] the verse and His saying: [And if they are inclined toward peace, then lean toward it; Quran 8:61] the verse, and he [Sallalahu alayhi wa sallam (peace be upon him)] made peace easily for 10 years. And therefore he tolerated for the Muslims weakening them from fighting or greed in their submission or in their payment of the *jizya* [poll tax] or other than it as being part of public interests.[10]

Not only did ibn Abd al-Wahhab not automatically declare jihad against *kuffar,* but he also permitted Muslims to live among them under the condition that the Muslims were permitted to practice and study their religion.[11]

This principle of peaceful coexistence was applied to both Muslims and non-Muslims, particularly Christians and Jews.

Although some today associate Wahhabism with fighting against Christians and Jews, in the style of Al-Qaida, this was not the vision of Muhammad ibn Abd al-Wahhab. In keeping with the teachings of the Quran and Sunna, ibn Abd al-Wahhab confirmed that Christians and Jews are to enjoy a special status and relationship with Muslims on the basis of their shared beliefs.[12] This relationship is to occur via the mechanism of the *jizya* payment, which results in the foundation of a contractual relationship under which Jews and Christians are referred to as *dhimmis:*

> And the eternal contract of the *dhimmah* is not permitted except by two conditions: The first of the two is the necessity of giving the *jizya* in every condition, the second: the necessity of the jurisdiction of Islam and . . . acceptance of what is judged by it for them from the discharging of truth and leaving what is forbidden according to the saying of the Most High: [And they are submissive/subdued; Quran 9:29].[13]

Once made, the Muslims cannot break this contract. In addition to military protection and the guarantee of their security, the *dhimmis* also have the right of religious freedom, including the right to raise their children in their own faith and, for *dhimmi* women, the right to retain their own faith when married to Muslim men. Ibn Abd al-Wahhab made it clear that "there is no exception and we do not know any variance."[14]

Similar to his discussion of *hadanah,* ibn Abd al-Wahhab provided scriptural support from both the Quran and Sunna for the permissibility of using the *jizya* as the mechanism for establishing the *dhimmi* relationship. In addition, he added historical precedent to the supportive evidence through the inclusion of *ijma* (community consensus):

> The basis for it and for the collection of the *jizya* is the Book [the Quran], the Sunna, and *ijma,* according to His saying: [Until they give the *jizya;* Quran 9:29] the verse, and the saying of al-Mughirah on the Day of Nahawanid: Our Prophet commanded us that we should fight you until you served God or you paid the *jizya.* Al-Bukhari narrated it. And the well-known hadith of Buraydah: "Have them contribute 13 properties." Muslim narrated it. And they agreed entirely about the permissibility of taking the *jizya.*[15]

Ibn Abd al-Wahhab further expanded the description of who qualifies for this relationship beyond Christians and Jews to include the following:

> Contracting it is not permitted except to the People of the Book and anyone [who have] a similar book. And the People of the Book are the Jews and the Christians and anyone who borrowed from their religion, like the Samaritans who adhere to the law of Moses, even though they differ from

them in the subdivisions of his religion, and the Christians, who differ among the Jacobites and the Nestorians and the Melchites and the French and the Romans and the Armenians and other than them from anyone who derives their origins from the law of Jesus. . . . And as for those who have a similar book, they are the Magis, this is a saying of many and according to Abi Thawr, they are among the People of the Book and their sacrifices and their women are permitted and this is a variance from the consensus. And what was narrated according to Ali that they have a book and an elevated status . . . and the Companions agreed about this.[16]

Because of his concern for following the example of the Prophet and the need to serve public interest, ibn Abd al-Wahhab included in his description of those who are entitled to the option of the *jizya* his worst ideological enemies—the Rafidah, the *kuffar,* and the *mushrikun:*

And he chose in the return of the Rafidah to take the *jizya* [from every division of the *kuffar* so that there would not remain a single one from the *mushrikun* of the Arabs after the laying down of the *jizya*], but that they would submit. . . . And the imam cannot reduce their treaty and renew the *jizya* upon them because the contract of the *dhimmah* is eternal. Umar contracted with them, and Ibn Uqayl chose to, permitting this according to placing *maslahah* over duration. Umar ibn Abd al-Aziz had done this and the shaykh [Ahmad ibn Taymiyya] chose it, and the contract was made for a certain time according to the Sahih. That is the oath of truce, the shaykh said . . . and if their truce is broken, it is not valid. The shaykh said: It is valid and is to be permitted and can work for *maslahah.*[17]

Once it is contracted, the truce relationship cannot be broken, even if the imam who originally contracted it dies or is dismissed.[18]

The protection for *dhimmis* extends even to those cases where they are captured during a jihad, provided that they are either already paying or promise to pay the *jizya.* According to ibn Abd al-Wahhab, both *maslahah* (public interest) and *ijtihad* (independent reasoning), as well as the Quran and Sunna, require that those *dhimmis* who are captured during jihad can neither be killed nor enslaved:

The captives from the Magis and the People of the Book who remain in the *jizya* . . . , the imam prefers this for them between killing and grace by other than compensation and sacrifice and enslavement. And according to Malik, like our *madhhab,* and about it grace is not permitted by other than compensation and a report according to al-Hasan and 'Ata' and Said bin Jubayr a distaste for killing captives. And he said: Benevolence is incumbent upon him or ransoming as he did for the captives of Badr and because God Most High said: [And thereafter is benevolence and ransoming; Quran 47:4]. And the Companions of Opinion *[Ashab al-rayy]* said: Therefore he desired to kill them, then enslave them not other than according to His saying [And kill the *mushrikun;* Quran 9:5] after His saying: [And thereafter is benevolence and ransoming; Quran 47:4]. And for us, benevolence and ransoming are permitted by the mentioned verse, and he [Sallalahu alayhi wa sallam (SAAS)] was benevolent toward Thamamah and Abi Uzzat al-Shayr and he said to the captives of Badr, "If al-Mat'am bin Ada is living, then I will ask them to repudiate their ties to him." And he ransomed the captives of Badr and other than them. And as for killing, he killed the men of the Bani al-Nadhir and he killed on the day of Badr al-Nadhr and Uqbah bin Abi Muit in captivity and he killed Aba Uzzah on the first day because all of a quality had been compensated for and anyone who did not decide for the *jizya,* he gave them the choice between death and benevolence and ransoming. The choice of choosing *maslahah* and *ijtihad* is not choosing greed.[19]

In addition, once the jihad has concluded, neither the property nor the freedom of the *dhimmis* can be taken due to the treaty relationship that exists: "And when the Muslims had power over the *Ahl al-Dhimmah,* they were required to restore to them their security of life and property and it was not permitted to make them slaves and we do not know any variance in it."[20]

Finally, if the enemy captures *dhimmis* who are paying *jizya* to the Muslims, the Muslims are obligated to ransom them, because the Muslims are obligated to protect their safety in exchange for receiving the *jizya:*

It is required to ransom the captive of the *Ahl al-Dhimmah.* Umar Ibn Abd al-Aziz and al-Layth said it because we assume as a duty their safekeeping according to their covenant and by taking their *jizya.* And the Qadi [ibn al-Qayyim] said: "It is necessary when the imam obliges it of them." If they were fighting and they were captured, this is incumbent upon him and this is stipulated in the writing by Ahmad [Ahmad ibn Hanbal].[21]

Ibn Abd al-Wahhab's writings make several points clear with respect to the *dhimmis.* First, the relationship becomes a binding contract via the mechanism of *jizya,* which, once paid, serves to maintain the contract in force, even in a case where the *dhimmis* are under enemy control. Second, certain religious groups, including but not limited to Christians and Jews, are entitled to a special relationship with Muslims in which their lives, property, freedom, and right to worship are guaranteed to the point where Muslims must be willing to fight to protect them or ransom them once captured. Finally, these writings provide a solid, indigenous religious basis for establishing formal relationships with non-Wahhabis. The question that remains is whether and how such teachings are being applied today in the Kingdom of Saudi Arabia.[22]

▓ Interreligious Dialogue Today

Although "officially" Islam is the only religion that can be freely practiced in Saudi Arabia today, unofficially, religious freedom is rising quietly, yet slowly. Evidence includes the increased number of people both within and outside the political and religious establishment who identify themselves as "anti-Wahhabis," official recognition of law schools other than the Hanbali *madhhab*,[23] official recognition of the Shia population and expansion of Shia rights to practice their religion, although not necessarily to teach it,[24] and the apparent incremental presence and recognition of Christianity.[25]

The slow yet steady rise in willingness to address relations with religious "others" has been endorsed by the Ministry of Islamic Affairs. Although Saudi Arabia does not yet formally participate in interreligious dialogue, it does engage informally in discussion with the Vatican's Council for Interreligious Dialogue.[26] In 2004, the ministry made its position clear in a book addressed to the West in which the kingdom's religious attitude toward Christianity and Judaism was outlined. This publication is remarkable because it reasserts Islam's broad respect for these monotheistic faiths and calls for formal dialogue with them because of their shared beliefs.

In language reminiscent of ibn Abd al-Wahhab's teachings on cooperation and treaty relations, the publication states:

> We Muslims will meet with Christians and Jews because all of us believe in God and His Books and His Messengers and the Last Day, and we believe in reckoning and Paradise and Hell, and we believe in human dignity and civil responsibility and the right of the freedom of choice, just as we believe in equality and justice and moral character, and we are in agreement on the majority of principles, although not political sects. And Muslims and Christians and Jews are the most powerful of people in relations [as in family relations] and harmony.[27]

The essay continues by discussing the common prophets to Muslims, Christians, and Jews, specifically mentioning Abraham, Moses, and Jesus, and the fact that Muslims share belief in the Torah and Gospels "and other than these two from the Heavenly Books."[28] At the same time, it notes that the same recognition of the Quran and Muhammad have not been forthcoming from many Christians, both historically and in the contemporary era, resulting in both the defamation of Islam and Muhammad and unnecessary enmity and hostility between faiths. However, rather than descending into further accusations, the author asserts that this circumstance offers an opportunity for interfaith dialogue with the purpose of correcting misunderstandings and misinformation and drawing back together those "divine messages and heavenly religions" under the broad umbrella of submission to God (al-Islam proper). This point is clarified via recognition of the common divine nature of these revelations: "And this designation is not limited to the last of the divine messages, but it is therefore generally for each according to what came by it as messages belonging to God."[29]

Support for these contentions is provided by nine Quran citations, all of which demonstrate the continuity of God's message in all revelations,[30] thus proving that "the Quran has given powerful confirmation that Islam is the name of every religion that was revealed by God."[31] Because the Quran recognizes the divine nature of other religions, the essay concludes by requesting a place for the Quran in interfaith dialogue on the basis that it "enfolds the prior messages as they were sent down from God's possession and increased by it much information and diverse religious observances and Sharia elaboration, so that human development and the civilizational journey can move forward."[32]

The desire for expanding dialogue and cooperation is clearly present. How this is to be carried out practically remains an open question.

Conclusion

Although Saudi Arabia historically has been portrayed as a country that resists interfaith dialogue and asserts its supposedly singular interpretation of Islam as the one and only correct interpretation, recent publications and national efforts to expand interfaith and intrafaith dialogue do not support this contention. Building on the foundations established by Muhammad ibn Abd al-Wahhab, the kingdom in recent years has given greater attention to the question of the status of both the Shias and the People of the Book.

The essence of the message remains the same as that of ibn Abd al-Wahhab—cooperative relations between Muslims, Christians, Jews, Shias, and even *mushrikun* and *kuffar* are not only possible, but desirable—while the mechanism of the implementation has changed—no longer the payment of the *jizya* in order to achieve *dhimmi* status, but mutual recognition of a shared divine revelation that results in a religious family in which Shias are recognized as Muslims, and Muslims, Christians, and Jews are all brothers and sisters. The theoretical theological foundations have been reasserted for expanded cooperation and peaceful coexistence. The main question for the future is whether political events will continue to overshadow these important theological reassertions and reinterpretations.

Notes

1. For example, the conflict between the so-called Chechen rebels and the Russian government derives its true inspiration from historical political grievances, notably the forced relocation of the Chechen population under Joseph Stalin's regime in 1944. For details, see James J. F. Forest, "Training Camps and Other Centers of Learning," in *Teaching Terror: Strategic and Tactical Learning in the Terrorist World,* edited by James J. F. Forest (Lanham: Rowman and Littlefield, 2006), esp. pp. 88–91. It is also important to note that many of these so-called Wahhabi movements derive their inspiration from militant offshoots of the Muslim Brotherhood, particularly

selective usage of the writings of Sayyid Qutb, and from selective usage of the writings of medieval scholar Ahmad ibn Taymiyya, rather than from the writings of Muhammad ibn Abd al-Wahhab. Al-Qaida is a prime example of this derived inspiration. For a detailed distinction of Wahhabism from Al-Qaida's ideology, see Natana J. DeLong-Bas, *Wahhabi Islam: From Revival and Reform to Global Jihad* (New York: Oxford University Press, 2004), esp. pp. 266–279. For analysis of the use of the term "Wahhabi" in a pejorative sense, see Alexander Knysh, "A Clear and Present Danger: 'Wahhabism' as a Rhetorical Foil," *Saudi-American Forum* no. 24 (2003). As one Saudi analyst describes use of the term "Wahhabi": "The media often describes any Saudi as Wahhabi, implying an association with intolerance, extremism, and backwardness. At the same time, though, the term is also applied globally for political ends to label orthodox Muslims even if they are from India, Indonesia, or the United States. Most of the time, the people being called Wahhabi may have never even heard of Muhammad bin Abdul-Wahhab. . . . Everything that the word Wahhabi stands for today goes completely against the monotheistic, just, peaceful system that Bin Abdul-Wahhab was striving for in Arabia." Abdalla M. Mohammed and A. Al al-Sheikh Mohammed, *Has Usama bin Laden Sprung from the Womb of Wahhabism* (Merrifield, VA: Saudi Studies Center, 2002), p. 4.

2. Evidence of the use of Wahhabi ideology to achieve political purposes is found in the alliance formed between ibn Abd al-Wahhab and Muhammad ibn Saud, particularly in letters subsequently sent to surrounding tribes, calling upon them to join the movement.

3. Both ibn Abd al-Wahhab and his followers used the term *muwahhidin.* Some of ibn Abd al-Wahhab's treatises are directly addressed to "Ya, Muwahhidin," indicating that *tawhid,* rather than loyalty to ibn Abd al-Wahhab, was the focal point of the faith. The emphasis on *tawhid* as the most important and central theme of ibn Abd al-Wahhab's teachings is apparent in the prominence of his treatise *Kitab al-Tawhid,* which was written as a catechism for his followers, explaining in detail the practical implications of belief in *tawhid* and how it was to be lived out in daily life. Muhammad ibn Abd al-Wahhab, "Kitab al-Tawhid," in *Mu'allafat al-Shaykh al-Imam Muhammad ibn Abd al-Wahhab* (Riyadh: Islamic University of Imam Muhammad ibn Saud, 1977). For a more detailed analysis of *tawhid* and ibn Abd al-Wahhab's theology, see DeLong-Bas, *Wahhabi Islam,* pp. 41–91.

4. For a discussion of Wahhabi-Ottoman relations and the development of Wahhabism in the nineteenth century, see David Commins, *The Wahhabi Mission and Saudi Arabia* (London: Tauris, 2006).

5. It is important to note here that, despite this not having been ibn Abd al-Wahhab's intent, some of his followers engaged in precisely these practices, particularly after ibn Abd al-Wahhab's withdrawal from public life in 1773. For details, see DeLong-Bas, *Wahhabi Islam,* pp. 243–256.

6. For full details, see DeLong-Bas, *Wahhabi Islam,* pp. 194–203. These points are also being emphasized by Saudi scholars in the aftermath of September 11, 2001. See, for example, Mohammed Ahmed and Mohammad S. Olimat, *Wahhabism: A Controversial Issue* (Merrifield, VA: Saudi Studies Center, 2002).

7. The Kingdom of Saudi Arabia has recognized the existence of *takfiri* ideology and the hatred it has brought in the aftermath of September 11, 2001. A 2004 Saudi royal study group found that the kingdom's religious studies curriculum "encourages violence toward others, and misguided the pupils into believing that in order to safeguard their own religion, they must violently repress and even physically eliminate the 'other.'" In response, the kingdom has worked to change the textbooks in favor of "tolerance" and "moderation." However, there remains concern about to

what degree these changes have been implemented, given that some current texts apparently still make assertions such as (1) Islam is the only "correct" religion and all other religions are false (first-grade curriculum); (2) while it is important to treat polytheists and unbelievers justly, one should still hate them (fourth-grade curriculum); and (3) it is forbidden to be a loyal friend to someone who either does not believe in God and His Prophet or fights the religion of Islam (fifth-grade curriculum). Nina Shea, "This Is a Saudi Textbook (After the Intolerance Was Removed)," http://www.washingtonpost.com, May 21, 2006. It should be noted that this article does not present a full analysis of the texts in question. More comprehensive analyses can be found in Eleanor Abdella Doumato and Gregory Starrett, eds., *Teaching Islam: Textbooks and Religion in the Middle East* (Boulder: Lynne Rienner, 2006).

8. For more detailed discussions of these terms, see DeLong-Bas, *Wahhabi Islam,* pp. 81–83.

9. Muhammad ibn Abd al-Wahhab, "Fatawa wa-Masa'il al-Imam al-Shaykh Muhammad ibn Abd al-Wahhab," in *Mu'allafat al-Shaykh,* p. 45.

10. Muhammad ibn Abd al-Wahhab, "Kitab al-Jihad," in *Mu'allafat al-Shaykh,* p. 398.

11. Ibid., p. 403. Nevertheless, ibn Abd al-Wahhab described living among the *kuffar* as acceptable but not desirable.

12. Christians and Jews are described in his writings as both "Ahl al-Kitab" (People of the Book, which refers to the existence of a commonly shared revelation) and "Ahl al-Dhimmah" (People of the Covenant, reflecting a contractual relationship based on payment of a special tax called the *jizya* by Christians and Jews to Muslims in exchange for exemption from otherwise mandatory military service; those who pay it are entitled to the military protection provided to Muslims).

13. ibn Abd al-Wahhab, "Kitab al-Jihad," p. 402.

14. Ibid.

15. Ibid., pp. 401–402.

16. Ibid.

17. Ibid., pp. 403–404.

18. Ibid., p. 404.

19. Ibid., p. 367. It is not clear who is meant by "the imam," although it is likely ibn Taymiyya. References to ibn Taymiyya typically occur under the reference of "the shaikh." Ahmad ibn Hanbal is referred to as "Ahmad."

20. ibn Abd al-Wahhab, "Kitab al-Jihad," p. 382.

21. Ibid., p. 397.

22. More detailed information about the contemporary Kingdom of Saudi Arabia, including analyses of Wahhabi thought and practice in theology and law, attitudes toward jihad, and the status of religious "others," can be found in Natana J. DeLong-Bas, *Jihad for Islam: The Struggle for the Future of Saudi Arabia* (New York: Oxford University Press, forthcoming 2009).

23. This initiative was the express wish of King Abdullah as expressed during the fifth national dialogue, of 2005, which addressed "us and others." For details, see Ebtihal Mubarak, "We Must Sort Internal Differences First," *Arab News,* December 15, 2005.

24. Achievements in the expansion of Shia rights include the following: the status of Shias within the kingdom was addressed during the national dialogue of 2003; Shias were permitted to campaign for office and vote in the municipal council elections of 2005; and Shias have been permitted to issue their own calls to prayer (which differ slightly from the Sunni call to prayer), to publicly mention the name "Ali," and to engage publicly in their rituals surrounding the martyrdom of Hussein.

Securing the right to campaign for and vote in elections was a particularly important step, because only citizens are permitted to vote. Because only Muslims can be citizens in Saudi Arabia, the right of Shias to vote and run for office marked official recognition of Shias as Muslims, rather than as *kuffar*. In addition, greater attention has been given in recent years to expanding job opportunities and improving education in Shia-majority areas. These practical measures have been praised by Shia leader Shaikh Hassan al-Saffar as critical to expanding the national role of Shias and to keeping the issue of the status of Shias a domestic, rather than an international, affair. See P. K. Abdul Ghafour, "US Under Fire for Double Standard on Religious Freedom," *Arab News,* September 20, 2004. At the same time, Shias still may not teach religious studies, hold sensitive government, educational, medical, or security positions, or publish religious tracts. Some school texts continue to teach that Shias are religious deviants and that their practice of shrine and tomb visitation is sinful. See "Saudi Shias Seek Greater Rights," http://www.aljazeera.net, September 27, 2005; Donna Abu-Nasr, "Saudis Vote in Historic Elections," *Boston Globe,* March 4, 2005; Donna Abu-Nasr, "Saudi Shi'ites See Promise in Local Elections," *Boston Globe,* March 3, 2005. For a historical discussion of the status of Shias in the kingdom, see Madawi al-Rasheed, *A History of Saudi Arabia* (New York: Cambridge University Press, 2002). For a politically and emotionally charged discussion of contemporary anti-Shia discrimination, see Asad Abu Khalil, *The Battle for Saudi Arabia: Royalty, Fundamentalism, and Global Power* (New York: Seven Stories, 2004).

25. I specify "apparent" because expatriate workers do, in fact, have the right to practice their religion discreetly. Certain non-Muslim religious holidays are being celebrated more openly, including Christmas. In December 2006, Christmas chocolates and tins of dates displaying Christmas trees were available for purchase in various malls in Riyadh.

26. See, for example, statements by Shaikh Saleh Al al-Shaikh on this question as published in *Al-Daawah* magazine since 2003.

27. Ibrahim Abd al-Rahman al-Bulayhi, "Call for Continuing from the Time of Common Mutual Understanding," in *Letter to the West: A View from Saudi Arabia,* (Riyadh: Ghainaa, 2004), p. 17.

28. Ibid.

29. Ibid., p. 18.

30. Verses cited: 2:127–128, 2:130–132, 3:83–85, 5:44, 3:52, 5:111, 10:90, 10:84, 28:53.

31. al-Bulayhi, *Letter to the West,* p. 20.

32. Ibid.

3

Wahhabism as an Ideology of State Formation

Khalid S. al-Dakhil

The Wahhabi movement, or Wahhabiyya, was born in the middle of the eighteenth century in Najd, or central Arabia.[1] It helped initiate a political and military campaign that ended in the creation of a state that in the early nineteenth century controlled four-fifths of the Arabian Peninsula. A movement that played such a historical role, and whose religious rhetoric was at the heart of its mission, was bound to become a subject of controversy and debate. Since the beginning, the Wahhabiyya has been narrowly defined, on either the basis of its apparent mission of religious reform, or the tribal characteristic of the social structure within which it arose. In both cases the conditions that preceded the movement are either discounted or ignored altogether.

The movement is widely assumed to be both religious and nomadic. It is also assumed that the movement originated in Najd, where religious conditions were presumably deteriorating, and was a response to that deterioration. It is therefore presumed that this movement was driven, almost exclusively, by a religious cause and in pursuance of purely religious objectives. This is not only the view of the Wahhabis and their followers, but also the predominant view, according to the literature, shared by Arabs, Muslims, and Westerners alike.

Simultaneously, the Wahhabiyya is characterized, especially in the non-Wahhabi literature, as nomadic in its social affiliation and political orientation. The driving force here is not primarily religion but *assabiyyah* (the feeling of tribal affinity), hence the movement's objective is assumed to be to impose the political dominance of a certain *assabiyyah:* the al-Saud vis-à-vis the others. The predominance of the tribe and nomadism in particular in the Najdi society before and during the time of the Wahhabis serves as the basis for this thesis.

Both the religious and the nomadic characterizations are considered to complement each other, especially by the advocates of the latter. The nomadic thesis acts as the sociological explanation for the religious characterization.

Nevertheless, the two theses are incompatible. To say that a movement adheres to a strict concept of the *sharia* and at the same time to insist that it is a nomadic movement is simply contradictory. Because the two theses epitomize two irreconcilable modes of living (whereas the religious representation of the movement is taken from the Wahhabi sources, the source of the nomadic characterization comes from methodological naiveté and cultural prejudice), the Wahhabiyya aimed to fundamentally alter the Najdi society. After the restoration of *tawhid* and the realization of a central state, it demonstrated a deep affinity with the land, and hoped fixed property would become an integral part of the social structure. In the nomadic mode of living, however, attachment is to the tribe and tribal ethos, not to the land.

Additionally, not only was the Wahhabiyya a *hadari* (urban) movement, and extremely anti-nomadic,[2] but it was also never attached to any particular tribe, nomadic or settled, in Arabia. Furthermore, the historical roots of the movement do not have anything to do with religion. The Wahhabiyya was a political force, the only political force of its time, pushing for the establishment of a central state. Both the religious and nomadic theses not only underrate the political nature and political role of the movement, but also negate the history of the movement altogether.

This chapter is an attempt to redefine the Wahhabi movement to demonstrate that it was not simply a religious reform movement obsessed with the question of *shirk* (association of others with the one true God), nor was it another manifestation of the nomadic mode of living for which Arabia is well known.[3] Rather, it was a powerful, political urban movement in the state formation process that was itself a product of this process and also helped push state formation to its logical conclusion.

The state formation process includes political, cultural, and social dynamics, the unfolding of which reflects the evolution of the concept of the state in a society: ideas, relations, institutions, ideologies, and eventually the state itself. This process had been taking place in Arabia, and in Najd in particular, long before the rise of the Wahhabi movement. By leading the way for the establishment of the state, the Wahhabiyya represented an advanced phase in that process. It is essential to reconstruct that history and make the case for its crucial relevance to the rise of the movement, the shape it assumed, and the role it eventually played in the history of Arabia.

The importance of religion in the rise of the movement is related to the fact that religion was the only educational and intellectual means available in the Najdi society of the eighteenth century through which novel ideas could be communicated. As such, religious discourse could in all likelihood be a condensed form of expression implying other political and social aspirations.

The Wahhabiyya is also presented as a nomadic movement because of the appearance of the tribe in the social structure of Arabia at the time. This too is misleading, because it is a static perception that fails to recognize the evolving, metamorphosing nature of the tribal structure. Advocates of the nomadic thesis could not decipher that the tribe in Najd was part of a state formation process. The nomadic tribe would eventually give way to a settled tribe. The process of settlement and resettlement was complicated, and assumed several and inter-twined phases: collective settlement, dispersive settlement, the rise of the au-tonomous towns, intensification of religious learning, the rise of the Wahhabi movement, and then the rise of the state.

These were the main dynamics of the state formation process in Najd up to the eighteenth century. In other words, the roots of the Wahhabiyya were not of a religious nature. They were political and social in character. At the same time, by initiating the idea of the state, and spearheading the campaign to re-alize that the Wahhabiyya was not just a product of the state formation process, the Wahhabiyya took the initiative to reshape the forces of that same process, and change the course of their history forever. Accordingly, the Wahhabiyya had a political message and a clearly defined political objective.

▓ Two Theses: Religion and Modernization

At this point, it is fitting to recall the conclusion of a paper on the expansion of the first Saudi state. After reviewing alternative answers to the question "why the [first] Saudi state appeared when and where it did," the author, Michael Cook, concluded that "the hypothesis that long-term historical change lies be-hind the emergence of the first Saudi state is . . . not to be dismissed. But we are perhaps on solider ground in regarding the event as an act of God."[4] This may have been an expression of sarcasm on Cook's part, or perhaps it was an act of desperation, or maybe both. Be that as it may, to attribute the rise of the state to "an act of God" is to dismiss history altogether. What Cook is suggest-ing here is nothing less than a theological finale that says more about his method than about the history of the state he was trying to explain. Cook's method, being empiricist historiography rather than historical analysis, was not ade-quate. However, Cook's conclusion is not unique. It reflects the state of most writings on the Wahhabiyya.

It is therefore important to subject the Wahhabiyya to historical and socio-logical analysis. Historically, understanding the Wahhabiyya's roots and nature is imperative for understanding the nature of the state it created. To understand this process, pre-Wahhabiyya history must first be analyzed. As will be shown later, most of those who have written about the movement removed it from its historical context and dealt with it on the basis of a set of premises and assump-tions irrelevant to that context.

The Religious Thesis

The proclaimed objective of the Wahhabiyya was the cleansing of all religious innovations and superstitious beliefs and practices said to have been widespread in Najd. The assumption is that by the eighteenth century, *shirk* (polytheism) was a common practice in the Najdi society. And being the major sin in Islam, *shirk* had to be wiped out. Embarking on such a mission prompted many to see the rise of Wahhabism as a religiously motivated response to deteriorating religious conditions. According to the proponents of this thesis, the rise of the movement can only be explained if it is seen as a religious call.[5]

The first and strongest advocates of this view were the Wahhabis, and chief among them were Hussein ibn Ghannam and Uthman ibn Bishr. Ibn Ghannam was a contemporary of Shaikh Muhammad ibn Abd al-Wahhab, and ibn Bisher lived through both the first and the second Saudi states. Both were from the same school, one that combined the profession of writing history with a religious perspective, and both were among the staunchest followers of the shaikh.[6] It is said that ibn Ghannam wrote his history in response to a request by Shaikh ibn Abd al-Wahhab himself.[7]

The opening of ibn Ghannam's history sums up the Wahhabi position this way: "At the inception of the 12th [18th] century most Muslims had fallen back into *shirk,* apostasized into the first *jahiliyah* [the pre-Islamic time, or the age of ignorance], and the light of faith had gone out of their souls. All of this was caused by the fact that the Muslims had been overcome by ignorance, and the capricious among them were so conceited that they chose to shove the book of God behind their back, and follow the path of their misguided fathers." The share of Najd in this rather grim state of religious conditions, according to ibn Ghannam, was great.[8] From this he concluded that the people of Najd were in the habit of practicing every type of *shirk.* Ibn Bishr affirmed ibn Ghannam's view when he indicated that the two types of *shirk,* the greater and the lesser, were very common in the Najdi society at the time.[9]

According to ibn Bishr, Shaikh ibn Abd al-Wahhab was appalled by the wide gap between the real, original meaning of *tawhid* as it was laid out in the Quran, and the Sunna of the Prophet, on the one hand, and the prevailing state of the people's beliefs and practices on the other.[10] The shaikh attributed this anomalous condition to the disappearance of the authentic and accurate meaning of the first pillar of Islam—professing the faith, or the *shahada:* "I bear witness that there is no deity but God, and Muhammad is the messenger of God." The *shahada* is the criterion that determines an individual's standing as a Muslim. The meaning of this pillar, said the shaikh, was not belief in God as the creator of the universe, for this was already taken for granted even by the *mushrikun* (polytheists) whom the Prophet Muhammad had fought in the seventh century. Believing in God at this level is called *tawhid al-rububiyah* (unity of God as the sole creator of the universe). By itself, this belief, although valid and mandatory, is not sufficient to make an individual a Muslim. Confessing the faith does not mean a belief in *tawhid al-rububiyah.* First and foremost it means a belief in *tawhid al-uluhiyah* (unity of God as the sole object of worship). The true meaning of the first pillar of Islam, and thus of the concept of *tawhid,* is the devotion of all forms of worship, with no exception, to God, and to God only, the one and indivisible.[11]

Shirk and the concept of *tawhid.* The shaikh's objective then was to close the gap between popular beliefs on the one hand and primary sources on the other, so that the true meaning of *tawhid* would be restored. From this the Wahhabi historians concluded that a movement with such a religious objective must be rooted in religious conditions and religious causes. However, for such an argument to hold, it must first be shown that religious conditions were deteriorating in Najd at the time. And since *shirk* is cited in the Wahhabi sources to be the principal indicator for that deterioration, the question is whether *shirk* (polytheism)—as defined in the Wahhabi sources—did exist in Najd in the eighteenth century, and whether the scale of that existence warranted the importance given to it in those sources.

The rise of the Wahhabiyya represents a historical shift on a large scale. The existence of *shirk,* cited as the explanatory factor in this case, must therefore have been on the same or similar scale. This is a matter of history and not of theory. On their part, the Wahhabis took the notion of *shirk* and its existence as a point of departure for their argument, when it was an open question, and not as an assumption on which to build an argument.

There are three basic facts about the Wahhabi movement: it was a religious movement, it emerged in the *hadari* (urban) milieu of the "autonomous towns" in Najd,[12] and it led the process of nation building in Arabia. These facts suggest immediately that the Wahhabiyya was a multidimensional movement. That it sought restoration of the true meaning of *tawhid* shows its religious content. But it is misleading to stop at that. The term *tawhid* is not simply a religious concept. It is a political concept too. The two types of *tawhid* testify to this. Restoring the *tawhid* that would give the Wahhabiyya its religious character could not have been achieved without the political authority of a state. The shaikh was keenly aware of this, and that is perhaps why he was pushing for a central state. According to both ibn Bishr and ibn Ghannam, the shaikh was carrying the political project of the state, looking for a sponsor from among the rulers of the Najd's autonomous towns.[13] *Tawhid,* which was at the center of the shaikh's movement, is too loaded a concept to be reduced only to its religious connotation.

In Arabic, the general meaning of the term *tawhid* is "to unify," as applied to peoples, tribes, and regions. The emphasis here is on the political connotation of the term. In Islamic theological lexicon, the word *tawhid* also means "to unify," but with a divine connotation of its own. Both meanings are reflected in the two types of *tawhid:* the unity of God as the creator of the universe, or *tawhid al-rububiyah,* and the unity of God as the sole object of all forms of worship, or *tawhid al-uluhiyah.* The first is a direct and unmediated relationship with God; hence it is a purely religious relation. The second is mostly mediated through the state, making it an overtly political relation. It is said that both concepts complement each other, yet it is only *tawhid al-uluhiyah* that makes one a Muslim. *Tawhid al-rububiyah,* on the other hand, is not sufficient by itself toward that end. In the Wahhabi political discourse, the two meanings come together, with the political unity being a precondition for the divine unity. If worship is to be directed solely to God, then political obedience is to be unconditionally given to one *wali ul amr* (the ruler). Shaikh ibn Abd al-Wahhab is quoted to have said: "For the unity of the community to be perfect is to give ear and obedience to whoever has the power to become its ruler."[14] The catchphrase in the Wahhabi literature says: "There is no religion without a *jama'ah* [community], and no *jama'ah* without an *imam* [a ruler], and no *imam* without obedience."[15] One sign of being faithful to God is to be faithful to the community. And to be faithful to the community is not to indulge in its public affairs, for this could lead to disobeying the ruler, something that could lead to *fitna,* or disorder.[16]

The political overtone of *tawhid al-uluhiyah* is obvious here. In the definition of this concept, the stress is on *ibadah* (worship), and the duty of devoting it solely to God. *Ibadah* is the ultimate expression of obedience. When obedience is given to God, *ibadah* takes the religious form of obedience. But then *ibadah* is not limited to religious deeds and rituals like praying and meditation, both of which can be performed exclusively on an individual basis. Rather, *ibadah* is a concept wide enough to include, among other things, the individual's social and political obligations, such as duties toward the community, especially toward the state, and toward the ruler in particular. The first obligation in this regard is to pledge an allegiance to a ruler,[17] and being obedient to the ruler is the second.[18] Clearly, both are political requirements, and both are to be fulfilled as complementary to one's religious obligations toward God. The two go hand in hand, and cannot be separated.

Since one's faith is not fully realized until one fulfills both types of *tawhid,* the implication is obvious: the relationship between the political and the religious is inextricable. In the case of the Wahhabiyya, the prerequisite for restoring the "true religious meaning" of *tawhid* is to restore the political *tawhid* of the society in the first place. And Najd of the eighteenth century was a disintegrating society.[19] It was on the verge of collapse. If it was a coincidence, it was a remarkable and indicative one that a movement whose discourse and objective revolved around the concept of political *tawhid* was born in a society heading in the direction of political disintegration.

The Wahhabiyya initiated the process of nation building in eighteenth-century Arabia. Indeed this was a declared objective of the shaikh all along.[20] That the movement embarked on such a mission is related to the fact that it was the product of a *hadari* (urban) environment. The notion of a central and inclusive state requires an inclusive vision as opposed to being politically and ideologically attached to a particular tribe. Taken together, all these historical facts make it clear that there is much more than religion to the Wahhabiyya. To reduce it to being only a religious movement runs counter to its nature and its real history.

The question of *shirk.* This brings us back to the issue of *shirk* and the extent of its existence in Najd, prior to the Wahhabiyya. The religious thesis does not fare better on this account. In fact, it is oblivious to the pre-Wahhabi history of Najd, which may explain that the thesis's stand on *shirk* cannot be reconciled with the basic and relevant observations from the movement's history. Consider the fact that opposition to the movement was not only religious, but also overwhelmingly of the same legal school as that of the Wahhabiyya itself—the Hanbali school. This means that religious schools or sects that accommodate or tolerate types of worship considered by the Hanbalis and the Wahhabis to fall within the religious category of *shirk* almost did not exist in Najd. That both the shaikh and his opponents shared the basic theological outlook on the issue of *shirk* makes it inconceivable that *shirk* was widespread among the laymen of the society without a religious authority to provide a point of reference for those people.

The second observation is that all local historical sources that were written prior to and during the early stages of the Wahhabi movement never referred to *shirk* as a phenomenon in the life of the Najdi people during or before the eighteenth century. These sources talked about wars, famines, natural disasters, epidemics, assassinations, and droughts. Yet they all failed to mention *shirk.* What is interesting is that these sources were entirely written by religiously educated people, the ulama, all of whom were from the Hanbali school. Why did these ulama not see in the social reality the same *shirk* seen by the Wahhabis?

It would seem that the differences between the Wahhabiyya and its opponents on this question were not as minor as suggested by the fact that they belong to the same school. To be sure, there were differences, and sometimes intense disputes, some of which are recorded.[21] But the thing to take note of about these disputes is that they were not over the existence of *shirk* and its extent in Najd. Rather, the main contentious issue in this theoretical dispute revolved around the question as to what constituted *shirk.* This was a theoretical question and the most likely reason for this is that *shirk* was too insignificant to become a subject of controversy. This also means that the differences between the two sides over the question of *shirk* were not over the basics of religion. And the fact that all the local sources concur on failing to take note of the existence of *shirk* could most probably mean but one thing, that *shirk* was not worth recording.

This is further supported by a third observation, which is perhaps the most significant of all: that almost all of Shaikh Muhammad's references to the sites of worship where *shirk* was presumably practiced were located outside of Najd.[22] It might be said that *shirk* for the shaikh and his followers was not limited only to tombs erected for saints. It also included superstitious beliefs and practices, belief in the ability of soothsayers, and the seeking of help from magicians. According to ibn Bishr, some of beliefs and practices were widespread in Najd at the time.[23] But this had been the case before and during the Wahhabi movement, and in fact has been the case since. Superstitious beliefs and practices have been a constant condition, and therefore cannot be legitimately used to explain the rise of the movement. The rise of the Wahhabiyya represents a significant shift in the history of Arabia. It cannot be explained by a constant condition showing no sign of change, not only in Arabia but also in Najd itself. It can only be explained by a corresponding shift in Najdi history and society at the time.

Yet the religious thesis never failed to be attractive. It was recently picked up by none other than renowned historian of Islam, Bernard Lewis. Lewis's motives and objectives are different from those of the Wahhabis. Despite this, however, he managed to share with them the same logic that attributes the rise of the Wahhabiyya to religious reasons. So if for the Wahhabis the reason was the spread of *shirk,* for Lewis it was the expansion of Christendom: "The rise of Wahhabism in eighteenth-century Arabia was in significant measure a response to . . . the retreat of Islam and the corresponding advance of Christendom."[24] Lewis, it should be pointed out, was the first to come up with such an explanation. Yet he could not provide any evidence for it. He could not make any reference to any source, especially Saudi or Wahhabi, to corroborate this rather innovative explanation. And this is not surprising, because there is not the slightest indication in the earlier and recent writings of the Wahhabis to remotely suggest that they were aware of any Christian advance, or that such an advance was felt in Arabia, or in Najd in particular.

It could be that because Lewis was writing in the context of the so-called war on terror, and because this war is implicitly premised on the notion of the "clash of civilizations," which in turn is heavily loaded with religious premises and reasoning, he could not escape approaching "Wahhabism" from this particular angle.[25] Even in this, he could not but invent reasons that are in tune with his time and interest and not with the history of the Wahhabiyya itself. In other words, Lewis was writing about an imaginary history of the movement.

The Modernization Thesis

The modernization thesis, on the other hand, focuses its analysis on the nomadic environment from which, presumably, the Wahhabi movement emerged. For this the Wahhabiyya was a tribal movement that led to a tribal state. Such a conclusion has become routine for the modernization theorists in dealing with the Wahhabiyya and the Saudi state. What distinguishes this thesis is its uncritical application of the Khaldunian model to the movement, so that it has become a means to reproduce ready-made stereotypes and clichés, both of which are by now redundant and meaningless. For example, Aziz al-Azmeh, one of those fixated on the Khaldunian model, reproduced the cliché that "the social and political dimensions of Wahhabite ideology is the setting of strict limits of exclusivity to a particular *'assabiyyah'* [tribal solidarity], thus rendering all that is external to this expanding *'assabiyyah'* social, political and geographical territory whose plunder and subjugation are legitimate, indeed incumbent upon members of this exclusive group."[26] Although this claim is central to al-Azmeh's argument, he has been unable to substantiate it by any reference to Muhammad ibn Abd al-Wahhab or any other Wahhabi source.[27]

But the thesis is best illustrated in a study about the state in the Arab East.[28] The Saudi state is included as one of the cases under the title "The Nomadic Wahhabi Base of the Saudi State."[29] The title itself is revealing, but the author, Mas'ud Dahir, insists on justifying its inclusion. The main reason is that the Saudi example illustrates how a nomadic tribe (i.e., the Saudi ruling family), in alliance with a nomadically based religious movement, succeeded in establishing its control over the cities. In the process, the nomadic tribe became urbanized. This is the most tedious replica of the Khaldunian formula. A minimal familiarity with the sources on Najd shows that Dahir was not reading the history of the state and the movement he intended to study. Instead, he was repeating to the letter what Abd al-Rahman ibn Khaldun had said more than 600 years ago about state formation in the Maghrib. Had Dahir studied the history of the Wahhabi movement, he would have realized that he was effectively reversing the course of its history. It is quite remarkable that a movement would take over the city within which it was born, and assume a nomadic characteristic, when it was anti-nomadic and its alliances were drawn exclusively from the *hadar* (dwellers) of the same city.

For modernizationist Muhammad ibn Abd al-Wahhab, he "considered it his life's purpose to mobilize the Muslims for the achievement of . . . a backward-looking utopia. He discounted all the civilizing elements in Islam in favor of the *norms and ways of life of the nomads.*"[30] Here not only is Wahhabi history misrepresented, but so too is the history of Islam itself.[31] What attracted the Wahhabis to the "original pristine purity" of Islam was the characteristically nomadic content of the latter.[32] Again the Khaldunian model is being replicated here without any reference to the history of the movement.[33]

The Wahhabi movement was not the first religious intervention in the history of Najd. From the records, we can only judge that it was the second religious intervention and that it was qualitatively different from the first. The first religious intervention was characteristically legal, and a depoliticized one. The Wahhabi movement was more extensive, in that it was both a religious and a political intervention, emphasizing ideological dimensions.[34] What is the significance of this difference between the two interventions? How was it related to changes in the pattern of settlement that led to the rise of the *hadari* community, in which the Wahhabiyya was born? Equally important is the timing of the Wahhabi movement with its political and ideological tendencies. Perhaps the most consistent and systematic application of the Khaldunian model to the Saudi state came at the hand of Ghassan Salame, who started his academic career as a specialist in the history of this state. For Salame, the Saudi state "has many reasons to attract Khaldunian attention, beginning with the desert, enclaved environment in which the state was born."[35] Why? Because one major factor behind the rise of this state was "a religious call," and the other was "a superior *assabiyyah*" that succeeded in defeating "other group feelings."[36] For Salame, the match between what ibn Khaldun said and what the Wahhabiyya did could not be more perfect. Yet in fact this is another, simple replica of the Khaldunian model being imposed on the Wahhabi history, simply because of the mere presence of religion and the tribe.

What Salame is saying here is astounding. For him the rise of the Wahhabiyya was in response to the need of the "superior *assabiyyah*" for legitimacy. But the chiefs of Al-Diriyya (much later to be known as the al-Saud),[37] by the time they had concluded their political pact with Shaikh ibn Abd al-Wahhab, were among the ruling families of the autonomous towns centuries before the Wahhabiyya. In other words, they belonged to the *hadari* community of Najd and not to its nomadic community. Besides, originally, the chiefs of Al-Diriyya, or Al-Muqrin, belonged to the tribe of Bani Hanifah, which is said to have settled in Al-Yamamah long before the rise of Islam.[38] By the eighteenth century, this tribe had already disintegrated and lost its unifying *assabiyyah*. Thus there is no reason to assume that, at the advent of the Wahhabiyya, Al-Muqrin represented a "superior *assabiyyah*." On the other hand, the leader of the movement, ibn Abd al-Wahhab, was from a different *assabiyyah* than that of Al-Muqrin. He was from another settled and disintegrating tribe, the Bani Tamim. It would be recalled that before going to Al-Diriyya, ibn Abd al-Wahhab went to Al-Uyayna seeking the support of its ruler, Uthman ibn Mo'amar, who, on the basis of the *assabiyyah* logic, was from the same tribe as that of the shaikh.[39] It was truly remarkable that, insofar as the shaikh's alliance with ibn Mo'amar crumbled, his alliance with Al-Muqrin proved to be the most durable in the history of Arabia. Where could the notion of *assabiyyah* be fitted here? Nowhere, for this movement was not responding to the political needs of a certain *assabiyyah*, particularly that of Al-Muqrin. Why then did the movement emerge at the time and place it did? That is the question Salame failed to address.

Both the religious perspective and the modernization perspective deal with the Wahhabi movement outside its historical context, but with a difference. The religious thesis, while based on the movement's history, is biased toward its religious premises, and thus tends to simplify the movement by reducing it to its religious dimension. The religious thesis augments its reductionism by failing to consider the pre-Wahhabi history. The modernization thesis, on the other hand, is based on both political and ideological prejudices, and methodological naiveté. As a result, most works informed by this thesis take the form of stereotyping and ready-made clichés rather than well-researched concepts and hypotheses. On that basis, the dominant themes in the literature on the Wahhabi movement are inadequate, to say the least.

The modernizationists do not seem to be aware that there was a pre-Wahhabi history. They keep replicating the Khaldunian model, simply on the basis that Arabia is known for its tribal structure, and the Wahhabiyya was a religious movement. For them, the presence of both, religion and the tribe, fit perfectly with what ibn Khaldun said about the role of *assabiyyah* and the religious call in the state formation. Yet despite the presence of religion and tribe within it, the Khaldunian model cannot accommodate the history of Arabia.

The Alternative

The alternative suggested here revolves around three themes. First, Wahhabism, far from being a tribal movement, was the product of processes of settlement and state formation that characterized the history of Najd until the first half of the eighteenth century, when the movement started showings signs of activity. It is assumed here that the relationship between the movement and the urbanization process was ongoing and interactive. It was a continuously unfolding process.

The urban characteristic of Wahhabism is shown in three features: the movement's universalistic message, the anti-nomadic content of that message, and the fact that the notion of a central state was the driving force behind it. The anti-nomadic attitude is the least-recognized attribute in the literature, even though this attitude is plainly displayed in the letters of Shaikh ibn Abd al-Wahhab. In those letters he consistently decries the religious conditions among the nomadic tribes. More than once, the shaikh declares that the life of the nomadic people is conducted on the basis of norms that flagrantly violate the basic principles of Islam. The shaikh says that the nomadic people deny, among other things, the day of judgment and the inheritance right of women. In doing so, according to the shaikh, they have committed apostasy and become *kuffar* (disbelievers).[40] Although the shaikh did not explicitly say so, it is clear that, for him, the deterioration of religious conditions among those tribes was related to their nomadic mode of living. Accordingly, bringing them back to abide by the *sharia* (Islamic law) required that they first abandon their nomadic way of life and settle in towns. And this signifies a *hadari* (urban) predisposition on the part of the movement's leader.

The second theme is that although Wahhabism was a religious movement, its origins were not religious at all. The movement's nature and its role, especially in the process that led to the establishment of the state, cannot be limited to the field of religion. On the contrary, the Wahhabi movement was multidimensional, both a religious and a political movement. True, it was on the basis of religion that once again the concept of the state was rejuvenated in the Arabian Peninsula, providing the political and the ideological forces to push the process forward. However, in playing such a tremendous role, religion was playing a unique role, and operating in a unique context. In central Arabia of the eighteenth century, religion was so hegemonic that it was the only source for education, discourse, and law. For the society to express itself, it had to do so through religious terms, religious symbols, and religious reasoning. In such a context, any political and social themes are often articulated through religious terms.

That the political, social, and religious themes in Najd at the time were so overlapping must be taken into consideration when studying the Wahhabiyya. It could be argued that, with religion enjoying such a hegemonic position to shape the cultural and political outlook of the Najdi society, the Wahhabiyya must have originated in a religious environment, and naturally assumed a religious nature and a religious role too. But this is misleading, for three reasons. First, it takes things at face value. Second, it is reductionist in its crudest form, in that it reduces the whole dynamics of the society and its culture to one dimension. Third, it dismisses out of hand the possibility that religion in this case was acting as an agent for other social and political forces in the society. In this sense, the religious discourse of the society, and in the movement at the time, have a subterranean text to them that needs to be brought to the surface. In other words, to limit the movement to its religious dimension is really to say nothing in the end.

In fact, religion was not the force from which other factors derived their dynamic in the process. On the contrary, religion was operating in a context from which it derived its dynamic and force. The third and most crucial theme of the alternative relates to the processes of tribal settlement, resettlement, and disintegration, the rise of the phenomenon of the Najdi towns, the spread of religious learning, or *fiqh,* and the growth of the towns into politically autonomous entities.[41] These social and political processes, operating in parallel, constituted the most salient feature of the history of central Arabia just before the rise of the Wahhabi movement. Historically, it was at the end of these rather tumultuous transformations that the Wahhabiyya was born. The turning point in those processes, and the most relevant for the rise of Wahhabism, was the drastic change in the patterns of settlement around the fifteenth century. First there was the pattern of "collective settlement," in which a tribe or a confederation of tribes would settle collectively as a tribal group. The population of each settlement in this case was drawn almost wholly from the same tribe. After that came the pattern of "dispersive settlement," in which members of the already settled tribes, especially families, would disperse and resettle.

The most distinct difference between the two patterns is that in the earlier pattern it was the tribe that was performing the act of settlement. In the later, dispersive settlement, this process was completely reversed. It was mostly families, departed from their tribes and roaming outside their tribal territories, that were looking for new settlement sites.[42] Thus the tribes disintegrated into smaller units as families scattered and territorial unity broke down.[43] As a result, the old society, based on the collective and unified structure of the tribe, gave way to a new society whose structure was primarily predicated on the family.[44] In the process, the *hadari* community of the autonomous towns came to replace the community of the tribes.[45]

It was this drastic and decisive change that paved the way for the Wahhabi movement to become a decisive political and social force thereafter. The movement came as a culmination of those long and interfaced processes, all of which were urban-instigated. The coming of the Wahhabiyya at that point was not an interruption. It was a continuity that carried on the process, pushing it to its logical conclusion. Settlement, resettlement, and the rise of the autonomous towns all were phases in state formation. Those phases took place almost simultaneously, and preceded the rise of the Wahhabi movement by almost 300 years.

Coming back to the notion that the Wahhabiyya was the second religious intervention, emphasizing *tawhid* (ideology) rather than *fiqh* (religious learning), shows that the movement's appearance was a sign that state formation was reaching an advanced phase of maturity in central Arabia. The mechanism of *fiqh* in the earlier religious intervention was needed to adjudicate legal problems arising from the earlier pattern of settlement. Ideology, on the other hand, came to meet the state's need for mobilization and legitimacy. And that is precisely where the political maturity manifested itself. If we are to reconstruct the historical trajectory that led to the Wahhabiyya and the first Saudi state, it would look like this: the collective pattern of settlement, dispersal, and disintegration of the tribe; the rise of the *hadari* community; the rise of the autonomous towns; the first religious intervention, based on *fiqh;* the second religious intervention, based on *tawhid* (the Wahhabiyya); and then the rise of the state.

By representing political maturity in the process, the Wahhabiyya brought the notion of the state to replace that of the tribe as the unifying force for the society. That process had been in operation for a long time, indicating that the Wahhabiyya was not an immediate or a coincidental response to the moment. Nor in this sense was the movement a reaction to a phenomenon of *shirk* or a replay of the old nomadic and tribal game. On the contrary, it continued the state formation process, giving it a new direction, and as such was a new force ushering in a new political era in the history of Arabia. By launching the notion of a central state, the appearance of the Wahhabi movement marked the beginning of the modern history of Arabia.

▨   Notes

1. The name of the movement in Arabic is "Al-Harakah al-Wahhabiyya." Its most common name in the literature is "Wahhabism." But because the movement's name in its original country, Saudi Arabia, is "Wahhabiyya," the latter will generally be used in this chapter.

2. Khalid al-Dakhil, *Social Origins of the Wahhabi Movement* (Los Angeles: University of California Press, 1998).

3. In the aftermath of September 11, 2001, the Wahhabiyya has become again a subject of political and ideological controversy. For some it is identified with terrorism. But the Wahhabiyya remains a state ideology that forbids any form of violent opposition to the ruler. Still, the Wahhabiyya cannot escape the effects of political Islam, nor the effects of terrorism. This is a new development that deserves to be treated on its own. The goal in this chapter is to try to come to grips with the original meaning and significance of the movement.

4. Michael Cook, "The Expansion of the First Saudi State: The Case of Washm," in *The Islamic World: From Classical to Modern Times,* edited by C. F. Bosworth, C. Issawi, R. Savory, and A. Udovitch (Princeton: Darwin, 1989), p. 676.

5. The religious thesis originated in the Wahhabi sources, primarily the writings of Shaikh ibn Abd al-Wahhab and his early disciples and followers. This section of the chapter relies on the writings of ibn Abd al-Wahhab, ibn Ghannam, and ibn Bishr. Variations of this thesis can be found in other non-Wahhabi sources, both Muslim and non-Muslim, as well. See, for example, Bernard Lewis, *The Crisis of Islam* (New York: Modern Library, 2003); David Commins, *The Wahhabi Mission and Saudi Arabia* (London: Tauris, 2006); Natana J. DeLong-Bas, *Wahhabi Islam: From Revival and Reform to Global Jihad* (New York: Oxford University Press, 2004).

6. Hussein ibn Ghannam, *Tarikh Najd,* edited by Nassir Addin al-Asad (Beirut: Shorouq International, 1985); Uthman ibn Bishr, *Unwan Almajd Fi Tarikh Najd* (Riyadh: Darat Almalik Abdul-Aziz, 1982).

7. ibn Ghannam, *Tarikh Najd,* p. 7.

8. Ibid., pp. 13–14.

9. ibn Bishr, *Unwan Almajd Fi Tarikh Najd,* pp. 33–34.

10. Ibid.

11. Muhammad ibn Abd al-Wahhab, *Kashf Ashubuhat,* translated by Mualafat Ash-Sheikh al-Immam Muhammad ibn Abd al-Wahhab (Riyadh: Islamic University of Imam Muhammad ibn Saud, n.d.), pp. 46–47, 50–53, 145–147, 155–157. The same idea with the same reasoning epitomizes the central theme around which all the writings of the shaikh revolve.

12. At the time, the most distinct political characteristic of Najd was the existence of separate and autonomous towns, each ruled by the founding family, or group of families, known as the *rou'asa* (chiefs). For more information on how these towns were established, see, for instance, Abdullah ibn Khamis, *Mu'jam al-Yamamah,* 2nd ed. (Riyadh: al-Farazdaq Press, 1980), esp. vol. 1, pp. 96, 193, 202, 264, 333–334, and vol. 2, pp. 29, 74, 96–97. Also see Ibrahim ibn Issa, *Tarikh Badhul Hawadith Alwaqiah Fi Najd* (Riyadh: Dar al-Yamamah, 1966), pp. 30–31, 50–51.

13. See the accounts of how the shaikh moved from Al-Oyaiynah to Al-Diriyya in ibn Ghannam, *Tarikh Najd,* pp. 84–88; and in ibn Bishr, *Unwan Almajd Fi Tarikh Najd,* pp. 38–43.

14. Abdulrahman Al-Qassim, ed., *Addurar Al-Saniya fi Alajwibati Annajdiya,* 16 volumes (Riyadh: no publisher, 2004), vol. 9, p. 6.

15. Ibid., p. 61.

16. Ibid., p. 84.

17. Many citations, especially those attributed to the Prophet Muhammad, stressing that the obligation of a Muslim to obey the ruler is an integral part of his obligations toward God, are detailed in ibid., vol. 9, pp. 10–13, 92–93.

18. Ibid., vol. 9, pp. 6–8, 23–29.

19. The main feature in all pre-Wahhabi sources is their constant account of political struggles within the Najdi towns, wars among the towns, assassinations, cyclical

droughts, and so forth. See, for instance, Ahmad al-Manqour, *Tarikh al-Manqour,* edited by Abdulaziz al-Khuwaiter (Riyadh: General Secretariat for Celebrating the Centennial of the Kingdom of Saudia Arabia, 1999); Muhammad ibn Rabiah, *Tarikh ibn Rabiah,* edited by Abdullah Ashible (Riyadh: Annadi al-Adabi, 1986).

20. ibn Bishr, *Unwan Almajd Fi Tarikh Najd,* pp. 38, 42. Also see ibn Ghannam, *Tarikh Najd,* vol. 1, p. 87. In the narrative of both sources, the shaikh was campaigning for the creation of a state in Najd.

21. For the views of the shaikh, see ibn Ghannam, *Tarikh Najd,* pp. 360–393; Muhammad ibn Abd al-Wahhab, *Ar-Rasaeil Ash-Shakhsiyah,* vol. 5 in the series *Mualafat Ash-Sheikh al-Imam Muhammad ibn Abd al-Wahhab* (Riyadh: Islamic University of Imam Muhammad ibn Saud, n.d.). For the view of his brother, who was one of the prominent opponents, see Suleiman ibn Abd al-Wahhab, *Al-Sawaiq al-Ilahiyyah Fi al-Radd Ala al-Wahhabiyyah* (Istanbul: Library of Ishiq, 1975).

22. References to *shirk* cases outside of Najd are an established pattern in the shaikh's letters. See instances in ibn Ghannam, *Tarikh Najd,* pp. 81, 83–84, 244, 335.

23. ibn Bishr, *Unwan Almajd Fi Tarikh Najd,* pp. 33–34. The manifestations of *shirk* that ibn Bisher enumerates here suggests that *shirk* in the Wahhabi sources refers almost exclusively to these types of behavior.

24. Lewis, *Crisis of Islam,* p. 121.

25. Consider this rather propagandist statement: "Wherever they [the Wahhabis] could they enforced their beliefs with the utmost severity and ferocity, demolishing tombs, desecrating what they called false idolatrous and holy places, slaughtering large numbers of men, women, and children who failed to meet their standards of Islamic purity." Lewis, *Crisis of Islam,* p. 122.

26. Aziz al-Azmeh, *Islams and Modernities* (London: Verso, 1966), p. 144.

27. See Aziz al-Azmeh, "Wahhabite Polity," in *Arabia and the Gulf: From Traditional Society to Modern States,* edited by Ian R. Netton (London: Croom Helm, 1986), p. 76.

28. Mas'ud Dahir, *Al-Mashriq al-Arabi al-Muasir: Min al-Badawah Ila al-Dawlah al-Hadithah* (Beirut: Mahad al-Inma al-Arabi, 1986). This entire book is an example of poor history; for the present purpose, see chap. 4, on the Saudi state.

29. Ibid., p. 273.

30. Bassam Tibi, *Arab Nationalism,* 3rd ed. (New York: Macmillan, 1997), pp. 88–89, emphasis added. Here, Tibi follows in the footsteps of his German mentor, Richard Hartman, in describing the Wahhabi movement in the same terms. Tibi does not cite any source, primary or secondary, on that movement. Further, he always borrows his conclusions from the German scholar, indicating that his understanding of the movement and its role are based on the findings of Hartman. Therefore, it appears that Tibi is not directly informed about the Wahhabi movement, and thus his views about it are not his own, but borrowed from the insights of others.

31. Tibi is showing here his ignorance of the movement, its history, and the history of the Arabian Peninsula as a whole. Tibi, *Arab Nationalism,* p. 89. The "House of Saud" were not then the rulers of the Arabian Peninsula. They were merely the rulers of the town of Al-Diriyya. And at that time, they were not known as the "House of Saud," Rather, the ruling branch in Al-Diriyya was known as the "al-Miqrin."

32. Islam was not a product of a nomadic environment. The urban roots and characteristics of Islam are no longer controversial. These issues were settled decades ago. Of the earliest works to call attention to this point was Eric Wolf, "The Social Organization of Mecca and the Origins of Islam," *Southwestern Journal of Anthropology* 7, no. 4 (1951).

33. In quoting Shaikh ibn Abd al-Wahhab, Tibi resorts to a German text by Hartman, instead of quoting the shaikh directly. As a result, the shaikh is quoted anachronistically as being part of the attack on "modernization" and "modernism." According

to Hartman, on the authority of Tibi, the shaikh once said, "I believe that the modernists have broken their link with the community and have cut themselves off from it. . . . I declare that every innovation in religious matters is modernism." Tibi, *Arab Nationalism,* p. 89.

34. Abdullah A. al-Bassam, *Ulama Najd Khillal Thamaniyat Qurun* (Riyadh: Dar al-Aasima, 1998). According to al-Bassam, the education of the Najdi ulama before the Wahhabi movement was almost exclusively limited to the field of *fiqh,* and they rarely ventured into other fields like *tafsir, hadeeth,* or *tawhid.*

35. Ghassan Salame, "Strong States and Weak States: A Qualified Return to the Muqaddimah," in *The Arab State,* edited by Giacomo Luciani (Berkeley: University of California Press, 1990), p. 34.

36. Ibid., pp. 35–36.

37. See al-Manqour, *Tarikh al-Manqour,* p. 56; Muhammad O. al-Fakhri, *Tarikh al-Fakhri,* edited by Abdullah al-Shible (Riyadh: General Secretariat for Celebrating the Centennial of the Kingdom of Saudi Arabia, 1999), p. 124; ibn Abd al-Wahhab, *Ar-Rasaeil Ash-Shakhsiyah,* p. 83. In these sources the last name used in referring to any member of this family is "al-Nuqrin."

38. ibn Issa, *Tarikh Badhul Hawadith Alwaqiah Fi Najd,* pp. 35–38; Hamad al-Jassir, "Ibn Arabi" (unpublished, 1993), p. 241. "Al-Yamamah" is an old name of Najd.

39. ibn Ghannam, *Tarikh Najd,* pp. 84–86; ibn Bishr, *Unwan Almajd Fi Tarikh Najd,* pp. 38–40.

40. ibn Abd al-Wahhab, *Ar-Rasaeil Ash-Shakhsiyah,* pp. 41, 209.

41. For more details and analysis of the processes of settlement and resettlement, see al-Dakhil, *Social Origins of the Wahhabi Movement,* chaps. 4–6.

42. al-Dakhil, *Social Origins of the Wahhabi Movement,* p. 154.

43. Ibid., p. 155.

44. All sources indicate that all the new towns were built and inhabited by families from different tribes. See ibn Issa, *Tarikh Badhul Hawadith Alwaqiah Fi Najd,* pp. 29–38. Here ibn Issa recounts how some of these towns were built, and by whom. He also indicates that family name started to become prominent, replacing tribal name.

45. al-Dakhil, *Social Origins of the Wahhabi Movement,* pp. 177–181.

4

Contestation and Authority in Wahhabi Polemics

David Commins

When Muhammad ibn Abd al-Wahhab launched his mission, he encountered stiff resistance from the ulama in Arabia and nearby lands. His views on monotheism and idolatry clashed with customary doctrine, so it was natural that scholars would refute them in epistles and treatises. According to the Saudi chronicles, his opponents chased him out of Basra and the Najdi town of Huraymila before he found political backing from the chief of Al-Uyayna. That backing proved short-lived and he had to move yet again, this time settling in Al-Diriyya, where he gained the support of its chief, Muhammad ibn Saud. In the next half century, ibn Abd al-Wahhab established his doctrine and implemented his vision of proper religious practice wherever Saudi power held sway. Indeed, he purged Najd of ulama opposed to his teaching and installed in their place men loyal to his doctrine. In achieving doctrinal hegemony, the Wahhabi movement forged a distinctive religious tradition that marked a rupture with Najd's historical tradition of religious scholarship and that built up its own mechanisms for asserting and maintaining its authority.

The Saudi conquest of Najd took decades to accomplish, and in its course, ulama waged a polemical campaign against the upstart movement. These same ulama belonged to a larger scholastic network encompassing Hijaz, Al-Hasa, Iraq, and Syria. Najdi shaikhs urged colleagues in Baghdad, Mecca, and Al-Hasa to rebut ibn Abd al-Wahhab, and Wahhabi authors dispatched epistles throughout Najd to vindicate their views. The critics of Muhammad ibn Abd al-Wahhab developed a repertoire of arguments to prove his errors on matters of excommunication *(takfir)* and idolatry *(shirk);* he and his successors responded with their own counterarguments to demonstrate that they were the ones adhering to the Quran and the Sunna. It seems almost inevitable that given the stalemate at the level of proof-texts, one side would denigrate the other's capacity for properly understanding God's word and the Prophet's tradition. Thus, very early in the formation of anti-Wahhabi discourse arose the accusation that Muhammad ibn Abd al-Wahhab lacked the scholarly credentials to draw conclusions from Islam's basic texts, and that it was his deficiency in this area that led him to erroneous views. As the polemical exchange persisted, it acquired a dimension that centered on the scholarly capacity of ibn Abd al-Wahhab, and that question became part of opposing narratives about his life.

In recent times, Wahhabi ulama have responded to an entirely different kind of challenge to the authority of their discourse. In the 1960s and 1970s, the writings and views of Muslim Brotherhood authors such as Sayyid Qutb gained a following in Saudi Arabia and the rest of the Muslim world. Even though the Wahhabi establishment endorsed the al-Saud's political alliance with the Muslim Brotherhood and related movements, the clerical leaders did not entirely approve of the Brotherhood's outlook. In fact, clerical leaders have expressed sharp criticism of major figures in the Brotherhood, like Qutb and Hasan al-Banna, and of Saudi ulama whose writings bear their imprint, like Salman al-Awdah.[1]

The Formation of a New Scholastic Tradition

In the two centuries preceding the rise of Wahhabism, religious scholarship in Najd was an extension of the early modern scholastic traditions of ulama in Cairo, Damascus, and the holy cities. The most eminent Najdi ulama were men who traveled to those cities as pupils in pursuit of learning. On their return, they transmitted the cosmopolitan scholastic tradition to central Arabia's oasis settlements. Thus, one of the earliest known religious scholars of Najd, Shaikh Ahmad ibn Yahya ibn Atwa (d. 1541), studied in Damascus with its prominent Hanbali teachers. When he returned from Syria, he became the most influential teacher of his era.[2] Ottoman Arab ulama exerted influence on Najd through their written works as well: Najdi ulama sought copies of manuscripts held in Damascus and Cairo to use in lessons. Furthermore, Arabian scholars wrote to their counterparts seeking fatwas on knotty issues.[3] To underscore the direction of cultural influence, the sources record no instances of religious pupils traveling from Syria or Egypt to Najd. It is true that most Najdi ulama followed the Hanbali *madhhab,* whereas Ottoman Arab ulama mostly followed the Shafii and Hanafi *madhhab*s, but there were Maliki and Hanafi ulama in Najd as well. Furthermore, Ottoman Hanbalism did not exhibit a tone of doctrinal rigor to set it apart from the other Sunni schools, a point on which scholars commonly stumble by anachronistically projecting Wahhabi doctrine onto all Hanbalis. Ottoman Hanbalism coexisted easily with other legal schools and counted devotees of Sufism among its foremost scholars.[4]

Well into the eighteenth century, Najdi and Ottoman ulama adhered to a religious outlook characterized by Sunni pluralism—coexistence among the legal schools and various Sufi orders. By 1800, the Wahhabis had remade Najdi scholastic life. Ottoman mosques and madrasas were no longer esteemed by Najdis as the cradles of authoritative learning but as incubators of idolatry. Ambitious Najdi religious pupils turned away from Ottoman towns and headed to Al-Diriyya.[5] Ulama who rejected Muhammad ibn Abd al-Wahhab's doctrinal views came under pressure to emigrate from Arabia when their towns fell to Saudi forces; they dispersed to Iraq and Hijaz, where they formed enclaves hostile to Wahhabi doctrine.[6] The upshot was a remaking of Najdi religious culture on the basis of allegiance to ibn Abd al-Wahhab's teachings.

Presiding over the reproduction of those teachings were the descendants of Muhammad ibn Abd al-Wahhab, collectively known as the Al al-Shaikh. When he retired from public life around 1773, he passed the mantle of religious leadership to his son Abdullah (1752–1826), whose daily lesson on quranic exegesis after the Friday noon prayer was attended by the Saudi ruler.[7] Each of Shaikh Muhammad's sons—Abdullah, Ali, Husayn, and Ibrahim—taught at a small school near their homes in Al-Diriyya.[8] In 1818, Shaikh Abdullah witnessed the first Saudi state's destruction and suffered exile to Cairo, where he died. The triumphant Ottoman-Egyptian forces exiled other members of the Al al-Shaikh as well, but with the revival of Saudi fortunes in the 1820s, one of Shaikh Muhammad's grandsons, Abd al-Rahman ibn Hasan, made his way from Egypt to Riyadh to reestablish the Wahhabi call. Religious leadership and authority to appoint mosque officials, teachers, and qadis remained in Al al-Shaikh hands well into the twentieth century. Given the prominence of kinship in Arabian culture, it seemed natural that religious leadership should remain the prerogative of the Al al-Shaikh, and it was reinforced by the scholarly achievement of individual members.[9] Thus, Abdullah ibn Muhammad ibn Abd al-Wahhab composed a number of influential theological and polemical works, and Al al-Shaikh leaders of the nineteenth century extended the doctrinal core with commentaries on *The Book of God's Unity* and further refinements of polemical arguments.[10]

Muhammad ibn Abd al-Wahhab and his descendants provided the leadership and the canon for the new scholastic culture of Najd, but it also needed a cadre of lieutenants to preach the doctrine. In the Saudi realm, Al-Diriyya and Riyadh attracted pupils; at the same time, fewer traveled to Ottoman lands for study, because securing positions as preachers, teachers, and judges required study under Wahhabi shaikhs. It is possible to trace this development with some exactness. In the second half of the eighteenth century, eighteen men traveled to Al-Diriyya to study, and all but one became qadis under the first Saudi state.[11] A similar trend occurred in the nineteenth century. Ten Najdi ulama born in the first quarter of the century went to Riyadh for religious studies, and nine of them became qadis under the second Saudi state.[12] Thirteen men from the same generation traveled to Ottoman centers to study: just three of them became Saudi qadis, whereas seven were clearly not Wahhabi; one settled permanently at Zubayr (a center of anti-Wahhabism).[13] The image that emerges is one where authority radiated from the Al al-Shaikh through their pupils to provincial towns at the same time that Najdis with Ottoman ties departed, resulting in the decline of study tours to Syria and Iraq.

If the Wahhabi mission's "staff" consisted of leaders from the Al al-Shaikh and their pupils, the "stuff" of the mission lay in its doctrine. Muhammad ibn Abd al-Wahhab's works gave Najdi religious scholarship a distinctive accent. In addition, the emphasis in religious writings shifted from a preponderance of jurisprudence to a closer balance between jurisprudence and doctrine. Mayy al-Isa reviewed religious writings for the period 1490–1740 and found twenty-seven works written by ten authors.[14] Within this small sample, sixteen items dealt with jurisprudence and only four dealt with doctrine. The jurisprudence works provided religious judges with practical guidance for such common matters as pilgrimage rites, religious endowments, and the like. Some of them fell into the genre of commentaries and abridgments of texts by earlier Hanbali authors from the central Arab lands. The most common sort of work was the compilation of fatwas.

Al-Isa's survey of religious writing in Muhammad ibn Abd al-Wahhab's lifetime reveals significant changes.[15] First, he dominated cultural production (at least in terms of treatises that have survived to the present). About half the treatises he wrote concern doctrine, one-quarter concern jurisprudence, and the remainder concern quranic exegesis, hadith, and other fields. While his doctrinal works broke with the Ottoman consensus, his works on jurisprudence hewed to custom, with abridgments of classic Hanbali works and a commentary on the same works that served as references for Hanbalis in Damascus and Cairo. Even a treatise on independent reasoning in jurisprudence *(ijtihad)* that is in the published collection of ibn Abd al-Wahhab's writings is not his original composition but an excerpt from medieval Hanbali author ibn al-Qayyim.[16] The effort to establish ibn Abd al-Wahhab's views on doctrine as dominant in Najd was successful, as only one doctrinal work from the pen of a contemporary Najdi opponent (his brother, Sulayman) has survived. In the nineteenth century, ibn Abd al-Wahhab's epigones dominated cultural production.[17] His son and grandson wrote eleven of thirteen doctrinal works from that period. Jurisprudence remained in "second place" after doctrine, with eight works composed during that period. The redefinition of doctrine had no impact on approaches to legal method and opinion, as Wahhabis used the same texts by ibn Qudama, al-Hajjawi, and their commentators as earlier Najdi ulama did.[18]

Commentaries on ibn Abd al-Wahhab's writings form another aspect of Najd's distinctive scholastic tradition. These commentaries, authored by his descendants, reinforced the authority of core ideas in *The Book of God's Unity* by broadening their textual foundations and expanding the discussion of proof-texts. In one collection of Wahhabi writings, ibn Abd al-Wahhab's foundational essay is 75 pages long, while his grandson Abd al-Rahman ibn Hasan's commentary on the essay covers more than 250 pages.[19] In commenting on one chapter, Abd al-Rahman buttressed the basic argument by paraphrasing its quranic verses, citing other verses with similar meanings, and referring to classical authorities like ibn Taymiyya, ibn Kathir, and ibn al-Qayyim.[20] This specimen of commentary indicates that the reproduction of Wahhabi discourse entailed, in one respect, the accumulation of additional layers of proof-texts and their discussion on top of the foundational texts.

By the mid-nineteenth century, the Wahhabi movement had thoroughly refashioned the scholastic culture of Najd, establishing new centers of learning, religious leadership, doctrine and canonical works, consensus on their authority, and patterns of travel by religious students. Saudi political power preserved this arrangement in Najd, but outside of that domain, anti-Wahhabi writers continued the polemical campaign that had accompanied the rise of the movement in the 1740s.

Challenging Muhammad ibn Abd al-Wahhab's Scholarly Authority

One of the early treatises against Muhammad ibn Abd al-Wahhab came from the pen of his own brother, Sulayman, himself a religious scholar.[21] Much of his treatise consists of point-by-point rebuttals of Shaikh Muhammad's views on idolatry and unbelief, but he begins by asserting that his brother lacked the qualifications to draw his own conclusions on such matters because he was not a *mujtahid,* an expert in religious sciences whose opinions believers may follow. Sulayman ibn Abd al-Wahhab cited Abu Bakr al-Harawi on the eleven qualifications of a *mujtahid,* including expertise in Arabic, quranic sciences, hadiths, *fiqh* (religious learning), and personal qualities (piety and honesty). If an individual lacked any one of these qualities, then he was not a *mujtahid.* To reinforce the point from the perspective of the Hanbali school, Sulayman cited Ahmad ibn Hanbal as stating that one must have memorized 400,000 hadiths to be a *faqih* (jurist). Sulayman contended that his brother lacked the qualifications for doing *ijtihad* and issuing fatwas. Even though ibn Abd al-Wahhab did not possess a single trait required for *ijtihad,* his opinion was popular with many uneducated folk. If challenged to discuss his views with scholars, he refused. Instead, he forced people to accept his opinions and asserted that whoever disagreed with him was an infidel. Essentially, according to Sulayman, ibn Abd al-Wahhab excommunicated Muslims and declared that he could do so on the basis of *ijtihad.* But his scholarly deficiency led him to repeat the same mistake committed by the Kharijites in early Islamic times, namely applying verses of the Quran to believers that rightly pertain to polytheists and People of the Book. Thus, Shaikh Muhammad famously declared the people of his time to be like the idolaters of the Prophet Muhammad's era.[22]

When it came to the crucial matter of setting a standard for discerning who was a Muslim and who was not, Sulayman cited hadiths to maintain that professing the *shahada* and performing the other pillars of Islam make one a believer. He also adduced a hadith about a slave woman who came before the Prophet seeking manumission. The Prophet asked her, "Where is Allah?" She replied, "In the heavens." Then he asked her, "Who am I?" She replied, "Allah's messenger." Then the Prophet concluded that she was a believer and was to be freed. As further evidence, Sulayman cited ibn al-Qayyim's view that, according to general Muslim agreement, if an infidel recited the *shahada*, then he had entered Islam.[23]

The essential issue was Muhammad ibn Abd al-Wahhab's view that most Muslims of his time were infidels. Sulayman asked his brother the origin of his idea that he could declare as infidels those who recited the *shahada*, performed the five prayers, paid zakat, fasted, undertook the hajj, believed in Allah, the angels, books, and messengers, and followed Islam's laws. How could he make their lands the Abode of War? What authoritative religious scholar (imam) had ever made such a claim? Pursuing the question of excommunication, Sulayman contended that his brother declared to be an infidel anyone who ascribed an associate to Allah. Sulayman agreed that the act of *shirk* made one an infidel, and that the Quran declared that Allah did not forgive *shirk*. But how could his brother categorize Muslims as polytheists for acts that he personally found objectionable? Through his own reasoning, not from any previous authority. Sulayman had already demonstrated that his brother lacked the qualifications to reach independent conclusions, and he noted that the follower *(muqallid)* could not rule on excommunication except in conformity to the categories established by the *mujtahids*. Therefore, he asked his brother if he could support his position by referring to consensus or the opinion of an authentic *mujtahid*.[24]

Because Muhammad ibn Abd al-Wahhab argued in his writings that *shirk* was prevalent in Najd, Sulayman had to address the question of how scholars defined *shirk*. He asserted that this was a matter that only scholars qualified for *ijtihad* could determine, and if they reached a consensus, then no one could depart from it. If Muhammad had a clear explanation from a scholar, then he should set it forth, and he (Sulayman) would obey it. Otherwise, Muslims were obliged to follow the consensus. So what was Muhammad's position? He asserted that even if someone professed the *shahada*, various practices could still render that person an idolater. Thus, calling on or making a vow to a dead soul, sacrificing to a being other than Allah, or seeking blessing by touching a tomb or taking soil from the ground nearby, were major acts of *shirk,* which removed the safeguard on one's blood and property. Sulayman argued that Muhammad had absolutely no authority for that position, and that the umma agreed that such judgments were the province of those with the rank of unrestricted *mujtahid.*[25]

It is well known that Muhammad ibn Abd al-Wahhab derived many of his positions on *shirk* from the writings of ibn Taymiyya and ibn al-Qayyim. Sulayman admitted that the two scholars indeed considered these practices to be *shirk,* and he agreed that it was proper to follow their position on the matter. The problem was that ibn Taymiyya and ibn al-Qayyim did not declare that these practices constituted major acts of *shirk* that resulted in removing one from the ranks of believers or that rendered the place where they occurred as a land of apostasy. Rather, they forbade such practices and placed them into the category of minor acts of *shirk.* Moreover, they maintained that these acts did not result in excommunication until individuals who performed them were presented with proof that they were guilty of *shirk.*[26]

Divine Inspiration and Muhammad ibn Abd al-Wahhab's Authority

Wahhabi ulama and their adversaries pursued their dispute during the nineteenth century. One critic who aroused the ire of Wahhabi ulama was Uthman ibn Mansur, an alim who served the second Saudi emirate as a qadi and composed a favorable commentary on *The Book of God's Unity.* It seems that he turned against the Najdi movement after studying in Iraq.[27] He wrote a treatise that prompted one of Muhammad ibn Abd al-Wahhab's grandsons to compose a brief history of the Wahhabi mission.[28] Shaikh Abd al-Rahman ibn Hasan was a pivotal figure in restoring the Wahhabi mission under the second Saudi state. He was already a young man at the time of Al-Diriyya's destruction in 1818, and he spent the next eight years in Cairo, where he studied at the Azhar. When Emir Turki gained power in Riyadh in 1824, Abd al-Rahman made his way there and led the religious establishment for the next forty years.[29]

Uthman ibn Mansur's offending treatise no longer exists, so Abd al-Rahman's essay *Al-Maqamat* is the only available source for it. Judging by Abd al-Rahman's work, ibn Mansur reiterated the charge that Muhammad ibn Abd al-Wahhab lacked scholarly training in Islamic sciences. Abd al-Rahman noted that ibn Mansur himself had no direct acquaintance with the details of Shaikh Muhammad's life and had merely parroted what some of his teachers in Iraq had told him. Abd al-Rahman used his essay as an occasion to vindicate his ancestor. He began the story of his grandfather's life with Sulayman ibn Ali, Shaikh Muhammad's own grandfather and the most famous jurist in Najd of his era. Among this man's pupils were his own sons, Abd al-Wahhab and Ibrahim, the first of whom became a respected qadi and the second an itinerant jurist who issued rulings on property transactions. Muhammad ibn Abd al-Wahhab, then, was raised in a family of scholarly distinction. Abd al-Rahman characterized Shaikh Muhammad's early education at home and in Medina as one focused on jurisprudence, until he traveled to Basra in order to learn more about quranic exegesis and hadith sciences. According to Abd al-Rahman, it was during Muhammad ibn Abd al-Wahhab's stay in Basra that he arrived at his critical insight. While ibn Abd al-Wahhab was studying with the town's ulama, God revealed to him aspects of His unity and attributes that had been hidden from others. It was this special divine inspiration that set Shaikh Muhammad apart from other scholars of his time and moved him to compose *The Book of God's Unity,* on the basis of hadith collections he found in Basra. Abd al-Rahman did not dryly impart this narrative, but spiced it with sarcastic asides that diminished ibn Mansur's learning. He remarked that ibn Mansur had boasted that he had met with leading scholars during his study tour in Basra and nearby Zubayr, but that in fact he had nothing to boast about, as he had gained no knowledge given his acceptance of the views of three slanderous anti-Wahhabi shaikhs.[30]

Muhammad ibn Abd al-Wahhab's next destination for study was Al-Hasa, where he sought the guidance of Abdullah ibn Fayruz and discovered the works of ibn Taymiyya and ibn al-Qayyim. Abd al-Rahman emphasized a tale of Shaikh Muhammad's perspicacious understanding of theology, as a demonstration of the new insight the shaikh had acquired during his stay in Basra. According to Abd al-Rahman, this episode in his grandfather's life was so widely known in Al-Hasa and Najd that ibn Mansur could not deny it except out of sheer enmity toward the mission. Shaikh Muhammad then returned to Basra (we do not learn what happened on this visit), and then headed home to Najd before undertaking the pilgrimage to Mecca. While performing the holy rite, God revealed to him the truth concerning the violation of God's unity when people worshipped objects instead of Him. Upon completing the pilgrimage, Shaikh Muhammad stopped at Al-Multazim and asked God to make religion clear once again through his own mission and to grant him acceptance from people. He joined a caravan bound for Syria via Medina, but a band of thieves robbed and battered him, forcing him to abandon his aspiration to study in Damascus. Instead, Shaikh Muhammad stopped in Medina, studied hadith and other Islamic sciences, and finally returned to Najd, where he found people committing idolatry by worshipping dead holy men, jinn, trees, and stones—a condition unpleasing to God. At that point, Muhammad ibn Abd al-Wahhab began his mission to call on others to devote all worship to God alone.[31]

An Anti-Wahhabi Biographical Dictionary

Abd al-Rahman ibn Hasan's account stands out for attributing his grandfather's doctrine to two instances of divine inspiration, at Basra and at Al-Multazim. The other early narratives from Saudi chroniclers ibn Ghannam and ibn Bishr make no comparable claim. Naturally, the anti-Wahhabi camp did not admit the possibility of divine intervention. Throughout the nineteenth century, its partisans reiterated Sulayman ibn Abd al-Wahhab's denial of his brother Muhammad's qualification for *ijtihad*. One critic gave the debate a new twist by denying the Wahhabi movement any place in the Hanbali scholastic tradition, in essence suggesting that Wahhabi ulama suffered from collective deficiency.

Muhammad ibn Abdullah ibn Humayd's biographical dictionary of Hanbali ulama excluded just about all Wahhabis from Hanbali ranks.[32] Ibn Humayd achieved this in several ways. First, his selection of Arabian Hanbalis in Muhammad ibn Abd al-Wahhab's lifetime (1702–1792) included twenty-four individuals who were either strong opponents of the reform movement or neutral toward it. Likewise, his selection of twenty-one Arabian Hanbalis for the nineteenth century consisted largely of the movement's adversaries. Second, ibn Humayd included narratives about Hanbali scholars who performed miraculous feats *(karamat)*, embraced Sufism, and partook in practices (visiting the graves of holy men and the prophets) that the Wahhabis regarded as forms of idolatry.[33] Third, ibn Humayd included only two Wahhabi shaikhs, but in both instances he obscured the connections these men had to the Wahhabi movement. Fourth, the few passages that deal with the Wahhabis leave the impression that they were treacherous, murderous, heretics lacking scholastic talent. For instance, ibn Humayd repeated the familiar charge that Muhammad ibn Abd al-Wahhab's father had differed with his son on doctrine. Furthermore, ibn Humayd reported that ibn Abd al-Wahhab ordered the assassination of his brother Sulayman, but that the latter was rescued by a divine blessing *(baraka)*.[34]

Contemporary Assertions of Wahhabi Authority

Since the beginning of the twentieth century, the Muslim world's religious landscape has undergone enormous changes, but Wahhabi ulama have not modified their doctrine or the scholastic grounds of their authority. Two changes are directly relevant to the standing of Wahhabi authority. First, the devaluation of ulama authority has probably diminished the impact of traditional anti-Wahhabi discourses. Of course, that development has affected Wahhabi ulama as well. Second, the writings of lay Islamist activists and authors have challenged ulama learning. It is true that these latter seldom criticize the Wahhabis. Indeed, for several decades, Islamist activists and the Wahhabis joined to combat secular and Western influences. Nevertheless, the popularity of Islamist ideas among young Saudis alarmed senior Wahhabi shaikhs in the 1980s and 1990s.

The roots of modern Islamist influence in Saudi Arabia go back to the 1950s, when Saudi Arabia offered refuge to members of the Muslim Brotherhood fleeing persecution at the hands of Arab nationalist rulers in Egypt and Syria. At that time, the kingdom was taking its first steps to create a national education system, but few Saudis had the training to staff the new schools. Members of the Muslim Brotherhood stepped in to become teachers at all levels of education and seized the opportunity to spread their views in schools and universities. Muslim Brotherhood teachers and professors introduced their Saudi pupils to the writings of the movement's leading thinkers, including Egyptian writer Sayyid Qutb.

Qutb eschewed traditional scholastic reasoning for a subjective approach that made him an original thinker and may account for the popularity of his works with young people whose outlooks reflected those of mass education, not madrasa learning. Wahhabi scholars displayed a cool attitude toward Qutb's writings because they contained what these scholars considered grave errors in doctrine and offensive characterizations of the Prophet Muhammad's companions. The preeminent Wahhabi shaikh of the early 1990s, Abdullah Abd al-Aziz ibn Baz, publicly faulted Qutb. For instance, on a doctrinal point pertaining to God's unity, Qutb interpreted the Quran's description of God sitting on a throne as a metaphor for God's hegemony over creation. The Wahhabis insist on a literal interpretation and reject anything else as a distortion of God's word. Ibn Baz also objected to Qutb's discussion of the first Muslim civil war, in which Muawiya defeated Ali. According to Qutb, Muawiya prevailed by resorting to deception and bribery, whereas Ali refused to sink to that level. Ibn Baz called this a repulsive slander against Muawiya, one of the Prophet's companions. Another terrible mistake in Qutb's writing, according to ibn Baz, occurred in his commentary on the Quran. The Egyptian writer interpreted a passage about Moses to suggest it meant that he represented an impulsive, hot-tempered leader; ibn Baz considered this an unforgivable slight of a prophet. In general, the Wahhabi shaikh lamented Qutb's influence on young people who were enamored with his books because of his smooth style and ability to stir emotions. Ibn Baz argued that they contained so many gross errors that they could easily lead astray anyone lacking deep training in religious sciences. Prominent Wahhabi shaikhs considered Qutb's errors to stem from a lack of formal training in those sciences and underscored that he was a literary critic well-versed in contemporary studies, but certainly not a religious scholar, and that religious pupils should avoid his writings in favor of books by recognized ulama. Thus, Shaikh Salih ibn Fawzan declared that Qutb arrived at his erroneous view of all Muslims as infidels because, unlike the ulama, he was unqualified to derive rulings from the Quran and the Sunna.[35]

Efforts to establish the authority of the Wahhabi tradition now extend into cyberspace, with websites dedicated to deflecting customary anti-Wahhabi criticisms, taking swipes at Islamic political movements, and setting forth Wahhabi doctrine as the true salafi way. One example will serve to illustrate this phenomenon. The website salafipublications.com presents an annotated English translation of Muhammad ibn Abd al-Wahhab's *Kashf al-Shubuhat*.[36] This treatise has long formed a mainstay of Wahhabi instruction and propagation.[37] Of particular interest are the annotations alluding to Islamists. Thus the annotator comments on discussions of *tawhid al-mutabaa* and *tawhid al-hakimiyya*. The first pertains to a group that strictly follows the Sunna in worship and transactions. The latter refers to a narrow domain of politics and politicians—activists in Islamic political movements, such as the Muslim Brotherhood and the Islamic Liberation Party. The annotator expresses disdain for these groups because they share a commitment to "innovated" forms of politics and the ideas of "innovators" like Sayyid Qutb and Hasan al-Banna. Such groups pay attention to the rulers of Muslim countries and they completely ignore the "Straying Heretical Innovators and the sects and groups of innovation such as Ikhwaan and Tabligh." Furthermore, according to the annotator, these groups incite rebellion against rulers and thereby cause harm to innocent folk. Their actions can only result in the sort of calamity that befell Algeria in the 1990s or in extreme movements such as the "Revolutionary Takfiris," who resemble the Kharijites.[38]

In a later section, the annotator observes that even though the Wahhabi mission has been active for over 200 years, most Muslims still do not properly understand monotheism and idolatry. The ranks of the uneducated include such Muslim Brotherhood leaders as Hasan al-Banna, Mustafa al-Sibai, and Said al-Hawa. The annotator urges believers to ignore "innovators" like the "Qutubite" Salman al-Awdah. He accuses al-Awdah of fomenting "Bolshevite revolutions" in Muslim countries and belittling efforts to spread the call to monotheism. He also refers to Muhammad al-Masari as "at-Takfiri at-Tahriri" (an allusion to the Islamic Liberation Party). He blames al-Masari for denouncing Muhammad ibn Abd al-Wahhab as a simpleton and for charging Wahhabi cleric Abd al-Aziz ibn Baz with "coming close to kufr."

▓ Conclusion

Initially, Wahhabi authority depended on the formation of a new scholastic tradition that displaced central Arabia's established scholastic tradition. The purging of ulama who held divergent views minimized contestation of the

Wahhabis' authority. Consequently, ulama who shared Sulayman ibn Abd al-Wahhab's assessment of his brother's qualifications for *ijtihad* migrated to neighboring Ottoman lands, leaving behind a hegemonic Wahhabi regime. During the nineteenth century, Saudi rulers enforced the Wahhabi ulama's ban on their adversaries. Ibn Humayd's biographical dictionary gave a novel twist to the attack on Muhammad ibn Abd al-Wahhab's standing as a scholar, but the Wahhabi ulama's tight control over religious institutions barred such critiques from their realm.

The modern Saudi state, however, has opened the doors wide to millions of Muslim and thousands of non-Muslim workers in order to develop infrastructure, economic enterprises, administrative bodies, education, medicine, and so forth. Therefore, the condition of isolation and exclusion that underpinned the Wahhabi ulama's monopoly on discursive authority no longer holds. Consequently, Saudis have been exposed to views that diverge from and even directly challenge Wahhabi doctrine. Broader changes in the production of culture have also facilitated challenges to the Wahhabi ulama's authority. The spread of print technology and the simultaneous withering of a scholastic culture based on the production of manuscripts opened the discursive field to authors whose educational formation lay in modern schools and universities rather than in ulama-pupil networks. The rise of the lay Islamist writer spawned a religious discourse that frequently contested the framework of meanings espoused by ulama.[39] Wahhabi ulama stand as ready as ever to defend their doctrine against both traditional polemics and Islamist assertions, in print and in cyberspace. Yet the Saudi domain's opening to millions of permanent Muslim residents and to electronic media spells the end of Wahhabi hegemony and the onset of a prolonged period of contestation among rival religious discourses within the kingdom.

▪ Notes

1. For a historical treatment of the Wahhabi movement, including discussion of polemics, see David Commins, *The Wahhabi Mission and Saudi Arabia* (London: Tauris, 2006).

2. The sources name fifteen Najdi ulama for the sixteenth century; five of them studied in Cairo and/or Damascus. It seems that their sojourns in cosmopolitan centers made them the most influential teachers when they returned to Najd. Uwaidah al-Juhany notes that there is a clear tendency for ulama who studied outside Najd to have the largest number of pupils coming from different towns to attend their lessons. In addition to ibn Atwa, al-Juhany discusses Ahmad ibn Musharraf (d. 1603–1604) as a man who studied in Damascus and then returned to Ushayqir to become an important teacher of the next generation of ulama. Uwaidah M. al-Juhany, *Najd Before the Salafi Reform Movement: Social, Religious, and Political Conditions During the Three Centuries Preceding the Rise of the Saudi State* (Reading, UK: Ithaca, 2002), pp. 129–132. On ibn Atwa, see Abdullah M. Mutawa, "The Ulama of

Najd from the Sixteenth Century to the Mid-Eighteenth Century," PhD diss., Los Angeles, University of California, 1989, pp. 104–109.

3. al-Juhany, *Najd Before the Salafi Reform Movement,* p. 134.

4. John Voll, "The Non-Wahhabi Hanbalis of Eighteenth Century Syria," *Der Islam* 49 (1972); George Makdisi, "Hanbalite Islam," in *Studies on Islam,* edited by Merlin L. Swartz (New York: Oxford University Press, 1981); George Makdisi, "The Hanbali School and Sufism," in *Actas iv Congresso de Estudos Arabes e Islamicos* (Leiden: Brill, 1971).

5. In the sixteenth and seventeenth centuries, Ushayqir was the major seat of religious learning in Najd. On the early preeminence and later decline of Ushayqir, see Mutawa, "The Ulama of Najd," pp. 90–92, 336; al-Juhany, *Najd Before the Salafi Reform Movement,* p. 134; Mayy bint Abd al-Aziz al-Isa, *Al-Haya al-Ilmiyya Fi Najd Mundhu Qiyam Dawat al-Shaykh Muhammad ibn Abd al-Wahhab wa Hatta Nihayat al-Dawla al-Saudiyya al-Ula* (Riyadh: Darat al-Malak Abd al-Aziz, 1997), pp. 144, 202–203, 209–210, 224.

6. David Commins, "Why Unayza: Ulama Dissidents and Nonconformists in the Second Saudi State, 1824–1865," paper presented at conference "Religion and Society in the Late Ottoman Empire," Los Angeles, University of California, April 12–13, 2002.

7. al-Isa, *Al-Haya al-Ilmiyya Fi Najd Mundhu Qiyam Dawat al-Shaykh Muhammad ibn Abd al-Wahhab wa Hatta Nihayat al-Dawla al-Saudiyya al-Ula,* pp. 252, 271.

8. Ibid., p. 277, n. 200.

9. When Abd al-Rahman ibn Hasan died in 1869, his son Abd al-Latif followed him as leader of the religious estate. When Abd al-Latif died in 1876, there appears to have been a hiatus in Al al-Shaikh leadership until his son Abdullah assumed the role in 1879, which he filled for over forty years until he died in 1922. Shaikh Muhammad ibn Ibrahim emerged as the next dominant figure, until his death in 1969. Also playing central roles in the mid-twentieth century were Abdullah ibn Abd al-Latif's brother Shaikh Umar ibn Abd al-Latif, as preacher at Riyadh's chief mosque, and Shaikh Abd Allah ibn Hasan, as chief qadi. On Abd al-Rahman ibn Hasan, see Abd Allah ibn Abd al-Rahman al-Bassam, *Ulama Najd Khilal Thamani-yat Qurun* (Riyadh: Dar al-Asima, 1998), vol. 1, pp. 180–201. On Abd al-Latif ibn Abd al-Rahman, see ibid., vol. 1, pp. 202–214. On Abd Allah ibn Abd al-Latif, see ibid., vol. 1, pp. 215–230. On Abd Allah ibn Hasan ibn Husayn ibn Ali ibn Husayn, see ibid., vol. 1, pp. 231–241. On Muhammad ibn Ibrahim, see ibid., vol. 1, pp. 242–263. On Umar ibn Abd al-Latif, see Abd al-Rahman ibn Abd al-Latif Al al-Shaykh, *Mashahir Ulama Najd wa Ghayrihim* (Riyadh: Dar al-Yamama, 1972), p. 144.

10. One of Shaikh Abdullah ibn Muhammad ibn Abd al-Wahhab's treatises is translated into English in J. O'Kinealy, "Translation of an Arabic Pamphlet on the History and Doctrines of the Wahhabis, Written by Abdullah, Grandson [sic] of Abdul Wahhab, the Founder of Wahhabism," *Journal of the Asiatic Society of Bengal* 43 (1874). Abd al-Rahman ibn Hasan and Abd al-Latif ibn Abd al-Rahman composed numerous treatises and dozens of epistles. See entries on them in al-Bassam, *Ulama Najd Khilal Thamaniyat Qurun.*

11. See David Commins, "Reinterpreting Wahhabism: The Formation of a Regional Religious Tradition," paper presented at the annual meeting of the Middle East Studies Association, Anchorage, Alaska, November 2003, app. 1.

12. See ibid., app. 2.

13. See ibid., app. 3.

14. al-Isa, *Al-Haya al-Ilmiyya Fi Najd Mundhu Qiyam Dawat al-Shaykh Muhammad ibn Abd al-Wahhab wa Hatta Nihayat al-Dawla al-Saudiyya al-Ula,* pp. 87–100.

15. Ibid., pp. 154–172.

16. Ibid., p. 165, n. 259.

17. Ibid., pp. 226–231.

18. Ibid., pp. 296–298.

19. Muhammad ibn Abd al-Wahhab, "Kitab al-Tawhid," and Abd al-Rahman ibn Hasan al-Shaikh, "Qurrat Uyyun al-Muwahhidin Fi Tahqiq Dawat al-Anbiya wa al-Mursalin," both in *Majmuat al-Tawhid al-Najdiyya,* edited by Rashid Rida (Riyadh: Al-Amana al-Amma li'l-Ihtifal bi-Murur Miat Am ala Tasis al-Mamlaka, 1999).

20. al-Shaikh, "Qurrat Uyyun al-Muwahhidin Fi Tahqiq Dawat al-Anbiya wa al-Mursalin," pp. 430, 432–433.

21. Suleiman ibn Abd al-Wahhab, *Al-Sawaiq al-Ilahiyya Fi al-Radd Ala al-Wahhabiyya,* edited by Ibrahim Muhammad al-Bitawi (Cairo: Dar al-Insan, 1987); al-Bassam, *Ulama Najd Khilal Thamaniyat Qurun,* vol. 2, pp. 350–355.

22. ibn Abd al-Wahhab, *Al-Sawaiq al-Ilahiyya Fi al-Radd Ala al-Wahhabiyya,* pp. 22–28.

23. Ibid., pp. 26–28.

24. Ibid., pp. 28–30.

25. Ibid., pp. 30–31.

26. Ibid., p. 31.

27. On ibn Mansur, see al-Bassam, *Ulama Najd Khilal Thamaniyat Qurun,* vol. 5, pp. 89–106; Muhammad ibn Uthman ibn Salih al-Qadi, *Rawdat al-Nazirin an Maathir Ulama Najd wa Hawadith al-Sinin,* 3rd ed. (Riyadh: Matbaat al-Halabi, 1989–1990), vol. 2, pp. 104–108.

28. Abd al-Rahman ibn Hasan Al al-Shaykh, *Al-Maqamat* (Riyadh, n.d.).

29. On Abd al-Rahman ibn Hasan, see al-Bassam, *Ulama Najd Khilal Thamaniyat Qurun,* vol. 1, pp. 180–201.

30. al-Shaykh, *Al-Maqamat,* pp. 5–6.

31. Ibid., pp. 6–7.

32. Muhammad ibn Abd Allah ibn Humayd, *Al-Suhub al-Wabila Ala Daraih al-Hanabila,* edited by Bakr Abd Allah Abu Zayd and Abd al-Rahman ibn Sulayman al-Uthaymin (Beirut: Muasassat al-Risala, 1996); for an introduction to ibn Humayd, see esp. vol. 1, pp. 11–70. Also on ibn Humayd, see al-Bassam, *Ulama Najd Khilal Thamaniyat Qurun,* vol. 6, pp. 189–204. For an extensive discussion of ibn Humayd, see David Commins, "Traditional Anti-Wahhabi Hanbalism in Nineteenth Century Arabia," in *Ottoman Reform and Muslim Regeneration,* edited by Itzchak Weismann and Fruma Zachs (London: Tauris, 2005).

33. On the mystical attainments of Ahmad ibn Yahya ibn Atwa of Al-Uyayna (d. 948/1542), see ibn Humayd, *Al-Suhub al-Wabila Ala Daraih al-Hanabila,* vol. 1, pp. 274–275. On Muhammad ibn Fayruz as "an exemplary Sufi," see ibid., vol. 3, p. 979. On Hasan al-Shatti's devotion to Sufi forms of worship, see ibid., vol. 1, p. 361. On Abd al-Jabbar al-Basri as "shaykh al-tariqa wa ustadh al-haqiqa," see ibid., vol. 2, pp. 443–444.

34. ibn Humayd, *Al-Suhub al-Wabila Ala Daraih al-Hanabila,* vol. 2, pp. 680, 686–694.

35. Isam ibn Abd Allah al-Sinani, ed., *Baraat Ulama al-Umma Min Tazkiyat Ahl al-Bida wa al-Madhamma* (Ajman: Maktabat al-Furqan, 2000). On Sayyid Qutb's popularity in mosques, see ibid., p. 7. On ibn Baz's views, see ibid., pp. 16, 20–21, 30–34. On other shaikhs' views, see ibid., pp. 35–37, 49–51.

36. http://www.salafipublications.com/sps.

37. The treatise is included in Husayn ibn Ghannam, *Tarikh Najd* (Riyadh, n.d.).

38. http://www.salafipublications.com/sps, "First Study," n. 3.

39. Dale F. Eickelman and James Piscatori, *Muslim Politics* (Princeton: Princeton University Press, 1996), pp. 43–45. Muhammad Qasim Zaman contends that the ulama have adapted to new circumstances, so that rather than viewing them as marginalized, we should instead view them as part of a new landscape of discursive practices and forms. Muhammad Qasim Zaman, *The Ulama in Contemporary Islam: Custodians of Change* (Princeton: Princeton University Press, 2002), pp. 54–59.

PART 2

Wahhabism and the Saudi State

5

Wahhabi Origins of the Contemporary Saudi State

John S. Habib

In this chapter, I treat the Saudi-Wahhabi state as the political expression of Wahhabism, itself, not as separate political entity in which Wahhabism flourishes as a protected religious ideology. By "Wahhabism," I mean the Hanbali school of jurisprudence as reflected in the writings and teachings of Muhammad ibn Abd al-Wahhab.[1]

The evolution of the state is considered in three distinct phases, the period 1902–1932, when the territorial conquests were completed and consolidated and Saudi-Wahhabi hegemony was imposed upon them; the period 1932–1945, when the tasks of forming a rudimentary Saudi-Wahhabi central government, unifying the disparate regions of the country, and creating a national Saudi-Wahhabi identity were undertaken; and the period 1945–1953, when the kingdom defined its strategic foreign policy objectives in the context of its Wahhabi mission.

From his adolescence, Abd al-Aziz ibn Abd al-Rahman, popularly known as ibn Saud, was driven by a passion to reconquer the lands that his ancestors had lost to their enemies in order to restore the Wahhabi persuasion of Islam as the only legitimate and permissible form of religious worship within them. To do this he had to heal intrafamily wounds, revitalize the Saudi-Wahhabi alliance, and create a full-time standing army. As he moved to create a modern nation-state, he also had to manage Wahhabi zealotry.

The contemporary state of Saudi Arabia was formally declared on September 23, 1932; its origins, however, go back to 1744, when Muhammad bin Saud, a minor prince of Al-Diriyya, a small town in Najd in central Arabia, championed the cause of Muhammad ibn Abd al-Wahhab, an itinerant, revivalist preacher from Al-Uyayna, a Najdi hamlet. Ibn Abd al-Wahhab, who came to be known by the religious title al-Shaikh, was bent on restoring the purity of Islamic doctrine to the nomadic and sedentary populations of Arabia, whom he believed had lapsed into non-Islamic and superstitious practices. The central doctrine of his teaching was the oneness of God; hence his followers came to be known as unitarians *(muwahhidin)*.

Together they forged an irrevocable alliance. Muhammad bin Saud pledged himself and his family to uphold and spread the Wahhabi persuasion of Islam. In return, ibn Abd al-Wahhab promised him dominion. The Sword and the political power that went with it would be the realm of Muhammad bin Saud and his descendants. The Book (the Quran) and the accompanying religious, moral, and educational authority would be the domain of Shaikh Muhammad ibn Abd al-Wahhab and the Al al-Shaikh, as his descendants came to be known. Each would be supreme but not absolute in its own sphere of authority, because each retained substantive checks on the authority of the other. Nevertheless, the lines of responsibility were clear and unambiguous. Each family respected them. Today, more than three centuries later, this alliance remains the keystone of governance in the kingdom.

From 1744 to the present, the Saudi-Wahhabi alliance ruled much of the Arabian Peninsula, with various degrees of control, except for two brief periods totaling about fifty years. The first Saudi state lasted from 1744 to 1818. Having conquered most of Arabia, Muhammad bin Saud installed a central government, imposed the practice of Wahhabi Islam, and instituted a reign of security and personal accountability in the peninsula heretofore unknown. Had the Saudis intended to exploit Wahhabism only as a vehicle to expand their political power in the Arabian Peninsula, they would not have continued their conquests, or riding the crest of Wahhabism, they would have extended their conquests beyond the peninsula while imposing Wahhabism only nominally or not at all. Instead the Saudis raided Iraq and territories known as Greater Syria *(bilad ashsham),* destroyed mosques and shrines, punished practices that were anathema to Wahhabi teachings, and imposed Wahhabism with a zeal that surpassed anything that the region had known before or has known since. It was not so much Saudi military territorial conquests in themselves that raised the alarm in the region, but rather Wahhabi fanaticism and excesses that accompanied them or that followed in their wake. The Saudi threat to raise the banner of Wahhabi Islam over Istanbul, the very heart of the Ottoman Empire, gave the sultan little comfort and no incentive even to contemplate accommodating the new religious challenge.

The Ottomans' interests were centered in Europe; for centuries they had abandoned the Arab territories as quagmires of little economic and even less political value to the empire. What passed as government was rule by local notables who were left to their own devices as long as they respected the nominal sovereignty of the sultan in the person of his resident Ottoman pasha or vali and maintained a modicum of security. Economically they were little more than patchworks of tax farms administered by Ottoman officials who awarded tax collection franchises to local notables, a percentage of which was the sultan's take. There is no need to elaborate on the rampant corruption, extortion, and violence that this system generated.

Any consideration that the sultan may have given to the thought of allowing the Saudis to govern the territories as his valis and bring order out of the political anarchy that prevailed there vanished in the face of Wahhabi defiance of his own political and religious legitimacy as sultan and caliph, respectively. The Ottoman viceroy in Egypt, Muhammad Ali, also viewed Wahhabi expansion as a menace to his own ill-concealed designs on Ottoman territories. He was only too willing, then, to accede to the sultan's urging that he check and repel the Wahhabi advance. In 1811 and for the next seven years, Muhammad Ali dispatched Egyptian military expeditions to Arabia, either under his personal command or under that of his sons, Tuson and Ibrahim. Overwhelmed by superior Egyptian military might, despite fierce resistance, the Saudi-Wahhabi forces retreated into the heart of their Najdi homeland, pursued by the Egyptians, who destroyed their capital at Al-Diriyya in 1818. After the Egyptian withdrawal, the Arabian territories reverted to their pre-Saudi-Wahhabi condition of political fragmentation and endemic insecurity.

While overambitious territorial acquisitions were a factor in the demise of the first Saudi state, Wahhabi fanaticism was the principal reason that led the Ottoman sultan and his Egyptian viceroy to confront and defeat it, two miscalculations that a Saudi prince yet unborn would not repeat. The Saudi state collapsed in 1818, but its flame had only been dimmed, not extinguished. The second Saudi state rose in 1824 from the ashes of the first, after only six years, on the strength of Wahhabi credentials won during the first state. It crumbled in total disarray in 1891. If the first state collapsed because of too much Wahhabi zeal, the second state was the victim of too little.

The troubles began in 1865, immediately after Abdullah became ruler following the death of his father, Faisal al-Turki. His brothers, Saud, Muhammad, and Abd al-Rahman, contested the succession. The ensuing internecine battles pitted brothers, uncles, nephews, and cousins against each other as they fought to extend their total control over all of the Saudi territories. The prestigious al-Rashid family of Hail in north central Najd, supported by the Ottomans, who nominally controlled parts of Arabia, exploited the rift, ousted the Saudis, and made the Saudi capital in Riyadh their own. In 1891 the last ruler of the second Saudi state, Abd al-Rahman, the youngest son of Faisal al-Turki, went into self-imposed exile with his adolescent son, Abd al-Aziz, taking refuge first among the al-Murrah Bedouin in eastern Arabia, then with the al-Khalifah ruling family in Bahrain, and finally with the al-Sabah emirs of Kuwait. The intra–al-Saud family infighting drained their energies, divided their ranks, and diverted them from their Wahhabi mission. It was a misadventure that a young prince would not repeat.

The third and contemporary Saudi state (1932–present) is the creation of that young, exiled prince who returned to his native land in the first blush of manhood, sword in hand, to reclaim the Wahhabi lands that his own father, whom he deeply revered, could not hold. Abd al-Aziz ibn Abd al-Rahman al-Saud was the central force that created the modern Saudi state. Dead now for more than fifty years, he is only as far removed from ruling the kingdom today as the legacies of his five sons who succeeded him as kings, Saud, Faisal, Khalid, Fahd, and Abdullah, the latter the reigning monarch. In sharp contrast to his nemesis, Hussein bin Ali, the guardian of the holy shrines at Mecca and Medina who established his dynasty and then sought an Arab kingdom to rule, ibn Saud sought Wahhabi hegemony and then established his dynasty to rule its territories.

▪ 1902–1932: Healing Intra–Saudi Family Rifts

After conquering Riyadh from the al-Rashid in 1902 with a legendary band of forty relatives, close friends, and trusted allies, ibn Saud embarked upon the mission of restoring the patrimony of his ancestors;[2] he needed to heal the fatal family rifts that had precipitated the fall of the second Saudi state. He liberated family members that the al-Rashid had taken prisoner, some of whom had fought against his father, Abd al-Rahman, during the internecine family wars. He restored their rights and privileges and integrated them fully into the national life of the kingdom. Known as the al-Arafa, a Najdi term that refers to camels taken as booty and then recovered, they were given full amnesty.[3] As direct descendants of his grandfather, Faisal al-Turki, they rank today among the most influential princes of the realm.

Since that reconciliation more than a hundred years ago, al-Saud unity has remained intact but not totally free of breaches, though none have been fatal.[4] Two are worth mentioning here. The decisions made in both cases required the official legal certification (fatwa) of the Wahhabi establishment (ulama) that they were carried out in accordance with Islamic law.

On November 2, 1964, about a hundred Saudi princes, with the advice and consent of the Wahhabi establishment, removed King Saud and installed his brother, Faisal, as ruler.[5] The deposed Saud, joined later by several brothers known as the "liberal princes," fled to Egypt, where Egyptian president Gamal Abdul Nasser gave them political asylum. There they promoted Arab nationalism of the Nasserist genre and agitated for the creation of a constitutional monarchy in Saudi Arabia. Eventually they recanted, and were allowed to return to the kingdom after being granted full amnesty and restoration of their rights and privileges. To further heal this particularly bitter breach of family collegiality, the Saudi government tacitly rehabilitated Saud by renaming Riyadh University as King Saud University.[6] Another breach of family unity was the ill-concealed opposition of senior Saudi princes and influential leaders of the Wahhabi establishment to allowing US military personnel to be stationed on Saudi territory to fight the war to liberate Kuwait (1990–1991).

Substantive differences over public policy still exist among influential members of the family, most notably over the speed and extent of internal social reform that is consistent with Wahhabi teaching. Rarely aired in public, their criticisms and suggestions are increasingly taking the form of op-ed pieces and letters to the editor that appear in popular Saudi Arabic- and English-language newspapers alongside those submitted by ordinary Saudi citizens, and as editorials in newspapers that are owned and published by Saudi princes.

Limiting Territorial Acquisitions

By 1913, ibn Saud's forces had brought all of central Najd and much of the Eastern Province (Al-Mantaqah al-Sharqiyah) under his control, but his territorial ambitions also extended to northern Najd, where the al-Rashid still held sway, to the Hijaz in the west, which for centuries had been nominally controlled by the Ottomans, and to parts of Arab territories that today constitute Iraq, Jordan, and Kuwait. Determined to avoid the overreaching territorial thrusts that contributed to his ancestors' demise, ibn Saud used force when it was a viable option, and resorted to patience and diplomacy when it was not. This strategy contributed to his growing stature as the single most powerful leader in the Arabian Peninsula, because as he would later boast, he "won his territories with his sword," or through statesmanship, tact, and wit, and was not beholden to a foreign power for them. A pragmatist, he consolidated each victory before moving on to achieve another. Recognizing that his warriors could never prevail against the British or Turkish military, their dedication and zeal notwithstanding, and that the paucity of his coffers limited his military options, he often resorted to dissimulation to achieve his goal of expelling the Ottomans from Arabia and to allay British fears of his encroachment on their territories. To the Ottomans, he signaled his willingness to recognize their nominal sovereignty over the territories where he held sway, without formally renouncing his own claims to them. In response in July 1914, the Ottomans issued a decree that named him Governor-General and Commander-in-Chief of Najd with the powers of a vali, but without the right to negotiate and sign treaties.[7] By December 1915, however, he felt strong enough to ignore that caveat and signed a treaty with the British that recognized him, his sons, and his descendants as the absolute authority over Najd, Al-Hasa, Qatif, and Jubail, as well as their dependencies, territories, and shores and ports on the Persian Gulf, and as the absolute chief of their tribes.[8] Absent mention of Iraq, Kuwait, or Jordan, this treaty constituted his tacit acceptance of the British presence there. As World War I loomed on the horizon, ibn Saud rebuffed generous Ottoman offers of money and arms and sided with the British instead. By war's end, his nemeses, the Ottomans, had been expelled from Arabia, his territorial acquisitions consolidated, his ties with the British strengthened, and his reputation as an Arab leader enhanced further. In contrast, the power of Britain's protégé Hussein bin Ali, on whom it had pinned its hopes for hegemony in the peninsula, was in tatters.

By 1922, the northern territories of Sakaka; Hail, the redoubt of the al-Rashid, erstwhile allies of the Ottomans; and Khaybar, located on the fringe of the Hijaz, were under his control. In violation of his treaty with the British, his Ikhwan contingents conducted ferocious raids into British-controlled territories in Iraq and Jordan, even as he unabashedly disavowed any responsibility when charged with aiding and abetting them. He used these raids to test Britain's will and capability to defend territories controlled by its Arab protégés, with an eye to extending his reach there if the British faltered. Unlike his ancestors, however, who paid heavily for it, he eschewed fanaticism in the pursuit of territory. Consequently, the excesses in human and material losses that accompanied these raids, and the intensity of the artillery and air power with which the British consistently repelled them, caused ibn Saud to order the Ikhwan to cease and desist, and he made them pay heavily when they did not.[9] This prompted a desperate reaction from the Ikhwan leadership. In a letter he wrote to Saud, future king and powerful Ikhwan leader Faisal al-Dawish expressed the reaction of most Ikhwan to his father's orders: "You have also prevented me from raiding the Bedouins. So we are neither Moslems fighting the unbelievers nor are we Arabs and Bedouins raiding each other and now you treat us with the sword and pass over the Christians, their religion and their forts built for your immediate destruction."[10] Ibn Saud was not swayed. He was able to stop most, but not all, of the Ikhwan raids into Iraq. The frayed but still extant British-Hashimite alliance precluded him from acceding to Ikhwan demands that they be allowed to bring Mecca and Medina under Wahhabi control. He checked their forays into the Hijaz itself, but he could not control their battles with Hussein bin Ali's forces in Khurma and Turaba, territories that were contiguous to and technically part of the Hijaz but whose population was predominantly Wahhabi. Their victories raised Ikhwan emotions to a fever pitch and increased their determination to subdue the Hijaz, with or without ibn Saud's approval. They also strained ibn Saud's relations with the British. He denied any responsibility for these crises also, but for the most part justified and supported Ikhwan claims that the battles were incited by Hashimite provocations. Since the Ikhwan almost always had the upper hand militarily, Hussein bin Ali could do little more than complain to the British and threaten once again to resign.[11] British feints to pressure ibn Saud by cutting off their aid were ineffective. The meager subsidies helped ease his financial woes, but no amount of money was likely to dissuade him from pursing his ultimate objective of uniting the Arabian Peninsula and imposing Wahhabism in it. Beyond that, British officers in Arabia were reporting to their superiors in Whitehall that ibn Saud had become too powerful to be treated cavalierly, as if he were a minor chieftain, and that it was very likely he would emerge as the supreme Arab power in the peninsula. They suggested that Whitehall might want to consider tilting more support to him and less to Hussein bin Ali. By war's end, Hussein's alienation of important elements of his Hijazi constituency through inept rule and shortsighted policies, the defection of many of his strongest supporters in the British foreign policy establishment who no longer considered him a viable instrument of British power in Arabia,[12] and his decision to deny Ikhwan the right to make the pilgrimage to Mecca, all sealed his fate. Armed with more justification than he needed, ibn Saud unleashed the Ikhwan. Their reputation for ferocity preceded them in the Hijaz and eliminated all but the most die-hard resistance. On September 1, 1924, Taif fell, followed by Mecca on October 14, 1924, and Jidda on December 23, 1925. In victory, ibn Saud entered Mecca not as a triumphant warrior but wearing the traditional garb of a pilgrim.

These conquests marked the limits of ibn Saud's territorial acquisition. In three decades, ibn Saud ended centuries of Ottoman presence in Arabia, rebuffed British efforts to establish hegemony in Arabia while winning their long-term friendship and goodwill, and established Wahhabism as the unique expression of Islam in these territories.

Revitalizing the ibn Saud–Abd al-Wahhab Compact

By committing himself to ensure the primacy of Wahhabi Islam, ibn Saud revitalized the Saudi-Wahhabi compact. His credentials as a devout Muslim and his determination to make Wahhabism the sole legitimate persuasion of Islam in the territories that he conquered guaranteed the unequivocal support of the Al al-Shaikh and the Wahhabi establishment, which was essential to endowing his rule with religious and political legitimacy. His marriage to Tarfa bint Abdullah bin Abd al-Latif Al al-Shaikh, reminiscent of Muhammad bin Saud's own marriage to Muhammad Abd al-Wahhab's daughter, tightened the traditional blood alliance of the two families. She became the mother of King Faisal, an Islamic scholar in his own right. His strong dedication to Wahhabism notwithstanding, he promulgated liberal reforms that advanced the education of women, modernized the Saudi fiscal system, and legitimized the use of television,[13] among others, in the face of strong opposition of some religious leaders and some members of the royal family.

Since the fatal events that caused the downfall of the second Saudi state, the al-Saud have never allowed their energies and attention to be diverted from their Wahhabi mission. The most powerful Saudi princes,[14] the most influential interests groups, and arguably the majority of the population all embrace it.[15] The Saudi government provides generous financial subsidies to Wahhabi groups abroad to help defray the cost of constructing mosques, schools, and religious educational institutions, while private citizens enthusiastically donate to Wahhabi charities and activities at home and abroad.

Wahhabism sets the rhythm of the national life of the kingdom. It defines the religious, social, and educational standards, including modest dress codes applicable to both men and women, compulsory daily attendance at congregational prayer, strict separation of the sexes, prohibition of the sale and consumption of alcoholic beverages, and the ban on coeducation and on public movie theaters. An agency of the state, the Organization to Do Good and to Avoid Evil (Hai'at al-Amr bi al-Ma'rouf wa al-Nahi 'an al-Munkar), enforces these standards through a cadre of religious police *(mutawwain)* who patrol the streets and public places, and have been known to penetrate the privacy of homes, and on occasion even to disrupt diplomatic gatherings where alcoholic beverages are being served.[16] When the organization was first established, its enforcers were literally volunteers with sticks and bamboo canes as their only weapons. Today they constitute a modern, well-equipped, and quasi-mobile uniformed force. While their capacity to arbitrarily intimidate and punish the citizenry with impunity for perceived anti-Islamic conduct has been curtailed somewhat in recent years, the organization remains a powerful instrument to maintain the pervasiveness of Wahhabi ideology in the kingdom today.

Creating a Permanent Military Force

Battles in the Arabian Peninsula were generally local in scope and limited in objective. Consequently, large standing armies were not necessary. Given that the sedentary population was tied to their urban or agricultural pursuits, the Arabian leaders traditionally recruited Bedouin levies to supplement their own forces and paid them with a share of the booty. Those who engaged the Bedouin, however, did so at their own risk, because they had the reputation of being fickle and unreliable. Detractors described them as "today a sword in the hand of the prince, a dagger in his back tomorrow."[17] Defenders extolled their unsurpassed hospitality to friend and foe alike, their chivalry in battle, their proud individuality and indifference to social class, and a natural dignity that defied their endemic conditions of grinding poverty. But these very qualities also made them unreliable allies. Their harsh, natural environment made opportunism a virtue, and loyalty to their nuclear and extended families a sacred duty. They paid for their freedom from central authority with an ascetic life where their needs were few. In good times they were indulgent, in bad they went without. While not adverse to wealth, they treated it with indifference: "Wealth belongs to God. We wake up poor in the morning and retire rich in the evening or we wake up rich and retire poor."[18] Beyond that, the modalities of nomadic life made adherence to the practice of the most fundamental precepts of Islam, cleanliness for example, virtually impossible: "How should we wash, and we need the water to drink?"[19] As lapsed Muslims, they had no ties to an ideology or religion that transcended their own individual needs or those of their narrow community.

Ibn Saud changed all that with the creation of the Ikhwan, literally "Brotherhood" (Harakat al-Ikhwan-Najd). His Wahhabi missionaries instilled in them dedication to Wahhabism that transcended their family and tribal ties, and that forgave traditional animosities, similar to the first Muslim converts who pledged their fidelity to the fledgling Islamic community above all others. They were exhorted to "cling to the rope of God and do not separate and remember that you were once enemies but by the grace of God you have become brothers."[20] After the noble tribes, notably the Mutair and the Utaybah, converted to Wahhabism, almost all others joined the movement. As Islamic brothers, they renounced their ingrained individualism and the pursuit of personal, material gain in order to advance Wahhabism. Already natural desert warriors, when fired with religious zealotry, they became so fearless that when a comrade fell in battle, they would cry out in anguish, "He beat me to heaven!" *(sabaqni fi jennah)*. Such was their courage that they attacked heavily fortified Ottoman and Hashimite emplacements, armed only with knives and swords, and sometimes with no weapons at all,[21] shouting their battle cries *(nakhwah):* "We are the people of the unity of God!"; "The winds of paradise are blowing, where are you who seek it!"; and "We are the knights of unity, brothers of he who obeys God, show your head oh enemy."[22]

Their transformation from lapsed Muslims to Wahhabi devotees began with ibn Saud's dispatch of missionaries who indoctrinated them in the fundamentals of Wahhabi Islam using the writings of Abd al-Wahhab, and catechisms tailored for their mentality.[23] They were taught that abandoning the desert for life in the town was a virtual reenactment of the Prophet Muhammad's own migration, or hijra, from Mecca to Medina, from the realm of polytheism *(dar al-kufr)* to the realm of faith *(dar al-Islam)*. They broke with centuries of Bedouin tradition, selling their flocks of camels and other livestock and settling by tribe in villages *(hujur)* that ibn Saud had built for them, about 222 in number.[24] There, provided with all their material needs, they retained their nomadic independence and detachment from the land and their capacity for instant mobilization. While awaiting ibn Saud's call to arms, they spent their time in congregational prayer at mosques and attended study sessions on religion and morality, some bearing on casuistry, where they learned, for example, that the length of the robe *(thobe)* must fall only at the ankles,[25] otherwise it was a punishable innovation *(bid'a)*.

Exercising strong influence in his court, they became the vanguard of his military elite, the singular most effective instrument of public security and vigilance in all of the conquered territories. They also were an albatross around his neck. They posed a major dilemma for him. They were indispensable to ibn Saud's mission of conquest, although he would not admit to this. They were brave warriors who asked little in return except to fight the infidels under his command in the name of God *(fi sabil Allah)*. Because they interpreted their Wahhabi instruction literally, their religious fervor often developed into zealotry and then into unrestrained fanaticism that translated into acts of terror against the innocent. They punished ordinary citizens severely for infractions of what they perceived to be un-Islamic conduct, no matter how petty. Such was their reputation for ferocity that the very mention of the word "Ikhwan" struck awe in the hearts of the people of Najd, fear among the non-Wahhabi Sunnis of the Hijaz, and sheer terror among the Shias of the Eastern Province, whom the Wahhabis regarded as infidels,[26] not even on a par with Christians and Jews who were protected as People of the Book (Ahl al-Kitab). The absence of modern communications gave them the freedom to attack perceived enemies, without ibn Saud's knowledge or authorization.[27] Their depredations and atrocities, especially against the inhabitants of Taif, infuriated him and ruptured his relations with them well before that breach had become public knowledge. He, himself, was not free of the disdain of fanatics among the Ikhwan who accused him of consorting with the Christians, usually British political officers, because he provided them food and lodging and other forms of hospitality on the rare occasion when they were guests at his court and encampments. Some Ikhwan publicly showed their contempt for these guests by covering their faces when their paths crossed, to avoid laying eyes on or exchanging glances with an unbeliever.

Not all Ikhwan were fanatical or inhospitable.[28] According to Amin al-Rihani:

> [Ibn Saud] puts the different Ikhwan to their right use; the sensible for service, the tolerant for commerce and foreign politics, the mad for battle. The case of the last class, however, becomes at times very critical. No he cannot always keep the brothers . . . under absolute control because of the vast distances in Najd and the primitive means of communication. In a word then, the Ikhwan are a power, a terrible power which must be regulated and put under a modern system of administrative control.[29]

Ibn Saud cautioned the Ikhwan against their arrogance and pointed out that he owed his power only to God,[30] and then to his sword:

> Think not, ya Ikhwan, that we consider you of much value. Think not that you have rendered us a great service and that we need you. Your real value, ya Ikhwan, is your obedience to God and then to us. And do not forget there is not one among you whose father or brother or cousin we have not slain. Aye, billah, it was by the sword that we took you, we conquered you, and that same sword is above your head. Beware, ya Ikhwan. Encroach not upon the rights of others. If you do your value and that of the deed are the same. We took you by the sword and we shall keep you within your bounds by the sword, in'shallah.[31]

An armed confrontation between ibn Saud and the chief leaders of the Ikhwan, led by Faisal Duweish and ibn Bijad of the Mutayr and Utaybah tribes, respectively, was inevitable. Generally, the Ikhwan perception of Arabia was narrow and naive, even more so their understanding of the world beyond its borders. Each Ikhwan leader expected to transform his own territory into an independent fiefdom to rule under the aegis of ibn Saud, as the supreme imam. They would be free to raid the Arab lands occupied by European infidels, take booty, and punish inhabitants who did not adhere to Wahhabi tenets. In contrast, ibn Saud had a broad vision of Arabia and its relationship to the outside world. According to Muhammad Jalal Kishk, he intuitively foresaw the collapse of two empires and the rise of another,[32] and formulated his policies accordingly.

When the revolt broke out at Sibylla in 1931, the results were never in doubt. Ibn Saud quelled the insurrection with ease, disbanded the movement, and punished the rebels. He left the *hujur* system intact, with each hijra administered by an elected tribal leader whom he approved or appointed. The loyal Ikhwan were formed into the White Army under the command of Majid bin Khathilah.[33] It subsequently evolved into the National Guard.

From the outset the Wahhabi establishment solidly supported ibn Saud. They saw Faisal Duweish's claims to be the champion of Islam and his demands to be allowed to raid the "infidel" British occupiers of Islamic lands in Kuwait and Iraq for what they were, quests for political ambition and for booty. Duweish, himself, confirmed this duplicity. After the Battle of Sibylla, he fled to Kuwait, where he sought political asylum from H.R.P. Dickson, the British consul. Reluctant to grant the request lest he anger ibn Saud, Dickson relented after Duweish removed his turban and placed it on Dickson's head, a traditional demand for refuge that could not be denied.[34] This decisive battle left the Saudi-Wahhabi establishment in uncontested control of the territories. The compact had come full circle.

1932–1945: Creating a Central Government

Ibn Saud was proud that his rule brought near absolute public security to the territories under his control, where even the humblest pilgrim on the way to Mecca had formerly been the potential victim of predators.[35] By 1932, he also brought incipient central government to the kingdom, made the Quran the nation's constitution, and made Islamic law *(sharia)* supreme, although some tribal and customary law compatible with the Quran and the *sharia* entered the new nation's legal system. But little else had changed. The country was poor and devoid of any known natural resources. Its public administrative infrastructure was primitive where it existed at all. Fragile, subsistence economies linked the nomadic tribes and small farmers and merchants of the villages and oases in a precarious interdependent relationship. The sources of the state's meager fiscal resources were receipts from the annual pilgrimages—the hajj and the umrah—customs duties, and the levy of taxes. Only the most rudimentary network of unpaved roads and tracks linked the major towns and cities, including Riyadh, the political capital, and Jidda, the country's major port and financial capital. Electricity was primitive and, when accessible, subject to outages; telephone and telegraph services were rare and even then available only to the elite in government and to a small cadre of privileged citizenry.[36]

The creation of the embryonic state added new challenges to old ones. The most difficult, perhaps, was creating a common identity out of a sedentary and nomadic population that was disparate in race, religion, social habits, customs, and education. While most Najdis celebrated the return to power of the Saudi-Wahhabi alliance, large parts of the population of the Hijaz and of Al-Hasa were deeply apprehensive about it.

The Hijazis feared that what they considered puritanical Wahhabi Islam would forcibly replace their less ascetic approach to religion. The prospect of rule from Najd, where the taciturn Najdis scorned the Hijazis because of their alleged moral laxity and the racial mixing that was pervasive there, frightened them.[37] But there were bright spots as well. Even before ibn Saud conquered the Hijaz, some prominent families and businesspeople, disaffected with Hussein bin Ali's ineffectual rule, had made known their support for him. After the conquest, he established close ties with them, with other elements of the business community, and with the political elite. He used them as bridges to the outside world, where they had long experience. Much to the relief of rank-and-file Hijazis, he retained intact the bureaucracy that had administered the Hijaz under Sharif Hussein bin Ali,[38] and ordered that Wahhabism be implemented gradually and enforced with restraint. These measures made Saudi rule less obtrusive and mitigated incipient attempts to oppose or thwart his rule in the Hijaz. Exaggerated claims that the demise of Hussein bin Ali's rule and the institution of Wahhabi rule in its stead would bring anarchy to the Hijaz proved to be unfounded.[39]

The large Shia population of Al-Hasa had little reason to welcome their new rulers and their worst fears were confirmed all too soon. Their civil liberties were severely restricted. They were systematically left out of the mainstream of Saudi public life, and they suffered discrimination in public welfare and social programs. Regulations against any manifestations of Shia Islam, public or private, were rigorously enforced.

Until his death in 1953, ibn Saud, with the assistance of several advisers, hardly more than six or seven, ruled the kingdom as a Bedouin chieftain with only a rudimentary administration. The Wahhabi establishment administered to the religious needs of the population, while the *sharia* courts adjudicated disputes and controversies. The White Army maintained internal security. A national army was not needed and existed virtually in name only. The central government was the overseer of a highly decentralized system; it adjudicated only the most serious of problems.

Although the kingdom was safe from exterior threats, ibn Saud's suspicions of potential Hashimite irredentist claims to the Hijaz gained credibility in 1946, when he received reports that the British were supporting a plot against him hatched by King Faisal and his brother King Abdullah, their protégés in Iraq and Jordan, respectively. He took the reports seriously enough to ask for President Harry Truman's intervention. The president responded quickly and favorably with a strong and unequivocal statement of support, which remains a pillar of Saudi-US relations today.[40]

1945–1953:
Formulating Strategic Policy Objectives

When ibn Saud launched his venture in 1902 to restore the supremacy of Wahhabism, Arabia was primitive, undeveloped, largely unmapped, and all but cut off from the outside world. At that time, he had little reason to think that the state that he hoped to create and the way of life of its people would differ measurably from life that prevailed in the previous two Saudi-Wahhabi states. But even as this internal Saudi condition prevailed into the 1950s and as late as the 1960s in some parts of the kingdom, the outbreak of World War II thrust the new nation into an alien world of conflicting religious beliefs and political ideologies. Although not nearly as evident then as it is now, the kingdom's geopolitical location and its yet to be tapped oil resources made it impossible for the kingdom to remain isolated even if it wanted to do so.

Ibn Saud did not create the kingdom alone and never claimed to have done so. He built it on a broad-based coalition of tribal, sedentary, and business interests. He recognized, more profoundly than most, perhaps, that the Saudi-Wahhabi alliance may have been the brightest, but it was not the only star in the firmament. Authoritarian government was one thing; autocracy was something else. For ibn Saud, coalition was consensus *(shura)*. It was the principal concept of governance at the beginning and it remained so until the end of his reign. He urged others to follow his example.[41]

But not all elements of his constituency were ready or even wanted to be a part of the new world order, and they were not limited to the Wahhabi establishment. Prince Faisal made this point to US officials during an official visit to the United States in 1945. He conveyed his father's hopes that the American government and people would understand that he had to be careful in introducing change in the kingdom to avoid giving the impression to the Saudi people that "His Majesty was leading them away from the traditions and virtues of their forefathers."[42]

Nevertheless, ibn Saud took concrete measures to demonstrate to the rest of the world that Wahhabi and Western ideologies were not inherently incompatible and could coexist and even thrive. Domestically, he opened up his country to oil exploration, to the expansion of trade, to Western technical and military training missions, and to hundreds and later thousands of expatriate Western experts and laborers. During World War II, he allowed the construction of a US air base in Dhahran that considerably reduced the time and distance of military flights between Europe and the Far East, and even considered allowing US troops to be stationed on his territory should that be needed to facilitate Allied victory. And to his own people he proved that this could be done while still respecting and protecting the strict Wahhabi character of the nation,[43] and the habits and customs of its people.

At the foreign policy level, he laid down principles that remain the core of Saudi foreign policy today:

1. The Arab nation and its people are one, but the international frontiers that separate them must be respected.
2. Protecting the rights of Palestinians in their homeland is an existential Islamic as well as an Arab responsibility.
3. Saudi Arabia and the United States share values as well as national interests that require a special relationship to ensure their mutual protection.[44]

Ibn Saud's death in 1953 marked the end of one era and the beginning of another in the life of the third state. Today, Saudi Arabia is confronted with the challenge of remaining true to its Wahhabi origins in a world that is increasingly suspicious of it.

▩ Notes

1. Ibn Abd al-Wahhab taught that the jurisprudence of Abu Hanifa, al-Shafii, and ibn Malik should be respected. See Salah al-Din al-Mukhtar, *Tarikh al-Mamalakat Al-Arabiya al-Sa'udiyah fi Madiha wa Hadirha* (Beirut: Dar al-Hayat, 1958), vol. 2, p. 146. His followers do not refer to themselves as "Wahhabis" but rather as the "People of the Unity of God" (Ahl al-Wahdah) and as *muwahhidin.*

2. Ibn Saud never lost an opportunity to make this point. The literature is laced with his references to these objectives. See Mohyiddin al-Qabesi, ed., *The Holy Qur'an & the Sword,* modified 4th ed. (Riyadh: Saudi Desert House for Publishing and Distribution, 1998).

3. Ibn Saud used amnesty and reconciliation as viable political tools that co-opted his enemies and mitigated opposition to his rule. He dealt compassionately

with Ikhwan leaders who rebelled against him in 1931. That same year, he met with his erstwhile enemies, Faisal bin Hussein, the Hashimite king of Iraq, and Faisal's brother, Abdullah, king of Jordan, but remained wary of them. His successors continued that policy. In 2005, Saudi Arabia's King Abdullah granted amnesty to Saudi and non-Saudi terrorists who had perpetrated bloody acts of violence in the kingdom against official Saudi and foreign targets.

4. For a discussion of the viability of the Saudi regime, see John Habib, *Saudi Arabia and the American National Interests* (Boca Raton, FL: Universal, 2003), chap. 11.

5. Gerald DeGaury, *Faisal: King of Saudi Arabia* (New York: Praeger, 1966), p. 133.

6. King Saud established King Saud University in 1957. King Faisal renamed it Riyadh University after King Saud was removed from power. In 1982 the Saudi government renamed it King Saud University.

7. Edward Grey to L. Miller, British Public Records Office, F.O. 371/2124, July 11, 1914.

8. Mission to Najd, "Treaty with Ibn Saud," Annex B, British Public Records Office, F.O. 271/4144, 1918.

9. For a full account of British responses to these raids, see John Bagot Glubb, *War in the Desert* (London: Hodden and Stoughton, 1960).

10. English translation of a letter "From Feisal bin Sultan Ed Doweish to Emir Saud," London, British Public Records Office, MSS, Vol. 37113736, Document E 3457, 1929.

11. Hussein bin Ali's complaints and repeated threats to resign as sharif began to wear on the British, causing one of his strongest Whitehall supporters to suggest calling his bluff and accepting his threat. See Hussein's "Memorandum on the Wahhabite Threat," to Allenby, Special High Commissioner in Egypt, British Public Records Office, F.O. 371/4146, n.d. (probably 1918–1919). For an insightful contrast of the political and diplomatic skills of Sharif Hussein and ibn Saud, see Joshua Teitelbaum, *The Rise and Fall of the Hashemite Kingdom of Arabia* (New York: New York University Press, 2001), pp. 223–224.

12. To H. Wingate (Cairo), London, British Public Records Office, F.O. 371/ 4144, Document no. 2390, January 5, 1919.

13. Ironically, King Faisal, a devout Wahhabi, was a victim of his own reforms. His defense of the use of television caused a small but violent incident in 1963 that cost the life of one of his paternal nephews who was among the protesters. In 1975, Faisal was assassinated at the hand of that nephew's brother.

14. "We are not prepared to undermine our cultural strengths or to adopt practices that do not suit us . . . we are developing our country within a context of faithfulness to our traditions." Prince Naif, minister of interior, and Prince Salman, governor of Riyadh, quoted in Milton Viorst, "The Storm and the Citadel," *Foreign Affairs* 75, no. 1 (1996): 107.

15. In private conversations in Riyadh and Tabuq in December 2005 and March 2006, young, university-educated professional Saudis working in the public and private sectors privately expressed to me their strong opposition to social reforms that are usually associated with the older generations, especially the public mixing of sexes and allowing women to drive.

16. I learned firsthand of several such instances in the late 1960s during my assignment to the US military training mission in Riyadh.

17. Amin al-Rihani, *Najd Wal Mulhaqatihu* (Beirut: Dar al-Rihani Lil Tabaa Wal Nashr, 1964), pp. 260–261.

18. Hafiz Wahhab, *Al-Jazirat al-Arabiyah Fil Qarn al-Ashrin* (Cairo: Matbaat al-Nahdat al-Misriyah, 1961), p. 295.

19. al-Rihani, *Najd Wal Mulhaqatihu,* pp. 260–261.

20. Surat al-Umran. See also Wahbah, *Al-Jazirat al-Arabiyah Fil Qarn al-Ashrin,* p. 293; also ibn Bishr, *Anwan al-Majd Fi Tarikh al-Najd* (Riyadh: Dar Bann lil Taba'ah wa Tajlid, 1953), pp. 14–15.

21. When I asked Ikhwan how they justified the risk of going to battle without weapons, they replied, "We counted on God to supply them."

22. Wahhab, *Al-Jazirat al-Arabiyah Fil Qarn al-Ashrin,* p. 295; Amin al-Rihani, *Muluk al Arab* (Beirut: Dar al-Rihani Lil Tabaa Wal Nashr, 1960), p. 82.

23. Abd al-Wahhab's treatise *Al Usul al-Thalathan Wal Adilatahu,* and Sulayman ibn Samhah Al-Nejdi's *Al-Hudiyah al-Sunniyah,* were used as catechisms. See also John Habib, *Ibn Saud's Warriors of Islam: An Interpretive Study of a Special Relationship* (Leiden: Brill, 1973), chaps. 3–4.

24. Habib, *Ibn Saud's Warriors of Islam,* p. 58.

25. Ibid., p. 54.

26. This fear existed as late as the mid-1960s when I was living in Riyadh. Some Ikhwan, easily identified by their dress, still lived there and in surrounding villages.

27. Amin al-Rihani, *Ibn Saoud of Arabia: His People and His Land* (London: Constable, 1928), p. 211.

28. Majid bin Khathila, emir of Al-Ghut-Ghut, the "notorious" Utaybah Ikhwan hijra, delivered the letter of revolt to ibn Saud. He befriended me in the 1960s and was a gracious host. When I asked how he, a devout Wahhabi and powerful Ikhwan leader, could permit his son and daughter to study in the United States, he replied, "Those were my days, these are theirs" *(Iyyami iyyamhum).*

29. al-Rihani, *Ibn Saoud of Arabia,* p. 211.

30. Ibid.

31. "I have become King of this country by the will of God." Ibn Saud quoted in al-Qabesi, *Holy Qur'an & the Sword,* p. 89.

32. The fall of the Ottoman and British empires, and the rise of US power. See Muhammad Jalal Kishk, *Al-Saudiyah Wal Hal al Islami* (London: Moody Graphics and Trans. Centre, 1961), chaps. 1–2.

33. Majid bin Khathilah was the chief of the highly feared Ikhwan hijra of Al-Ghut-Ghut, whose very name terrified the people. In his tent, pitched just beyond the ruins of Al-Ghut-Ghut, surrounded by rows of tribesmen, young and old, I asked him if the legend was true that on the eve of the Battle of Sibylla he had handed the official Ikhwan notice of revolt to ibn Saud personally without saying "peace be on you" *(assalaam alaykum),* in keeping with Ikhwan practice not to address infidels with that Islamic greeting. Reluctantly he admitted it was true. When I asked how ibn Saud had punished him for his role in the revolt, he replied: "Oh, he knew how to punish a man, all right. He ordered Al-Ghut-Ghut destroyed, never to be rebuilt, but even worse he had the hair on my head and beard shaved. I was so humiliated I hid in the wilderness until it grew back."

34. Muhammad al-Manna, *Arabia Unified* (London: Hutchinson Benham, 1980), p. 132.

35. "Today security prevails throughout the entire country. . . . I am not saying this to boast of it but to point out that we . . . are part of the forces of Allah." Ibn Saud quoted in al-Qabesi, *Holy Qur'an & the Sword,* p. 89. See also al-Rihani, *Ibn Saoud of Arabia,* p. 218: "A camel may have succumbed to its heavy burden and was dying. The owner would go away and come back in three days with a new camel. The old camel would be dead but the merchandise would still be there."

36. These conditions existed as late as 1970 when I was living in Riyadh.

37. al-Manna, *Arabia Unified,* p. 23. These characterizations refer to the Hijaz prior to its conquest by ibn Saud.

38. Teitelbaum, *Rise and Fall of the Hashemite Kingdom,* p. 223.

39. Colonel C. E. Wilson to Major Young, London, British Public Records Office, F.O. 371/4147.

40. "Preservation of integrity and security of Saudi Arabia is one of basic objectives of U.S. in Near East. . . . In case Saudi Arabia should be the victim of aggression or should feel that it is seriously threatened with aggression and should bring its case before the UNO, USG will live up meticulously to obligations when it signed the charter." Acting Secretary of State to the Minister in Egypt (Tuck) for Eddy, *FRUS,* January 19, 1946, p. 738.

41. "We want Shurah to combine Sunna with Allah's command in the Quranic Verse." Ibn Saud quoted in al-Qabesi, *Holy Qur'an & the Sword,* p. 66.

42. "Working Meeting," Faisal, Green, Henderson, *FRUS,* vol. 3, 1945, pp. 1002–1003.

43. Habib, *Saudi Arabia and the American National Interests.*

44. Ibid. The British believed that because of their long relationship with ibn Saud, they, not the Americans, should have a privileged position in the kingdom. "What am I to believe when the British tell me that my future is with them and not with America? . . . That America after the war will return to her preoccupation in the Western Hemisphere? . . . On the strength of this argument they seek a priority in Saudi Arabia. What am I to believe?" *FRUS,* vol. 8, 1945, p. 8.

6

The Annexation of the Hijaz

William Ochsenwald

The integration of the Hijaz in western Arabia with other regions controlled by the Saudi dynasty has been a slow, precarious, and complex process, often involving resistance by the Hijazis. Nevertheless, during the initial period of Saudi rule, from 1926 to 1939, the Saudi royal family, based in the Najd in central Arabia, and their religious allies, the Wahhabi ulama, were relatively successful in eliminating opposition and co-opting many Hijazis, even before the arrival of post–World War II oil revenues. The process of regional integration, including both resistance and the successful means to overcome it, has continued ever since.

Religious discourse was one of the most important elements used by the Saudi regime in all phases of this process: the advent of the new administration, the creation of the state, and the legitimization of the ruling dynasty. To further this purpose, the Najdi ulama wanted the population of the Hijaz to convert to the Wahhabi version of Islam.[1] The Saudi ruler, Abd al-Aziz ibn Abd al-Rahman al-Saud, known in the West as ibn Saud, endorsed this goal, but also often chose to adopt pragmatic policies, seeking to obtain security through gaining the acquiescence of the population to a slow transformation of Hijazi society.

The historical background of the Hijaz before the Najdi-Saudi conquest of 1924–1925 provided a framework that both hindered and favored the new rulers. Since the foundation of Islam in the seventh century, the three major cities of the Hijaz—Mecca, Medina, and Jidda—had been far more cosmopolitan, wealthy, and externally oriented than Najd. While Najd was often an independent area, the Hijaz usually was incorporated into large Muslim empires, including, for the four centuries before World War I, the Ottoman state. During the Ottoman era, a brief period of Saudi control of the holy cities in the early nineteenth century had been marked by turmoil and the imposition of harsh religious control. These factors suggested that the Saudi rulers from the 1920s onward would face many problems in ruling the Hijaz, since Najd lacked the financial, military, and political resources available to the Ottomans, while earlier Saudi rule had been unpopular. On the other hand, the independent Hashimite Kingdom of the Hijaz, from 1916 to 1925, had proven such a disastrous endeavor that almost any alternative would have been considered an improvement.[2]

In central Arabia, the young Abd al-Aziz had come into power on the basis of several factors, both secular and religious, including his leadership skills, his family's status, and his strict adherence to the Wahhabi version of Islam. Abd al-Aziz came to be seen as the "guardian of ritualistic Islam" and therefore the legitimate ruler. This role was expressed through implementing zakat and jihad, and obtaining obedience through both voluntary and compulsory means.[3] Saudi identity was based on the community of those who accepted the leadership of the ruler, his dynasty, and the Wahhabi ulama's interpretation of Islam.

The religious basis of Saudi rule in the Hijaz was clearly stated by Abd al-Aziz, who had taken the title of sultan, in a decree published in late 1924 in the first issue of the new Meccan newspaper *Umm al-Qura*. Abd al-Aziz said that the reason for coming to the holy places was to serve God and that the basis of law would be the Quran.[4] The Hijazi ulama issued a statement supporting the new regime, and the sultan pledged to meet regularly with them. He recognized the distinctiveness of the Hijaz: God had exalted it by placing the Kaba there.[5]

In addition to this concept of religion as the basis of government, Saudi actions in regard to the pilgrimage and to the commanding of good and the forbidding of evil showed that religious values, institutions, and practices were playing a major role in creating some acceptance of the new regime, despite the Wahhabi ulama's excessive zeal. The hajj, or pilgrimage, was the single most important religious, social, economic, and governmental event in the Hijaz. Before the advent of large oil revenues, the pilgrimage provided the chief source of revenues for those who governed the Hijaz. The new Saudi regime successfully administered the pilgrimage and thereby greatly increased the willingness of urban Hijazis to accept the Saudi dynasty.[6] However, despite the success in managing the pilgrimage, there was a realization among many Hijazis that their interests were distinct from, and sometimes contradictory to, the interests of Najdis. In an attempt to overcome this sentiment, Abd al-Aziz said in 1926 that the Hijaz belonged to the Hijazis, and that, in accordance with their wishes, he would assume the title of king and ensure the safety and peace of the holy places and roads, but that the affairs of Najd and the Hijaz would be kept strictly separate.[7]

This chapter examines a few of the more important features of political, religious, and social interactions in the Hijaz: religious zeal, opposition groups, use of the military and police, establishment of new institutions, and adoption of new symbols of authority. Secular methods for integrating the Hijaz with Najd are also briefly addressed.

Religious Zeal

The Saudi regime in the Hijaz implemented a number of religious rulings to enforce rigorous Wahhabi strictures. Even more alarming initially was the unauthorized massacre of civilians when the Ikhwan forces took Taif on September 5, 1924. This revived fears among Hijazis that the harsh circumstances of the first Saudi period of control over the Hijaz might be repeated. However, Abd al-Aziz's extension of control was thereafter more gradual and careful. Most Hijazis initially welcomed Saudi stability, the end of combat, and the enforcement of law and order, but they also were uneasy about Wahhabi zealotry. Through the appointment of Wahhabi ulama as religious officials, Abd al-Aziz gained an important means for influencing the Hijaz, though subsidiary posts were still filled by Hijazi ulama.

The new administration soon demonstrated its rigorous policies. The directorate for *sharia* affairs was given responsibility for courts, waqfs, and mosques, including the Meccan Haram. Abd al-Aziz first appointed Abd Allah ibn Bulayhid of Najd (1867–1940) as Grand Qadi of the Hijaz, headquartered in Mecca. But the relatively lenient ibn Bulayhid was replaced around 1927 by the more rigorous Abd Allah ibn Hasan ibn Husayn Al al-Shaikh (b. 1870), who served until his death in 1959.[8]

The new administration ordered that all Muslims (meaning men and not women) must pray together and strictly observe the times of prayer. Smoking and drinking alcohol were prohibited. The first violation of this prohibition would result in a prison sentence, while subsequent violations would lead to exile. Prohibitions were issued against picnics, dancing, taking oaths in the name of the Prophet Muhammad, and burning candles at tombs. Local Hijazi ulama had to accept Wahhabi doctrine on the sources of law and on *tawhid* (belief in God's unity). The Committee to Promote Virtue and Prevent Vice issued orders to prohibit public mourning of the dead, the shaving of beards, and the wearing by men of gold or silver ornaments.

The use of religious police in the Hijaz was justified by Muhammad Bahjat al-Baytar (d. 1976), a young theologian originally from Damascus. Administrative control over the religious police, their relations with the regular police force, and the regulations under which the religious police operated varied. Abd al-Aziz permitted increased rigor by the religious police in 1927–1928 and 1931, but he, and especially his son and viceroy Faisal, often limited their powers. While some Hijazis participated in the work of the committees and the religious police, these were dominated by Najdis.[9]

Rules reflecting extremely strict Najdi Wahhabi views on the moral conduct of women were established. For example, women were prohibited from visiting tombs, and had to be escorted by a male relative when traveling in the evening. Earlier condemnation of amulets, mourning, fortune-telling, and other elements of unofficial Islam heavily affected women, who were banned from participation in most religious rituals. So, for instance, while both men and women were ordered not to mourn the dead, men could publicly participate in carrying a body to the site of burial, but women were not permitted to participate in the funeral cortege.[10]

Saudi administrators banned a wide variety of items and behaviors. For instance, both phonograph players and liquor were forbidden. Public executions designed to carry out the *sharia* and to deter crime took place throughout the Hijaz, including in the holy city of Mecca, thereby departing from the custom of earlier rulers. The Saudi administration publicly condemned what it considered religious vices.

Additional measures taken by the authorities to privilege Wahhabi discourse in the Hijaz involved religious architecture, education, and publishing. The Grand Qadi went to Medina, where he procured a fatwa condemning the use of domes over tombs.[11] Most of the domes over the tombs of prominent early Muslim leaders were then destroyed. Religious teaching in Mecca was limited in 1928 to certain sites; only government-authorized teachers could legally give lessons.[12] However, few students studied with the Wahhabi ulama resident in Mecca; instead, most Hijazis preferred to study with Hijazi teachers. Only Wahhabi religious principles were to be taught in the schools and mosques. Advance permission from the government was required before publication of the Quran or hadiths. Publishers were threatened by fines or even imprisonment if they published books containing what the government deemed superstition, heterodoxy, and heresy. Booksellers had to register and supply a list of their inventory to the authorities. The government and the religious establishment also condemned sorcery, magic, intoxicants, gambling, eating pork, and sodomy.[13]

The new regime in the Hijaz banned the performance of most Sufi rituals and apparently banned most, but not all, Sufi orders. Sufi leaders moved away from the holy cities. Fragmentary evidence suggests that Sufis continued privately teaching in Mecca and Medina, but their ceremonies were held in secret with small numbers of people.[14]

Saudi authorities usually treated Shia Muslims as inferior to Sunnis. Apparently, Shias of the Saudi state in the Hijaz were not treated as repressively as the Shias living in Al-Ahsa, but relatively little is known about Hijazi Shias for the period 1926–1939. Shias were buried in locations separate from those of Sunnis. The regime prohibited public Shia religious ceremonies, though private ceremonies in unmarked buildings persisted. Shias were excluded from formal study at the Medina Haram. With no local training facilities for Shia ulama, Shia students had to leave Saudi Arabia for study in Iraq or Iran. No separate courts existed for Shias, and building mosques intended for Shias was forbidden.[15]

In addition to such changes in the treatment of religious groups as a result of formal regulations, there were other changes in religious praxis that were strongly encouraged though not actually mandated. Formerly the call to prayer had differed from town to town, with calls to prayer in Mecca and Medina more elaborate than those in Najd. Now only the Wahhabi version of the call to prayer was employed. Most important, the *mawlid* ceremony, commemorating the birth of the Prophet Muhammad, formerly celebrated with great enthusiasm in the Hijaz, continued semi-secretly after 1926, since the Najdi ulama frowned upon it.[16]

Yet during this same period of rigorous regulations, Abd al-Aziz was also periodically trying to moderate the severity of his ulama to decrease the tension resulting from their desire to impose Wahhabi ways on the Hijazis. In speeches to pilgrims and others, Abd al-Aziz often emphasized the need for Muslim unity.

Committees established to enforce the new regulations did not always do so rigorously. An example is that horse racing remained permitted, perhaps because the king and the royal court patronized it.[17] Just a few months after crackdowns, phonograph records and alcohol were once again widely available in Jidda, and in Mecca prayers were less often observed, more people smoked cigarettes in the streets or water pipes inside shops, and there was public singing of songs.[18]

Initially, the Meccan Haram saw the replacement of a variety of Sunni imams leading prayer services with just one imam, a Wahhabi. By October 1926, protests led to a new ruling whereby two Wahhabi imams had a superior status, but imams from the Hanafi, Maliki, and Shafii rites also served. However, by mid-1929 this situation had been revised once again, so that all Muslims prayed together and three imams using only the Hanbali rite led them.[19]

In the later 1930s, measures were taken once again to promote the application of rigorous Wahhabi views in the Hijaz, including a ban on any three-dimensional representations of living creatures, such as children's dolls. In 1938, playing cards were banned. Despite such decrees, people continued to behave in ways that were even more frowned upon than children playing with dolls, as demonstrated by foreign sailors who visited Jidda on overnight leave to find prostitutes. Allegedly *'araq,* a potent alcoholic beverage, was secretly distilled in Mecca.[20]

Despite such defiance and popular opposition among Hijazis and some foreigners, governmental regulations, religious practices, and behavioral patterns mandated by the king and the Saudi administration prevailed. In the course of time Wahhabism came to seem less objectionable to urban Hijazis, especially in comparison to the problems endured by the population during the last years of the Ottoman Empire and during the period of Hashimite rule.

▨ Opposition to Saudi Rule

Saudi authorities consolidated their rule in the Hijaz by suppressing individuals and groups who favored other possible rulers, whether these challenges came from outside or inside the Hijaz. King Abd al-Aziz deftly maneuvered international Muslim opinion to forestall external intervention, while seeking the backing of Great Britain. Internally, the king faced limited resistance among the nomadic tribes and the urban dwellers.

The nomadic tribes of the Hijaz remained relatively calm in the first years of Saudi rule, until the drought of the late 1920s and the economic depression of the early 1930s created terrible hardships and the preconditions for widespread discontent. In the one major case of a tribal anti-Saudi uprising, Hamid ibn Rifada of the Billi in May 1932 entered the Hijaz with several hundred fighters. He came from Egypt via Transjordan, almost certainly with the aid of Transjordanian authorities and possibly with support from King Fuad of Egypt, Hashimites in Iraq, and various Hijazi exiles living in Egypt. Sections of the Billi, Huwaytat, Juhayna, and Atiyya tribes joined ibn Rifada, bringing his forces up to about 1,500 men. Abd al-Aziz mobilized between 5,000 and 10,000 fighters from Najd, as well as sections of the regular Hijazi army, and decisively defeated ibn Rifada on July 30, 1932. The Saudis killed ibn Rifada, two of his sons, and hundreds of his troops. Despite this success, it can safely be assumed that Wahhabi proselytizing had not yet fully reached the more distant parts of the Hijaz.[21]

The government also suppressed possible internal public criticism of the regime by establishing regulations against opponents. The administration outlawed meetings held for the purpose of circulating rumors or conspiring against the state. The punishment for such activities was imprisonment for two to five years or exile from the Hijaz. Any meeting, no matter what its purpose, required a report to the government and advance approval.[22] This extraordinary constraint on social interaction showed that the Saudis worried about the loyalty of the Hijazis. Similarly, the government enacted strict controls over book and newspaper publication in April 1929, while in 1935 Saudi Arabia issued regulations prohibiting the import, sale, and possession of firearms.[23]

The exiled Hashimite sharifs who were now rulers of Transjordan and Iraq had left behind relatively few backers, but still owned some real property. Abd al-Aziz agreed with the British on December 17, 1925, to guarantee the personal safety of those sharifs who resided in the Hijaz. Disputes over Hashimite property in the Hijaz lingered on for years until finally resolved in 1933, when the king removed all restrictions on the property of the sharifs. In May 1926, Sharif Muhsin al-Mansur, uncle of former king Ali, was arrested and sent to Riyadh. Then thirty-four other Hijazis were arrested for treason. This group included Sayyid Ahmad Saqqaf, former lord chamberlain to King Ali. The conspirators had supposedly been meeting in secret and planning the overthrow of the Saudis, while corresponding with persons in Yemen and Egypt.[24] Border tensions with Transjordan and Iraq, and Transjordanian support of the ibn Rifada revolt, also made the Saudis suspicious of the Hashimites.

Many Hijazis who did not favor a Hashimite restoration nevertheless still wanted a decentralized Saudi state, so that the interests of the Hijaz could receive more attention. There were also occasional public indications of anti-Saudi feeling, as in the appearance of a large notice, on the walls of Mecca's post office, asking why Syrians should administer the Hijaz and why Hijaz money was going to Najd. In August 1927 the government arrested twenty-three persons, six of whom held positions in the Hijaz administration, charging them with anti-Saudi conspiracy.[25]

Internally, the ulama of Najd had been intent on "Wahhabization," but nearly all Hijazis, most foreign pilgrims, and Muslim religious officials abroad, were opposed to this goal. The imposition of Najdi patterns in the Hijaz, already somewhat unpopular, became even more of a problem during the Great Depression. A conference of Hijazi notables and merchants in 1931 criticized extravagant spending, called for a government budget, opposed using Hijazi revenues for subsidies to Najdi tribes, and expressed a desire for a more powerful and elected consultative council. While the king rejected these demands, private pressure from the viceroy, high officials, and Hijazi notables later in 1931 did lead to some reforms, including increased powers for Faisal as viceroy of the Hijaz.[26]

Perhaps the most widespread anti-Saudi activity was a conspiracy led by businessmen Husayn Tahir al-Dabbagh and his brother Muhammad. In 1927, Husayn al-Dabbagh founded in Mecca an antimonarchical group; in 1928 he was exiled. His views were endorsed by exiles in Egypt, who in the late 1920s organized the Hizb al-Tahrir al-Hijazi (Hijazi Liberation Party, also called Al-Ahrar al-Hijazi), which favored the liberation of the Hijaz from Saudi rule and the establishment of representative government. The group was financed by rich exiled Hijazi businessmen, Transjordanian leaders, and possibly prominent Egyptians. This conspiracy had connections to Iraq, Transjordan, Asir, and Yemen, and enjoyed some support within the Hijaz itself. Arrests in June 1932 quashed local support, as sixteen accused members were exiled to Najd, though the king soon pardoned them. A former head of the regular army, Fawzi al-Qa'ukji, was arrested in Mecca on suspicion of involvement with the conspiracy. In 1932, the Saudi authorities formally banned political parties.[27] In November 1932, an uprising in Asir led by members of the Idrisi family, but with links to Yemen and the Dabbaghs, broke out. By January 1933, Saudi forces had crushed most of the opposition in Asir. However, Husayn al-Dabbagh remained abroad until 1942.

The failure of the opposition—the ibn Rifada tribal revolt, local unrest in Mecca, and the Dabbagh group—can be attributed in large part to poor organization, unclear goals, crosscutting purposes among their sponsors, leaks of plans to the Saudis, and British opposition. King Abd al-Aziz's policy of clemency was also a success. He often welcomed back former exiles and even appointed some of them to government positions. Moreover, Saudi rule in the Hijaz was not as deeply unpopular as the various opponents had expected.[28]

However, criticism of the regime also took the form of widespread accusations of corruption directed against high officials. Critics cited the lack of a distinction between the state's finances and those of the royal family. Opposition to Saudi rule centered even more often on the Najdi-Wahhabi regional and religious orientation of the royal family. In addition, some Hijazis favored their own regional values, customs, and beliefs—their own Hijazi identity, as opposed to a putative Saudi identity based on Najdi values.

■ Use of the Military and Police

The security of the state in the Hijaz depended initially on the Ikhwan, but they were ordered to return to their home bases outside the Hijaz in 1926, though they would later be recalled as needed. The Ikhwan forces were curbed by early 1930,[29] but the fiscal crisis of the 1930s meant that it was difficult to find money for their replacements—the army and police.

For both Hijazis and pilgrims visiting the holy cities, maintaining security along the pilgrimage routes was crucial. In order to do this, the nomads of the Hijaz had to be placated.[30] The means King Abd al-Aziz employed to gain security along the pilgrim routes included personal persuasion, appeals to religion, dispensing money and gifts,[31] settling border disputes involving nomadic tribes, and most important of all, the occasional use of force. In January 1926, Abd al-Aziz summoned the leaders of the tribes to Mecca, where he divided the pilgrimage routes among them. Each leader was responsible for guaranteeing security in a particular area, and assumed a collective obligation for the actions of all tribal members. The tribes would have to accept the *sharia,* pay the alms tax, go on jihad when summoned by the king, and protect travelers, who would no longer have to pay protection money. Raiding was outlawed. On the other hand, the king would provide the tribes with subsidies.[32]

Recruitment for the regular army was broadened to include urban Hijazis, with town shaikhs ordered to supply men, though no formal conscription system was established. By late 1926, the army in the Hijaz numbered about 2,000 but still consisted almost entirely of Najdi irregulars. The Saudis recruited some soldiers and officers from the forces of former king Ali, and also hired a number of former Ottoman officers. Troops were formed into three regiments—artillery, machine-gunners, and infantry.[33] By 1932, official figures for the whole country showed 1,800 in the regular armed forces, 12,700 in the camel corps, and 26,800 in garrisons, plus 1,400 frontier guards.

Foreign observers rated the Saudi regular army as ineffectual. In late 1934 the government announced the opening of a military academy in Mecca that would offer training for officers. Regular soldiers, as opposed to tribal irregulars, were to wear uniforms. Responsibility for the army was in the hands of Abd Allah Sulayman, the minister of finance, while the police were under the control of Emir Faisal. By 1939, some elements in the Saudi government seemed to prefer a small regular paid army as opposed to relying chiefly on tribal forces, but the regime still remained dependent upon tribal and urban-based levies from Najd for most of its available forces.

The poorly armed police had to undertake a variety of tasks in regard to public security. Religious police had a separate organization and duties; they were widely unpopular because of their rigorous enforcement of Wahhabi strictures. The regular police were used to control the routes between the major cities—foreign travelers had to show passports to the police, and at the gates of Medina police examined the identity papers of those wishing to enter the city.[34] Police also carried out public executions and lashings in towns and cities, usually on Fridays, as a deterrent to crime.[35]

The army and police provided the means for controlling the Hijaz. However, successful rule depended also upon positive acts designed to build institutions, create symbols of sovereignty, and encourage uniformity between Najd and the Hijaz.[36]

■ Secular Institutions, Symbols, and Uniformity

The Saudi administration tailored the state's secular institutions and policies to help secure its rule in the Hijaz. By 1932 the government even felt confident enough of its authority to conduct a census of the males living in the Hijazi cities, although with the assurance that the census would not be used for conscription or taxation.[37] The Saudi regime also reorganized certain secular government agencies, such as those dealing with customs, municipalities, health, and schools.

Three important symbols of secular sovereignty were Saudi passports, postal stamps, and coins. Authorities first issued passports in 1926. New Saudi postage stamps appeared in 1926 and 1934. The Saudi regime minted in Mecca several small copper coins in 1925–1926, and silver riyal coinage was introduced in 1927–1928.[38]

Personal identity was organized in the new nationality law of 1926. Thereafter, all former Ottoman subjects born in the Hijaz were Hijazis, all persons born thenceforth in the Hijaz were Hijazis, and every resident not carrying valid documents proving his or her foreign nationality was also a Hijazi.[39] The 1926 regulation on Hijazi nationality as amended in 1931 assumed that all Hijazis were Muslims. While these regulations helped to define Hijazi legal identity, controls over foreign visitors also defined identity by excluding the "other," the non-Hijazi. All foreigners had to have a guarantor in case there should be any claims on the person when she or he left the country. Only pilgrims who came just for one short visit were exempted from this requirement. By 1938, foreigners needed a permit to stay in Saudi Arabia for more than one year. Some foreign Muslims objected that the Hijaz was no longer the land of all Muslims, but rather was becoming the exclusive domain of the Saudis.[40]

Official regulations and policies were supplemented by measures designed to achieve royal control over the Hijaz through changes in basic social values and customs. Perhaps marriage was the most important religiously sanctioned social custom. According to British sources, in 1930 the government sent the Hijaz's Majlis al-Shura a "measure ordaining compulsory marriage for all upon reaching maturity [with the] excess female population of Nejd . . . to be mated with the bachelors of the Hejaz." This unusual proposal apparently had no practical consequences, but it reflected a real need of the state.[41] It should be noted in the context of marriage that King Abd al-Aziz did not marry into any of the prominent Hijazi families.[42] Unfortunately there is little evidence as to how many nonroyal Najdis married Hijazis.

In addition to marriage patterns, Hijazis expressed their identities through clothing. Hijazi attire differed from that of other Saudi regions. However, Najdi styles became predominant after the Saudi conquest, at least for officials, when the government required its male workers in the Hijaz to wear the Najdi-style headdress. Najdi ulama wanted their Hijazi counterparts to wear head coverings that would reflect a Najdi sensibility. In June 1937 the government issued an order via the town crier that all Muslim Saudi men in Jidda must wear beards and not shave them. Hijazi women had worn veils of pale colors, but now they had to wear black veils.[43] Thus Hijazi women were obliged to wear external clothing that obscured any possible regional variations between Saudi women coming from different parts of the kingdom. However, it seems likely that most people, in their clothing as well as in their culinary customs, music, and styles of residential architecture, preserved at least some of the heterogeneity of the Hijaz, thereby reflecting an identity separate from that of Najd.[44]

Among all the factors tending toward the elimination of Hijazi local identity, religiously linked institutions and government practices were the most important. However, military might, patronage networks, the creation of national symbols and customs, and regulations defining citizenship all played a role in the solidification of Saudi rule in the Hijaz.

▪ Conclusion

The Saudi use of religion in the Hijaz between 1926 and 1939 helped establish the dynasty's control over the region even before the advent of oil riches.

While Wahhabi zealotry offended the Hijazis, King Abd al-Aziz was also sometimes able to adopt pragmatic policies that somewhat mitigated the harshness of Wahhabi practices. His excellent management of the pilgrimage was one of the greatest factors in the somewhat grudging acceptance of Saudi rule. By 1939, Hijazis and Najdis still regarded themselves as separate people, with Najdi dominance often resented by Hijazis.

By 1939, Saudi national identity did not yet exist to any substantial extent in the Hijaz. Instead, subjects of the Kingdom of Saudi Arabia, a nascent nation whose name was based upon that of the royal family and which contained the holiest Muslim sites, held many other identities and loyalties. Hijazis belonged to overlapping categories and interest groups based on family, gender, tribe, religious sect, economic group, and cultural background, to name just a few. Political identity was uncertain, amorphous, and changeable. However, the new Saudi regime, in the short time between 1926 and 1939, had made substantial strides toward reducing overt opposition in the Hijaz, both through the use of armed force and by peaceful means.

Building upon a reasonably able provincial administration, minimal revenues, new methods of transportation and communication, British support, and the personal abilities of the king, the Saudi regime ruled the Hijaz despite the problems posed by the Great Depression. Nevertheless, substantial opposition to Saudi rule still persisted, certainly among restive tribal groups, but also among families who had been linked to the earlier Ottoman and Hashimite regimes.

In certain senses the Hijaz remained substantially different from other regions. The basic character of the inhabitants was different, with the urban populations of the Hijaz having a more cosmopolitan background and diverse interests as compared to the townspeople of Najd.

While the Saudi monarchy united the Hijaz with Najd through the person of the king, administratively the Hijaz enjoyed a special status arising from its earlier history and its religious role. Factors linking together the provinces of the Saudi realm included some common institutions, a growing closeness in religious matters, joint interests in the success of the pilgrimage and the economy, and a fear of any great alteration in the political structure that might lead to chaos, anarchy, and civil or international wars. Even those who were unhappy with Saudi rule seldom favored Hijazi independence or secession.[45] Increasingly, Hijazis became reconciled to Saudi rule.

The union of the various provinces into one political unit had been symbolically expressed in September 1932 when the king changed the state's name from the Kingdom of Hijaz and Najd and Its Dependencies to the Kingdom of Saudi Arabia. The separate names of Hijaz and Najd were thus eliminated from the official designation of the state. Gaining first the acquiescence and later the more willing acceptance of the Hijazis to Saudi rule was a slow and difficult process, but one that was substantially under way by 1939.

Saudi rule in the Hijaz was subsequently made difficult by the uncertainties and adverse economic circumstances posed by World War II. However, after 1945, royalties from oil operations in eastern Arabia made Saudi Arabia enormously rich. While governmental spending of the oil money favored Najd, large sums also flowed to the Hijaz and especially to its merchant families. Saudi religious policies in the Hijaz after 1945 continued to be reflected both in successful management of the pilgrimage and in the imposition of zealous and often unpopular Wahhabi interpretations of Islam. This unpopularity decreased somewhat with a dramatic improvement in educational opportunities, both for men and women, which helped spread Wahhabi or neo-Wahhabi values and views in the region.

Open opposition in the Hijaz to Saudi rule was almost nonexistent, except for the unsuccessful rebellion by religiously inspired rebels who seized the Meccan Haram in 1979. Partially in reaction to that event, the Saudi government emphasized even more strongly the religious policies and credentials that helped earn it acceptance among most Hijazis.[46] Beneath the surface, however, a sense of the separateness of Hijazi cultural identity lingered on, separating the Hijaz from other Saudi regions. In the 1990s, largely in reaction to Saudi Arabia's military dependence on the United States, radical critics from the Hijaz such as Osama bin Laden launched passionate religious criticisms against the Saudi ruling elite. However, the Saudi government maintained its firm control in the Hijaz region, in part due to the religiously based and secular policies, institutions, and procedures that had been put in place during the period 1926 to 1939.

▓ Notes

Parts of this chapter were delivered at the 2004 and 2005 meetings of the Middle East Studies Association. A lengthier discussion of certain aspects of the chapter may be found in William Ochsenwald, "Islam and Loyalty in the Saudi Hijaz, 1926–1939," *Die Welt des Islams* 47, no. 1 (2007).

1. Most Saudis rejected the term "Wahhabi," arguing that so-called Wahhabism was simply a stronger version of the unitarianism in which all Muslims believed. In 1929, Wahhabis were termed "followers of ibn Hanbal and ibn Taymiyya" by Hafiz Wahba. See Hafiz Wahba, "Wahhabism in Arabia: Past and Present," *Journal of the Central Asian Society* 26, no. 4 (1929): 58. Nevertheless, since the term "Wahhabi" was so widely used, I will employ it in this chapter. This term is not intended to have any derogatory connotations.

2. Useful sources for the pre-Saudi history of the Hijaz include William Ochsenwald, *Religion, Society, and the State in Arabia: The Hijaz Under Ottoman Control, 1840–1908* (Columbus: Ohio State University Press, 1984); Hasan Kayali, *Arabs and Young Turks: Ottomanism, Arabism, and Islamism in the Ottoman Empire* (Berkeley: University of California Press, 1997); Joshua Teitelbaum, *The Rise and Fall of the Hashemite Kingdom of Arabia* (New York: New York University Press, 2001).

3. Madawi al-Rasheed, *A History of Saudi Arabia* (New York: Cambridge University Press, 2002), p. 51.

4. *Umm al-Qura,* December 15, 1924, p. 1.

5. *Umm al-Qura,* December 19, 1924, pp. 1, 3.

6. The pilgrimage is discussed at length in Ochsenwald, "Islam and Loyalty in the Saudi Hijaz." Also see David Commins, *The Wahhabi Mission and Saudi Arabia* (London: Tauris, 2006), p. 78.

7. Robert L. Jarman, ed., *The Jedda Diaries, 1919–1940,* 4 vols. (Melksham: Archive Editions, 1990), Great Britain, Foreign Office, E 1399/367/91, S. R. Jordan to Austen Chamberlain, February 4, 1926, monthly report for January 1926. Security for pilgrims as a justification for Saudi rule over the Hijaz would continue to be cited by later Saudi rulers. See James Piscatori, "Managing God's Guests: The Pilgrimage, Saudi Arabia, and the Politics of Legitimacy," in *Monarchies and Nations: Globalisation and Identity in the Arab States of the Gulf,* edited by Paul Dresch and James Piscatori (London: Tauris, 2005), p. 224.

8. Jarman, *Jedda Diaries,* E 1399/367/91, Jordan to Chamberlain, February 4, 1926. For a general discussion of the early Saudi administration of the Hijaz, see Abdullah al-Uthaymin, *Tarikh al-Mamlaka al-Arabiyya al-Saudiyya,* 4th ed., pt. 2 (Riyadh: Maktaba al-Ubaykan, 1998), pp. 300–304; on the new qadi, see p. 313.

9. Ayman al-Yassini, *Religion and State in the Kingdom of Saudi Arabia* (Boulder: Westview, 1985), p. 69; Guido Steinberg, *Religion und Staat in Saudi-Arabien: Die Wahhabitischen Gelehrten, 1902–1953* (Wurzburg: Ergon, 2002), pp. 411–413, 568–573; Commins, *Wahhabi Mission and Saudi Arabia,* pp. 94–95. For a detailed discussion of the committees and their functions, see Michael Cook, *Commanding Right and Forbidding Wrong in Islamic Thought* (Cambridge: Cambridge University Press, 2000), pp. 181–187.

10. *Umm al-Qura,* December 26, 1924, p. 1; Jarman, *Jedda Diaries,* E 5083/644/91, H. G. Jakins to Chamberlain, November 6, 1927; Jarman, *Jedda Diaries,* E 4470/484/92, F. H. W. Stonehewer-Bird to Cushenden, August 31, 1928; Eleanor Abdella Doumato, *Getting God's Ear: Women, Islam, and Healing in Saudi Arabia and the Gulf* (New York: Columbia University Press, 2000), pp. 38–40, 222.

11. Werner Ende, "The Nakhawila: A Shiite Community in Medina Past and Present," *Die Welt des Islams* 37 (1997): 318; Steinberg, *Religion und Staat in Saudi-Arabien,* pp. 537–539.

12. Jarman, *Jedda Diaries,* E 4286/484/91, Stonehewer-Bird to Chamberlain, August 3, 1928. See also Mai Yamani, *Cradle of Islam: The Hijaz and the Quest for an Arabian Identity* (London: Tauris, 2004), p. 120; Steinberg, *Religion und Staat in Saudi-Arabien,* pp. 281–286.

13. Jarman, *Jedda Diaries,* E 2686/94/91, Jakins to Chamberlain, May 1, 1929; Steinberg, *Religion und Staat in Saudi-Arabien,* p. 551; Doumato, *Getting God's Ear,* p. 239.

14. Mark Sedgwick, "Saudi Sufis: Compromise in the Hijaz, 1925–40," *Die Welt des Islams* 37, no. 3 (1997); Steinberg, *Religion und Staat in Saudi-Arabien,* pp. 553, 561; C. A. Nallino, *Raccolta di Scritti Editi e Inediti* (Rome: Istuto per l'Oriente, 1938), vol. 1, p. 95, esp. n. 2; Commins, *Wahhabi Mission and Saudi Arabia,* p. 79.

15. For a discussion of Shias in and near the city of Medina, see Ende, "Nakhawila"; for Shias in the east, see Commins, *Wahhabi Mission and Saudi Arabia,* pp. 75–76.

16. Steinberg, *Religion und Staat in Saudi-Arabien,* pp. 546–547; al-Yassini, *Religion and State in the Kingdom of Saudi Arabia,* p. 48; Yamani, *Cradle of Islam,* pp. 114–115, n. 27; p. 220, n. 20; p. 223. However, it should be noted that Yamani does not clearly date the beginning point of the changes.

17. Jarman, *Jedda Diaries,* E 5333/715/25, A. S. Calvert to Simon, August 4, 1934. See also Steinberg, *Religion und Staat in Saudi-Arabien,* pp. 419–421; on p.

548 the author indicates that Faisal issued a decree in July 1929 allowing Meccans to play music, but only outside the city, such as during picnics or similar outings.

18. Jarman, *Jedda Diaries,* E 4333/557/25, Calvert to Hoare, July 1, 1935; Evelyn Cobbold, *Pilgrimage to Mecca* (London: Murray, 1934), p. 197; Steinberg, *Religion und Staat in Saudi-Arabien,* p. 548.

19. Jarman, *Jedda Diaries,* E 6655/367/91, Norman Mayers to Chamberlain, November 3, 1926; Nallino, *Raccolta di Scritti Editi e Inediti,* p. 91; Steinberg, *Religion und Staat in Saudi-Arabien,* pp. 544–545; Jarman, *Jedda Diaries,* E 4713/94/91, W. L. Bond to A. Henderson, August 22, 1929; al-Yassini, *Religion and State in the Kingdom of Saudi Arabia,* pp. 74–75.

20. Jarman, *Jedda Diaries,* E 4331/580/25, A. C. Trott to Eden, July 1, 1937; Reader Bullard, *Two Kings in Arabia: Letters from Jeddah, 1923–5 and 1936–9* (Reading, UK: Ithaca, 1993), pp. 61, 168; Steinberg, *Religion und Staat in Saudi-Arabien,* p. 573; Jarman, *Jedda Diaries,* E 7045/580/25, A. C. Trott to Eden, November 6, 1937; Jarman, *Jedda Diaries,* E 3188/720/526/7, R. Bullard to Halifax, April 1, 1938.

21. Jarman, *Jedda Diaries,* E 4944/1197/25, C. G. Hope Gill to John Simon, September 8, 1932, monthly report for July and August 1932; al-Uthaymin, *Tarikh al-Mamlaka al-Arabiyya al-Saudiyya,* 4th ed., pt. 2, pp. 240–242, 577. See also Joseph Kostiner, *The Making of Saudi Arabia, 1916–1936: From Chieftaincy to Monarchical State* (New York: Oxford University Press, 1993), pp. 74–75, 154–158.

22. Jarman, *Jedda Diaries,* E 3198/367/91, Jordan to Chamberlain, May 1, 1926, monthly report for April 1926.

23. Jarman, *Jedda Diaries,* E 7476/557/25, Calvert to Hoare, December 1, 1935, monthly report for November 1935.

24. Jarman, *Jedda Diaries,* E 3790/367/91, Jordan to Chamberlain, June 1, 1926, monthly report for May 1926.

25. Jarman, *Jedda Diaries,* E 4115/644/91, Stonehewer-Bird to Foreign Office, September 1, 1927, monthly report for August 1927.

26. Kostiner, *Making of Saudi Arabia,* pp. 148–150.

27. Jarman, *Jedda Diaries,* E 4944/1197/25, Hope Gill to Simon, September 8, 1932, monthly report for July and August 1932, pp. 158–163. See also Anita L. P. Burdett, *King Abdul Aziz: Diplomacy and Statecraft* (Chippenham: Archive Editions, 1998), vol. 2, pp. 548–549; *Umm al-Qura,* July 1, 1932.

28. Kostiner, *Making of Saudi Arabia,* pp. 158–163.

29. Commins, *Wahhabi Mission and Saudi Arabia,* pp. 80–93.

30. *Umm al-Qura,* January 23, 1925, p. 1, cites the failure of security along the pilgrimage routes as one of the main problems of the former Hashimite regime.

31. Ugo Fabietti, "State Policies and Bedouin Adaptations in Saudi Arabia, 1900–1980," in *The Transformation of Nomad Society in the Arab East,* edited by Martha Mundy and Basim Musallam (Cambridge: Cambridge University Press, 2000), p. 84.

32. Jarman, *Jedda Diaries,* E 191/367/91, Jordan to Chamberlain, March 1, 1926, monthly report for February 1926. See also Abdulaziz H. al-Fahad, "The Imama vs. the Iqal: Hadari-Bedouin Conflict and the Formation of the Saudi State," in *Counter-Narratives: History, Contemporary Society, and Politics in Saudi Arabia and Yemen,* edited by Madawi al-Rasheed and Robert Vitalis (New York: Palgrave, 2004), p. 74, n. 117.

33. Al-Uthaymin, *Tarikh al-Mamlaka al-Arabiyya al-Saudiyya,* 4th ed., pt. 2, pp. 337–338.

34. Cobbold, *Pilgrimage to Mecca,* pp. 39, 41, 120, 244. See also Kiren Aziz Chaudhry, *The Price of Wealth: Economies and Institutions in the Middle East* (Ithaca: Cornell University Press, 1997), p. 59.

35. Jarman, *Jedda Diaries,* E 3963/902/25, Andrew Ryan to Simon, July 3, 1933, monthly report for June 1933.

36. Kiren Aziz Chaudhry emphasizes that the state was built first then the economic elites (and others) participated with it in constructing a national market and a sense of common values and identity. See Chaudhry, *Price of Wealth,* p. 44.

37. Jarman, *Jedda Diaries,* E 3903/1197/25, Ryan to Simon, July 17, 1932, monthly report for May and June 1932.

38. al-Uthaymin, *Tarikh al-Mamlaka al-Arabiyya al-Saudiyya,* 4th ed., pt. 2, p. 322; Ami Ayalon, "The Hashemites, T. E. Lawrence, and the Postage Stamps of the Hijaz," in *The Hashemites in the Modern Arab World,* edited by Asher Susser and Aryeh Shmuelevitz (London: Cass, 1995), pp. 25, 30; H. C. Mueller, "Notes on the Maria Theresa Dollar in Saudi Arabia," February 1, 1956, in *Mulligan Papers* (Washington, DC: Georgetown University Library), file 8/25.

39. Jarman, *Jedda Diaries,* E 6655/367/91, Mayers to Chamberlain, November 3, 1926, monthly report for October 1926.

40. Jarman, *Jedda Diaries,* E 1699/509/172/3, Bullard to Halifax, March 1, 1938. For the 1938 citizenship law, see Nallino, *Raccolta di Scritti Editi e Inediti,* pp. 148–149. Saudi policy in regard to citizenship and landownership in some ways paralleled that of the Ottoman administration of the Hijaz.

41. Jarman, *Jedda Diaries,* E 5396/92/91, Hope Gill to Henderson, September 19, 1930, monthly report for July and August 1930.

42. Michael Herb, *All in the Family: Absolutism, Revolution, and Democracy in the Middle Eastern Monarchies* (Albany: State University of New York Press, 1999), p. 40.

43. Mai Yamani, "Changing the Habits of a Lifetime: The Adaptation of Hejazi Dress to the New Social Order," in *Languages of Dress in the Middle East,* edited by Nancy Lindisfarne-Tapper and Bruce Ingham (Richmond: Curzon, 1991), pp. 58–59.

44. Mai Yamani discusses more recent times than those covered in this chapter, but some of her observations may be applicable to the period 1926–1939. See Mai Yamani, "You Are What You Cook: Cuisine and Class in Mecca," in *A Taste of Thyme: Culinary Cultures of the Middle East,* edited by Sami Zubaida and Richard Tapper (London: Tauris Parke, 2000).

45. Kostiner, *Making of Saudi Arabia,* p. 184.

46. William Ochsenwald, "Saudi Arabia and the Islamic Revival," *International Journal of Middle East Studies* 13, no. 3 (1981); William Ochsenwald, "Saudi Arabia," in *The Politics of Islamic Revivalism,* edited by Shireen T. Hunter (Bloomington: University of Indiana Press, 1988).

7

State Power, Religious Privilege, and Myths About Political Reform

Gwenn Okruhlik

The deeply conservative nature of Saudi Arabian society is often used to explain the absence of meaningful political reform. This is a convenient myth. The idea of social conservatism as an inhibitor of political reform is propagated by the regime in order to preserve the political status quo. The ruling family structures the playing field to this end, providing space for socially conservative forces to thrive while limiting space for others. It does so to deflect attention away from explicitly political issues toward sociocultural issues. This plays out in especially interesting ways with regard to women. Thus I demonstrate in this chapter the codification of social absurdity, much of which is focused on gendered issues. I argue that this has marginalized the regime from much of the domestic constituency as well as from much of the umma. In a larger sense, though, this chapter is about the idea of Wahhabism and its relation to nation making.

My purpose is fourfold. I seek to de-mythologize conservatism in Saudi Arabia; to examine the conflation of law, tradition, and politics as they relate to gender; to articulate the irony of *al-islah* (reform), that is, to argue that present reforms serve to consolidate power; and finally, to suggest that there is an internal tension between Wahhabism and nation making.

The latter is especially interesting because, indeed, the debates in Saudi Arabia are about the big questions. Competing narratives articulate the prevailing norms that form the very bases of political and social life. These encompass the relationships among the state, ruling family, religion, and citizenry. More precisely, it is a contest over the substantive terms of citizenship, or the appropriate distributions of rights, obligations, and resources and the appropriate uses of force and wealth. Citizenship *(muwatana)* and nation (umma) are sites of privilege, exclusion, and marginalization.[1] Among diverse populations such as that of Saudi Arabia, full and equal inclusion is a sensitive subject. This is especially true, and complicated, where an exclusionary religious orthodoxy is fused with state power. In short, there is an internal tension between the exclusivity of Wahhabism and the imperatives of inclusionary nation making. The regime is far from neutral and has effectively pushed the citizenship debate into the social realm and away from its distinctly political dimensions. Reform is carefully choreographed to consolidate the ruling family's centrality in national political life and reassert its authority. Understanding Wahhabism, and its relation to power, is central to all four objectives of this chapter. It is my starting point.

Understanding Wahhabism

Observers use "Wahhabism" variously, thus conceptually obfuscating an already complicated reality. The term has multiple connotations so that substantively it refers variously to text, contemporary practice, or social manifestations. Further, it is often used differently by believers and nonbelievers, inside and outside Saudi Arabia, and its meaning varies before and after 2001.[2] The ideas of Wahhabism and salafism are often used interchangeably; indeed, the two are so conflated in policy briefs, scholarship, and journalism that they are effectively devoid of analytic content. While Wahhabism and salafism share outward signs of piety, they are analytically quite different phenomena. This is not mere semantic gymnastics but intended to capture important trends for purposes of sound analysis about power. They differ in message, politics, and ideological ends.

I use the term "Wahhabi" sparingly, only in reference to the official religious orthodoxy in Saudi Arabia.[3] As official orthodoxy, Wahhabism refers to the state creed embodied in the relationship between the ruling family and the ulama (religious scholars) whom it appoints—for example, those who serve on the Council of Senior Ulama (Hay'at Kibar al-Ulama) or in education and the judiciary. Their religious judicial opinions (fatwas) often hold less credibility and authority with individual believers because of the extraordinarily close relationship they maintain with the ruling family. Over time, the ulama were bureaucratized and made subservient to the ruling family.[4] Many Muslims, liberals and conservatives alike, charge that the official ulama codified accretions to the way of the Prophet and his companions that have nothing to do with Islam. They developed overly strict codes of behavior. Wahhabi orthodoxy today is arguably quite different from the original teachings of Muhammad ibn Abd al-Wahhab.[5]

I use the term "salafis" to refer to believers in society, whether within Saudi Arabia or in the international Muslim community, who follow the way but are not tied to the state ulama, whom many criticize. For the salafis, a return to the pious ancestors bypasses the accretions of Wahhabi ulama who were appointed by the state. Salafis prefer a direct link to the text; for them, the accretions of state ulama corrupt the pure message. While salafis have strict codes of behavior in faith, morals, rituals, and social affairs, believers look to many individual writers of fatwas to deal with complexities of modern life rather than to a single authoritative body. In a general sense, salafis are often seen as more open and tolerant than the Wahhabi orthodoxy, as many seek new ways of being Muslim in the contemporary world. Salafis are at least uncomfortable with, and often in opposition to, the official Wahhabi orthodoxy of Saudi Arabia, and see it as a central problem in the wider Muslim community. Their practice of religion is largely private.

As these social and religious practices assume explicit political expression, another term used is "neo-salafism" *(salafiyyun al-judud),* to describe those who seek to promote political change through social change. This is a fine, porous line and people draw it at different places. There are multiple avenues of neo-salafism, from progressive advocacy of pluralism, legal reforms, and elections, to intolerance to the extreme end of armed jihad. Islamist expression became an especially important part of society in the prolonged absence of expression, association, and assembly, and it was the only way to express dissent. In the protected space of Islam, ideologies were forged and networks constructed.[6] In general, adherents promote a discourse of resistance to domestic corruption and to foreign hegemony. In Saudi Arabia, they criticize the absolutism of the ruling family, and the official relationship between the al-Sauds and the state ulama. More precisely, their criticism is not aimed at the message of ibn Abd al-Wahhab but at the marriage between the al-Sauds and Wahhabi orthodoxy and at dependence on the United States, whose foreign policy they contest.

Orthodox "Wahhabi" Exclusivity

Islam, as mediated and propagated by the regime in Saudi Arabia, is exclusive and bounded, official and static, orthodox and state-centric, with clearly defined rules about what is permissible and what is prohibited. The message that emanates from official orthodoxy is mostly about a narrow reading of the text. It insists on a strict conformity in belief and behavior, and it is the state's responsibility to enforce proper behavior. It does not welcome local interpretations that vary across time or space. There is only a single religious truth, and the religious establishment claims it.

This could be a source of strength, since all Muslims share certain core, unchanging beliefs. The problem here, however, is that core beliefs have been supplemented by human interpretation and accretions. Under the guise of purity and authority, Saudi Arabia's official orthodoxy advances a rigid code of behavior in daily life that governs dress, decorum, ritual, sex, pets, and toys—a code that may not provide much meaning to citizens or to far-flung members of the global umma. As many Saudi Arabians point out, various restrictions on behavior, codified by state-appointed religious authorities, have little to do with the Quran, yet have been written in stone. These accretions reflect a particular time and a particular place—a time of patriarchy and authoritarianism inside Saudi Arabia and a place of dependence on outside powers for protection.

Official ulama in Saudi Arabia rely upon exclusive religious sources and are limited by a strict and authoritative interpretation of text. Such jurisprudence and quranic exegesis may be definitive for some believers, but others within Saudi Arabia and certainly in the broader umma now question the very idea of a single set of official interpreters. This fragmentation of religious authority highlights the complications for any aspirant to spiritual leadership in the umma if they adhere to an exclusivist, official interpretation of Islam. The regime has shown itself neither capable nor willing to lead with a broader message of tolerance and social justice.

De-Mythologizing Conservatism

It is often argued that Saudi Arabian society is more conservative than the ruling family, that princes who seek to initiate progressive change are held in check by a deeply conservative society. This is open to doubt for three reasons. First, political attitudes cannot be inferred from social attitudes. Much of Saudi Arabian society is generally conservative in social and religious affairs, particularly in the center of the country, less so along the coasts. Nevertheless, there is no necessary connection between religious devotion, social behavior, and political beliefs. One does not always imply or lead to the other. There are political liberals who are social conservatives, and social liberals who are political conservatives. Social conservatism and religious devotion do not translate into support for political authoritarianism. Conservatism has been mythologized in order to reinforce the status quo. Saudi Arabian society is diverse and can largely be characterized as devout in religious terms, traditional in social norms, and mostly apolitical in terms of activism. Yet most citizens have a desire for fair distribution of resources and the rule of law. It is state officials who propagate the idea of simple linear movement from religious conservatism to social conservatism to political conservatism or even support for political authoritarianism.

Second, it is the ruling family that systematically empowers the most conservative elements of society, giving them institutional and public space in which to operate—for example, in the sprawling bureaucracy and the educational arena. For decades, other voices were forced to remain on the periphery of discourse and power. The state is not a neutral vessel. Instead, its authoritarian representatives structure the playing field so that only one voice is heard and only one voice is safe to support.

Third, the problem in Saudi Arabia is not conservative interpretations of Islam, conservative clerics, or those who follow ibn Abd al-Wahhab. The difficulty lies in the monopoly that extreme "Wahhabi" doctrine has over the interpretation of religion and its fusion with state authority. Although denied, many people argue that *al-madhab al-Wahhabi* is indeed the sect and jurisprudence *(fiqh)* of the state.[7]

The sociopolitical consequences of Wahhabi orthodoxy stem from its official tie to the state and the subsequent imposition of belief on others. The regime enforces compliance with conformist codes in the country through law and through the institution of the religious police, the *mutawwain*. For the most part, only those who practice Wahhabi orthodoxy are rewarded with institutional and bureaucratic positions of authority. As a result, it dominates the public discourse, even as Islam is diversely practiced in private. This is the link between authoritarian politics and religious coercion.

Further, the problem is not with conservative morality but that the very idea of morality has been trivialized. It is conflated with the codification of social absurdities, demonstrated by religious rulings that regulate the plucking of eyebrows, the use of nail polish, and the length of gowns, rather than grapple with explicitly political issues that revolve around distributive fairness, governmental accountability, and social justice.

The Slippery Slope: Conflating Law, Tradition, and Politics

In the official narrative on citizenship in Saudi Arabia, there is a conflation of religious law, social tradition, and political authoritarianism. It often seems impossible to tell where one ends and the other begins. The official narrative meticulously weaves together the power of Islam and the al-Saud family as protector of Saudi Arabia's moral integrity. It equates the modern state with the fusion between the ruling family and a particular manifestation of Islam. The official narrative has produced a civic mythology in which citizenship has four social and economic components: family, personal behavior, Islam, and economic welfare.

The first component, identity with and loyalty to one's family, is of critical importance. Loyalty to the family structure is linked with loyalty to the state under the al-Sauds; the private family reinforces the public family. The second component, expected norms of social behavior, is defined fairly rigidly, and women bear the brunt of social expectations. Some behavior is declared taboo on religious grounds *(haram),* while other behavior is circumscribed by social norms of shame *(ayb).* This fuses social norms and religious interpretation.[8] The state, in turn, identifies itself with this fusion. The protection of a woman's honor is aligned with the protection of the family unit, which, as society's core institution, is expected to serve and obey the state. The third component refers to the regime's association with Islamic values. The regime promotes itself as the protector of the faith. The Quran is Saudi Arabia's constitution, and the *sharia* is the law of the land. The regime merely upholds these through its association with Wahhabi ulama. The fourth component of citizenship concerns the population's access to material benefits provided by the state. This economic aspect was added during the frenzied growth spurred by the oil boom of the 1970s. Citizenship, then, was expressed through cultural, social, and economic qualities, but devoid of political rights. Neither inclusive nor mutable, this dominant narrative could not absorb differing popular perspectives.

This conflation of religious law, social tradition, and political authoritarianism is given even more weight through the idea of *sadd bab al-dhara'i'*. The phrase has potent meanings and manifestations.[9] Literally, it refers to "the blocking of the means." In practice, it is interpreted so broadly that it is a "slippery slope." It has at least three mutually supporting dimensions: the religious-legal, the familial and social, and in the largest sense, the metapolitical, in terms of battles about the relationship between state, ruling family, citizen, and religion.

First, the slippery slope is a justification utilized by ulama in legal rulings. For example, the late shaikh Abdullah Abd al-Aziz ibn Baz, Grand Mufti on the Council of Senior Ulama, stated: "The Pure Law forbids those acts that lead to forbidden acts and considers those means to be forbidden also."[10] Behavioral prohibitions have been legalized, justified, and codified through the use of this extension. In Saudi Arabia, any behavior that is not explicitly permitted by *sharia* can be prohibited. There is another view. In other countries, that which is not explicitly prohibited by *sharia* is permitted.

Second, in everyday familial and social relationships, the slippery slope means that brothers, fathers, husbands, and fathers (*mahram,* or guardians) have a good deal of leeway with which to confine the female members of their family (how they dress, where they walk). Here, anything that leads to that which is *haram,* is itself *haram,* and anything that may lead to temptation is forbidden. This is why unrelated men and women cannot mix. Gender segregation is profound. An eloquent, if simple, lament about the effect of the slippery slope on the lives of ordinary Saudi Arabians came from a Riyadhi man: "It's just that . . . this is not normal." His was not an intellectual critique or a legal dissection, just the pained fear of a father raising several children under suffocating artificial constraints.[11] It can be used to prohibit most any behavior that the ulama (or male family members) desire to restrict. If this practice is undone, patriarchy cannot be so easily wrapped in religion. The notion of a slippery slope reflects an Islam saddled with the accretions of a state-appointed religious officialdom. After all is said and done, the danger of the slippery slope is in its ambiguity and its elasticity.

Third, the slippery slope is used in national political struggles. The issues at hand are such things as the lack of accountability of the government, corruption, injustice, and authoritarianism. But the battles are often played out on the issues that surround women. The idea of the slippery slope is most potent on the most outwardly visible issues, like driving, the mixing of men and women, guardianship, and covering. It is not that these issues are necessarily the most vital issues to women—indeed, they are not for many women—but they are outwardly visible issues and therefore vulnerable to "the blocking of the means."

In Saudi Arabia, conservative beliefs are not the issue; their codification and coercive imposition are. Ideas of social justice and political accountability are not peculiar to Western liberals. Indeed, in critiquing the harsh sentences imposed on the three men who called for a constitutional monarchy, writers have specifically invoked Islam to defend freedom of expression, debate, and tolerance of divergent opinions.[12] In sum, neither the al-Saud family nor "Wahhabism" alone is the full story. Rather, it is the excesses of each, the fusion of both, and the exclusion of all others that inhibits meaningful nation making.

Saudi Arabia's political landscape encompasses many ideas of the nation and of citizenship. Islamists of multiple shades, hues, and nationalities—and the tenuous network between some of them—offer some of the most articulate counter narratives to the official version of belonging, making them vital to political discourse. Unfortunately, it also makes them targets of the regime's efforts to co-opt, coerce, or neutralize alternative voices. Many Saudi Arabian citizens have sought to expand the tightly closed public space. The most effective among them creatively negotiate around and through authoritarian strictures to broaden the space for political contestation.

■ The Irony of *Islah:* Reform That Consolidates Power

A perennial problem in Saudi Arabia is that, once the government finally moves to institute a change, after years of study and committee work, social forces on the right and on the left have typically moved far beyond what is implemented. The regime's actions are always too little, too late, and often represent lost moments of opportunity. The irony of *al-islah* is that, for the most part, "reform" consolidates the power of the al-Saud family in political life.[13] The regime structures the playing field, through severe controls on space and participation, to reward acquiescence.

The basic law introduced in 1992 established a consultative assembly *(majlis al-shura)* and provincial administrations. Nevertheless, it also consolidated the centrality of the ruling family rather than broadening political participation. The *majlis* remains fully appointed and has only an advisory role. The number of *majlis* members has recently increased, but the expansion was designed for the assembly "to represent all tribes." Yet a significant portion of the population is not tribal, and even if it were, this justification casts light on parochial identities rather than on something larger and more inclusive.

The press has been given more leeway since 1998, but still faces red lines that cannot be crossed. Primary among these are direct criticism of the ruling family, the official religious establishment, and especially the fusion between them. Another example of how the regime structures the playing field is found in the national dialogue forums *(muntadiat al-hiwar al-watani)*. Initiated by Abdullah in June 2003, these forums turned out to be a venue for controlled dialogue to direct frustrations into acceptable channels, rather than for meaningful communication between social forces and the ruling family. The meetings held thus far have addressed vital issues, but they tend to be long on recommendations and short on implementation.[14] The formal recommendations are all politely positive, including the recognition of all sects (including the Shias), the equality of citizens, and the need to search "for ways and means to link fatwas and religious edicts with realities on the ground."[15] Still, people are cynical. One Saudi bemoaned that they often "invite the wrong people"—less effective or nonrepresentative individuals. "It is the usual rhetoric; everything still must go through the government. The dialogue is non-threatening and confidence building."[16] It is above all an effort to marginalize the extremists and thus consolidate their position. Another Saudi said, "The ironic thing is that the religious people adopted an *al-mani* [humanist] platform! But they [humanists] weren't allowed to participate in the dialogue!"[17]

In April 2005, elections were held throughout the country for municipal-level councils. There was marked ambivalence about these elections in many quarters in Saudi Arabia: only about 25 percent of the overall eligible electorate voted. The turnout was higher in the eastern part of the country, where the Shia minority resides; they effectively used the elections to assert their presence. In the months preceding the actual casting of ballots, civil servants were warned, in no uncertain language, that they would face disciplinary measures, including the loss of their jobs, if they criticized state policies or any governmental programs.[18] To say the very least, this pressure inhibits democratic dialogue. Women were not allowed to participate at all. The elections themselves were for only half of the council seats; the government finally appointed individuals to the remaining half of the seats in December 2005.

According to an activist who has worked in elections for years, "We had elections forty years ago! And they were for 100 percent of the seats on the council!" One man lamented that "the struggle was never about this. People did not get into this fierce struggle for this . . . not for half of municipal councils."[19] The councils were concerned with issues such as street paving, the size of billboards, and parking. Even though these are certainly important issues, especially in Saudi Arabia, where the development of infrastructure has not kept pace with the rate of population growth, activists feared that these meager reforms distracted people from the larger issues at hand, such as the lack of freedom of expression. Although for dissenters the elections were only a means to an end, from the regime's perspective the elections were a means *and* an end, aimed at defusing dissent and satisfying international pressure.

In these unwieldy elections, voters had to choose perhaps six candidates from a ballot of several hundred. Instant messaging and e-mail were used to circulate so-called golden lists *(al-qawa'im al-dhahabia)* of candidates, those individuals whom religious leaders deemed acceptable and portrayed as "pleasing to God." These candidates swept most of the elections. The credentials of the winners were certainly not in doubt; by all accounts, these individuals were highly competent. Nevertheless, there are different ways to interpret what has been called "the Islamist sweep." For many supporters of the winning lists, the results show how democracy works. They would argue that democracy reflects a society and that their society is conservative; that the "golden list" candidates played the game better and won, and that other contenders were incompetent.

Yet in reality the explanation may be more complex. In short, the playing field is not level in Saudi Arabia; the ruling family structures it to their advantage. Each time that people who are focused on meaningful political change put forward potential leadership, the individuals are arrested, jailed, or intimidated. For the duration of the campaign and elections, some of the most articulate nationalist reformists were in jail. The ambivalence and cynicism surrounding the elections arose because they took place without the supporting norms of freedom of expression and assembly. People are prohibited from criticizing the status quo, especially the fusion of official religious orthodoxy with the state. Although there is some room to discuss social issues, political discussion is met with intimidation.

In March 2004, thirteen reformists were arrested after they promoted the idea of a constitutional monarchy in a petition and then met to form a human rights association. Most of these men were eventually released after they signed a pledge to avoid discussing politics in public. Three men refused to sign and remained in jail; they were charged with threatening national unity, challenging those in authority, criticizing the educational system, and inciting public opinion. Their trial started and stopped several times and was eventually conducted behind closed doors. The men were handed down strict sentences in May, ranging from six to nine years. Some were released only after pledging not to engage in public politics again. Others remained in jail long after the municipal elections were over, until Abdullah had assumed leadership. The problem is not the winning candidates. They smartly took advantage of a political opening and consciously sought to expand a previously closed space; they campaigned and mobilized support. The problem remains the regime, which refuses to open protected space for all contenders, representing all social groups and all political orientations.

In February 2007, once again, ten reformists were arrested when they met to discuss such things as elections, freedom of expression, a culture of rights, and the formation of a political party. One was released for reasons of deteriorating health. The rest remain in detention without trial as of mid-2008. In late 2007, a Saudi court sentenced a prominent political activist, Abdullah al-Hamed, to six months in prison after he encouraged women to protest the detention of their relatives being held by the state. As well, a popular Internet blogger, Fouad al-Farhan, was detained for four months without charge and his blog was blocked. Television and newspaper journalists have also been recently targeted anew.

Reassertion of Regime Authority

The completion of municipal elections notwithstanding, observers suggested that, on the one hand, the legitimacy of the ruling regime was on trial, even to the point where cracks appeared in the state apparatus. They pointed to such issues as the domestic jihadist campaign, the string of assassinations in Al-Jouf, and a military that includes many oppositional Islamists. On the other hand, the same people painfully acknowledged that the regime successfully reasserted itself. How can cracks in the state occur simultaneously with a reassertion of the ruling family's authority?

Saudi Arabian social forces are engaged in a fight to fashion a moral order. The moral foundation of the regime remains on shaky ground. A just political economy would contain corruption, cease princely land grabs, attach accountability to *sharia* and civil law, and end arbitrary governance. The ruling family, however, has yet to reassert itself in moral terms or alter the behavior of some family members. Instead, it has reasserted itself through coercive power and material wealth. The ruling family has arrested and jailed liberals, nationalists, and participants in network politics; it has also co-opted some articulate members of the *sahwa* (the Islamic "awakening") and of the "rationalist" Islamist trend.

Most important, Saudi Arabia's rulers have also renewed their relationship with the official religious orthodoxy and with *sahwa* clerics. Indeed, the clerics whom the regime has empowered may later become the official ulama of the state. These men may be the *sahwa al-sultan,* so to speak. They are part of the state discourse in its fight on terrorism, providing it with the intellectual and cultural means to fight jihad. If and when these clerics become part of the state, they risk losing their voice and credibility with the population. Once co-opted by the state, the shaikhs will no longer be able to challenge the prevailing (im)moral order over which the ruling family that appointed them presides. Hence their co-optation will later become a source of popular dissent.

What allows the regime to hinder the social forces engaged in nation making? How does the regime frame its reform efforts to make them fit the legitimate cultural repertoire?[20] In its renewed relationship with religious authorities, the regime postures itself as what may be called the "guardian of virtue and custodian of change." This is reminiscent of its response to the events of 1979. When the ruling family feels threatened, it empowers the very forces that may pose a great challenge to them. This seems to be a reaffirmation of the old civic mythology and its emphasis on the al-Saud family as protector of the moral integrity of the nation. Once again, the regime uses this mythology to both enhance its Islamic credentials and keep its traditional religious constituency happy, and to take the steam out of oppositional religious forces.

Deflecting Attention from Internal Politics

When the ruling family renews its relationships with religious orthodoxy and *sahwa* clerics, it placates those who are troubled by changes to the domestic social order, especially in matters of gender, education, and religious practice. Nevertheless, it is important to recognize that only the sociocultural aspects of the *sahwa* are given safe space in the country. The political aspects of the *sahwa* are instead directed outward—for example, to Iraq, Chechnya, or Afghanistan. The consequence is that the debate over political reform is deflected to foreign issues rather than focused on domestic issues. In the context of regional crises, it has proven relatively easy to deflect attention outward.[21] Another manifestation of deflecting energy outward is found in the controversy over the publication of cartoons in Europe that were defamatory toward the Prophet Muhammad.

At the same time, the permissible domestic debate is about social issues, such as gender, media, globalization, and "reforming Wahhabism," rather than about the more difficult, explicitly political issues, such as reforming the al-Saud or the fusion of official religious orthodoxy with the state. It is much easier to offer an intellectual critique of the excesses of official religious orthodoxy than it is to talk about the excesses of some ruling family members or, most important, the fusion of Wahhabi orthodoxy with the ruling family.

There was a vibrant time from 2002 through early 2004, when fear of state retribution for political activism declined. Social forces took advantage of the intense international attention paid to their domestic circumstances and took more chances in pushing for political change. This vibrancy was squelched, however, with a crackdown once the regime felt secure that international attention was diverted to the war in Iraq. With the arrests of reformists in March 2004 and again in February and November 2007, activists became increasingly frustrated and worn down. Still, a loose national reformist network continues to press for change. Some people are co-opted, others are in abeyance, and many hope for the eventual resilience of the network. Religious television programming has increased significantly. The regime has made dubious moves, jailing reformists, appeasing conservative religious authorities, empowering the social *sahwa,* and frightening the vast majority of the population into silence. Saudis are concerned that "everybody went underground when the regime cracked down—the critical question remains, how will people emerge from underground? In what form? Last time [after the wave of arrests in 1994], they went underground and emerged as jihadis."[22]

Social forces try to lay the groundwork for political rights and a more inclusionary polity—beyond Wahhabi orthodox exclusivism—but the state blunts such efforts. Using its coercive power and material wealth, the regime seeks to diminish or neutralize any collective sense of being not directly dependent on it. Given uncertainty about the future of the region, especially the prolonged war in Iraq and US threats against Iran, there is concern about a potential resurgence of local identities, based on region, tribe, sect, or other forms of community, that may provide a sense of security in crisis. For the short term, it appears that rapid economic growth has absorbed some of the concern, at least on the surface.

The regime has returned to its quadruped of tried-and-true methods: coercion, co-optation through disbursement of oil revenues, renewed relations with religious orthodoxy, and playing social forces against one another. At the same time, the negative aspects of the rentier condition have been resurrected: skyrocketing oil prices generate more revenue, which may be used to co-opt dissenters and placate the population's material wants without addressing the messy political and social problems.

▪ The Politics of Resistance and Reform

There is of course much intra-salafi debate. It exists also within the official Wahhabi establishment, but to a more limited degree. How this internal debate matters depends on who replaces long-entrenched Wahhabi ulama. It was rumored that some senior members would retire, even though job tenure is usually for life. The orientation of new replacements would indicate the prospects for real reform or, alternatively, the perpetuation of the status quo. If more tolerant, less rigid people replace retiring ulama, then the anger and resentment long directed at the official ulama may begin to wane. New, innovative ulama may liberate Islam in the country from the heavy weight of official Wahhabi interpretive rulings that have trivialized the religion. What is needed is either multiple ulama (no single official voice except in *fiqh*) or an official ulama that demonstrates more tolerance for diversity and less tolerance for social absurdities wrapped in the logic of the slippery slope. For now, neither appears likely. Throughout 2006 and 2007, on the streets and in the courts, people continued to confront the surreal enforcement of absurdity by the *mutawwain*. Mostly, the ruling family remained on the sidelines.

Abdulaziz al-Fahad, a prominent attorney and intellectual in Riyadh, argues that Wahhabism is in fact making a transition from exclusivism to accommodation. It is an important argument. The Gulf War fatwa that invited US troops into Saudi Arabia "demonstrates an ideology that is more interested in practical politics than in ideological rigor."[23] The fatwa was a compromise made to preserve the state. This is indeed likely and significant. One could also suggest that the pragmatic accommodation to the ruling family and the United States in the official fatwa became the problem. In any case, the process of accommodation that al-Fahad eloquently describes must continue, but must also be directed inward, toward accommodating different points of view and expression within Saudi Arabian society, not just accommodating a foreign hegemon.

Whatever change does occur in Saudi Arabia, the Wahhabi establishment is not likely to be easily dismantled; however, particularly rigid individuals within it may be marginalized in the national discourse as more moderate salafi thinkers are brought aboard. The best that many hope for is to preserve the importance of the purity of belief of the early ancestors, minus the suffocating religious and social accretions by fatwa. The insertion and assertion of moderate salafis who are more persuasive and less coercive, and who are more accepting of pluralism within and without Saudi Arabia, could be a step in the right direction. But neither salafis nor Wahhabis can be the only voices represented in the ulama. The ulama and all public institutions must represent the plurality of people in Saudi Arabia. That is why loosening the hold of Wahhabi orthodoxy can be only one part of a package of reforms. It is clearly not enough as a singular objective. Unless religious reform goes hand in hand with structural political reform, it remains vulnerable to manipulation.

Political reforms will remain a sticking point even if religious exclusivism and stifling social codes are loosened. Those changes must be coupled with legal, institutional, and normative protections for the rights of free expression, association, and assembly. This is especially true for women, whose rights have often been curtailed in times of crisis or sacrificed as bargaining chips in negotiations. Women are full citizens. The population of Saudi Arabia is diverse in principled orientations and social practices. All citizens—across gender, sect, region, and ideology—must be afforded such protections. In rewriting the narrative on citizenship and belonging, explicitly political rights and protections must be guaranteed.

■ Conclusion: Wahhabism and Nation

Many Saudi Arabians do not question the coexistence of religion and the state. Instead, they ask which manifestations of religion have what relation to the state. Islam is part and parcel of an entire discourse on progress and nation. Debates in Saudi Arabia are imbued with moral dimensions. In Saudi Arabia, conservative beliefs are not the issue; their codification and coercive imposition are. As noted previously, neither the al-Saud family nor Wahhabism alone is the full story. Rather, it is the excesses of each, the fusion of both, and the exclusion of all others that inhibits meaningful nation making. There seems to be an internal tension between the exclusionary practices of official Wahhabism and nation making amid an empirically diverse society. An exclusionary religious nationalism cannot capture a diverse nation.

Wahhabism, as mediated by the regime, is authoritative and static, official and state-centric, exclusivist and bounded, concerned with specific delineations of *halal* and *haram* behavior. At the same time, both the Saudi Arabian domestic population and the umma have become ever more nuanced as a space of movement and contestation, negotiation and interpretation. As wider Muslim discourse grows more eclectic, less centered, less authoritative, and more concerned with dialogue, reform, and pluralism, the official orthodoxy and, in turn, the discourse of state and religious authorities in Saudi Arabia, remain concerned with narrower, official "Wahhabi" precepts of right and wrong, innovation and misguidance.

If Islam is a living experience that moves and breathes across time and space, can there be such a thing as an alternative interpretation of Wahhabism that provides for a more flexible and pragmatic negotiation of daily life? Just as there is no essential, immutable Islam, even as people insist they uphold the doctrine, perhaps there is no essential immutable Wahhabism. Can Wahhabism be reimagined in a way that tolerates pluralism, or would it then, in fact, be something substantively different? Wahhabi orthodoxy that is transmitted outward through *dawa* becomes something quite different in far-flung corners of the umma. While it provides meaning, structure, and belonging, the mutated frame of reference is about the transformative power of tradition, not the perpetuation of the status quo. The message of purity that has resonated so widely is not Wahhabi exclusivism but salafism that is

beyond a state and beyond a regime. It rejects officialdom. Wahhabi orthodoxy may have fueled a debate, but it did not lead the debate. What it became
instead was the subject and object of that debate. The Wahhabi frame of reference became something quite different in the ways it was received precisely
because exclusivity does not make a nation in a diverse world.

Notes

1. On citizenship and nation making, see Suad Joseph, "Introduction: Gender
and Citizenship in Muslim Communities," *Citizenship Studies* 3, no. 3 (1999); Suad
Joseph, ed., *Gender and Citizenship in the Middle East* (Syracuse: Syracuse Univer-
sity Press, 2000); Nils Butenschon, Uri Davis, and Manuel Hassassian, eds., *Citizen-
ship and the State in the Middle East* (New York: Syracuse University Press, 2000);
Sarah Radcliffe and Sallie Westwood, *Remaking the Nation: Place, Identity, and Pol-
itics in Latin America* (New York: Routledge and Kegan Paul, 1996); Sheila
Croucher, "Perpetual Imagining: Nationhood in a Global Era," *International Studies
Review,* no. 5 (2003). On myths, see Rogers Smith, "Citizenship and the Politics of
People Building," *Citizenship Studies* 5, no. 1 (2001); Madawi al-Rasheed, "God, the
King, and the Nation: The Rhetoric of Politics in Saudi Arabia in the 1990s," *Mid-
dle East Journal* 50, no. 4 (1996).

2. For different takes on Wahhabism, see Hamid Algar, *Wahhabism: A Critical
Essay* (Oneonta, NY: Islamic Publications International, 2002); Aziz al-Azmeh,
Islams and Modernities (London: Verso, 1996); David Commins, *The Wahhabi Mis-
sion and Saudi Arabia* (London: Tauris, 2006); Natana J. DeLong-Bas, *Wahhabi
Islam: From Revival and Reform to Global Jihad* (New York: Oxford University
Press, 2004); Khaled Abou el-Fadl, *The Great Theft: Wrestling Islam from the
Extremists* (San Francisco: Harper, 2005); Abdulaziz H. al-Fahad, "From Exclu-
sivism to Accommodation: Doctrinal and Legal Evolution of Wahhabism," *New York
University Law Review* 79, no. 2 (2004).

3. My preference is to avoid the word altogether. It is used here only to emphasize that the trends that are troubling today are part and parcel of the regime rather
than a reflection of free social expressions. "Regime" refers to the nexus of power
between the al-Saud and the official ulama and its apparatus, a relationship that
waxes and wanes over time but is nonetheless of long standing.

4. For discussion, see Rayed Khalid Krimly, "The Political Economy of Rentier States: A Case Study of Saudi Arabia in the Oil Era, 1950–1990," PhD diss.,
Washington, DC, George Washington University, 1993; Guido Steinberg, "The Wahhabi Ulama and the Saudi State: 1745 to the Present," in *Saudi Arabia in the Balance: Political Economy, Society, and Foreign Affairs,* edited by Paul Aarts and Gerd
Nonneman (New York: New York University Press, 2005).

5. Muhammad ibn Abd al-Wahhab was the leader of a religious revival movement in the center of Saudi Arabia, the Najd, in the early eighteenth century. Followers
of his teachings do not usually refer to themselves as "Wahhabis," as that implies worshipping someone—a human mortal—other than God. That word was not widely used
in Saudi Arabia until after 2001, when it pervaded the discourse in the West. Because
monotheism *(tawhid al-ibada)* is central, their preference instead is to call themselves
"unitarians" *(muwahhidin),* the "People of Unity" (Ahl al-Tawhid), or more commonly,
"salafi," to emphasize that they follow the early practices of pious ancestors *(al-salaf
al-salih).* They ascribe to a religious purity. Followers are exclusionary, carefully

drawing boundaries to distinguish believers from others, whether Muslim or non-Muslim. Believers, in turn, reject sectarian divisions and schools of thought that divide Muslims; they perceive only one, true Islam. In principle, they view different interpretations as a deviation from the straight path. In practice, they adhere to a certain ritual austerity and emphasize actions that are *haram* (prohibited) or *halal* (permitted). To believers, *bid'a* (innovation in religious concepts) is wrong; indeed, they promote a relatively strict code of conduct based on *sharia,* the hadith, *fiqh,* and *ibadat* (rituals of worship) that, because it is right, serves devotion on earth and, ultimately, salvation. Followers are generally antagonistic to Sufi rituals, the worship of saints *(awliya),* folk religious traditions, including superstition and animistic practices, polytheism, and the association of any person or thing with the worship of God *(shirk).* This means prohibitions on visiting graves of saints or celebrating the birthday of the Prophet Muhammad, things defined as unbelief *(kufr).* Their beliefs may be evident in outward social expression such as the degree of covering for women, whether or not a man wears an *igal,* the length of men's *thobes,* or beards, or gender segregation.

6. See Gwenn Okruhlik, "Making Conversation Permissible: Islamism in Saudi Arabia," in *Islamic Activism: A Social Movement Theory Approach,* edited by Quintan Wiktorowicz (Bloomington: University of Indiana Press, 2004); Gwenn Okruhlik, "Empowering Civility Through Nationalism: Reformist Islam and Belonging in Saudi Arabia," in *Remaking Muslim Politics: Pluralism, Contestation, Democratization,* edited by Robert W. Hefner (Princeton: Princeton University Press, 2005), pp. 189–212.

7. Hamad Saleh al-Misfr, "Ittako Allah Ya ma'shara al Kodatt Fi Ahkamikum" [Fear God, Oh Judges, As You Make Decisions], *Al-Quds al-Arabi,* May 23, 2005. Al-Misfr asks, "Do the judges [who sentenced the three men] know what they are doing or are they ordered by the sultan?"

8. Saddeka Arebi, *Women and Words in Saudi Arabia* (New York: Columbia University Press, 1994), p. 284.

9. Several interviewees discussed the central problem of "the blocking of the means," and how to unravel its damage: Dammam, July 2003; Riyadh, July 2003; Jidda, May 2003; Riyadh, July 2003.

10. "Islamic Fatwa Regarding Women," compiled by Muhammad bin Abdul-Aziz Al-Nusnad, translated by Jamal Al-Din Zaraboro (Saudi Arabia: Darussalam, 1996), pp. 310–313.

11. Personal interview, Riyadh, July 2005.

12. In the article "Ittako Allah Ya ma'shara al Kodatt Fi Ahkamikum," al-Misfr refers to *"al amen al fikri fi sunnat Allah,"* the security of ideas in the way of God. See Muhammad Mafouz, "Watania wa 'Adala al Siyasia" [Citizenship and Political Justice], *Majala al-Kalima,* May 27, 2005.

13. A version of this argument appears in Gwenn Okruhlik, "The Irony of Islah (Reform)," *Washington Quarterly* 28, no. 4 (2005).

14. The seven meetings held thus far have focused on national unity (Riyadh, July 2003), fighting extremism (Mecca, January 2004), women and education (Medina, June 2004), youth expectations (Dhahran, December 2004), world cultures (Abha, November 2005), education improvement (Al-Jouf, November 2006), and work and employment (Qassim, April 2008).

15. King Abdulaziz Center for National Dialogue, http://www.kacnd.org.

16. Personal interview, Jidda, June 2003.

17. Ibid.

18. Hebah Saleh, "Saudi Warning to Critical Civil Servants Dents Hopes of Political Reform," *Financial Times,* September 16, 2004.

19. Personal interviews, Riyadh, July 2005.

20. On the notion of a legitimate cultural repertoire, see Rhys Williams and Timothy Kubal, "Movement Frames and the Cultural Environment: Resonance, Failure, and the Boundaries of the Legitimate," in *Research in Social Movements, Conflict, and Change,* edited by Michael Dobkowski and Isidor Wallimann (Stamford: JAI, 1999).

21. The United States is complicit in this deflection. It emphasizes reforms of education, banking, and the World Trade Organization. It does not press for meaningful and explicit political power sharing. On the US role in this process, see Ali al-Ferdan, "The Prison of Reformers and the Reality of the Saudi Government," *Arabian News,* May 16, 2005.

22. Personal interview, Riyadh, July 2005.

23. al-Fahad, "From Exclusivism to Accommodation," pp. 516–517.

8

Religious Revivalism and Its Challenge to the Saudi Regime

Toby Craig Jones

Salman al-Awdah and Safar al-Hawali rose to prominence in the early 1990s as leading members of the *al-sahwa al-islamiyya* (the Islamic "awakening"), a loosely affiliated network of religious scholars that brazenly challenged the power of the ruling al-Saud family and Saudi Arabia's political order. Led by the charismatic al-Awdah and the fiery cleric al-Hawali, the *sahwa* scholars initially earned renown inside Saudi Arabia for their bold criticism of the decision by the country's leaders to invite the US military into the kingdom in response to Saddam Hussein's invasion of Kuwait in 1990. The presence of hundreds of thousands of non-Muslim soldiers in the heart of Islam's "holy land" set off a firestorm of malcontent. The *sahwa* preachers crested to popularity by fanning the flames of public opprobrium.

Since the mid-1990s, al-Awdah and the former anti-Saudi figures of the *sahwa* have undergone a series of transformations. Most notably, they have abandoned their onetime support for radicalism and support for figures such as Osama bin Laden. They also no longer operate on the front line of political dissent against the ruling al-Saud. The shift in behavior and political tone can be partly explained by the Saudi government's harsh crackdown on the *sahwa* in the 1990s. But the transformation of the *sahwa* is also attributable to a number of other factors, including their desire to remain relevant in a complex domestic religious and political arena. This chapter explores some of the transformations of the *sahwa* as well as the ways in which, and the terms by which, symbolic figures like Salman al-Awdah are competing in an increasingly crowded spiritual and political marketplace inside and outside Saudi Arabia. In particular, I examine the role of the "new" media—the Internet and satellite television—in the remaking of the *al-sahwa al-islamiyya.*

▓ Foundations of the *Sahwa*

While al-Awdah and his peers achieved particularly high levels of visibility and popularity in the 1990s, the *al-sahwa al-islamiyya* first gained a foothold in Saudi Arabia in the 1960s.[1] But it was only after the dramatic events of 1979 that the network and its ideas began to flourish. In November that year a group of hundreds of anti-Saudi religious militants led by Juhayman al-Utaybi, a former member of the National Guard turned radical ideologue, stormed and occupied Mecca's Grand Mosque. The rebels, having smuggled scores of light weapons into the holy sanctuary, fortified the mosque and held off Saudi military and police for days. With guidance from a team of French commandos, Saudi special forces eventually rooted al-Utaybi and his followers from the mosque's elaborate underground complex of tunnels and hidden rooms, killing those who resisted.[2]

Despite efforts to suppress and control the flow of information about what transpired in Mecca, the occupation and subsequent siege of the mosque sent shock waves throughout the kingdom. Following closely on the heels of Iran's revolution and overlapping temporally with bloody demonstrations of Shia discontent in Saudi Arabia's Eastern Province, the violence in Mecca portended the very real possibility of sustained instability and ongoing threats to Saudi power.[3] Unnerved by the specter of more widespread opposition and especially by the fact that radicals were attacking the regime's Islamic credentials—claiming that the al-Saud had forsaken their faith in favor of Western materialism—Saudi Arabia's rulers moved to preempt future challenges to power in two ways. First, the government unleashed its police power, cracking down on known and suspected radicals. Authorities beheaded al-Utaybi and sixty-two of his followers in cities around the kingdom, sending a clear signal that it no longer tolerated dissent. Second, and much more important, the state set out to bolster its Islamic bona fides, empower Islamic conservatives, and co-opt the message of Islamist critics and rivals. As Gwenn Okruhlik has noted, Saudi leaders "sought to bolster the legitimacy of the ruling family by appropriating the power of Islam."[4]

The effort to reinvent the family's Islamic credentials had its roots in Saudi history. Since the late eighteenth century, successive leaders from the al-Saud had relied on religious scholars for their political legitimacy. Adherents of the cleric Muhammad ibn Abd al-Wahhab bestowed upon the al-Saud their blessing in exchange for total oversight of religious, cultural, and social affairs. In the early twentieth century the Wahhabi clergy not only endorsed the political power of the al-Saud, but also actively recruited religious warriors (the Ikhwan) to assist in the consolidation of what would become a Saudi empire on the Arabian Peninsula. But the relationship between the paramount Wahhabi religious figures and the Saudi state had transformed over the course of the century, with the clerics being subordinated to the will of the royal family and bureaucratized in the increasingly sprawling political system.[5] In addition to the profligate ways of the royal family and their embrace of Western models of economic and social development, it was the relegation of the clergy to secondary status that energized radical tendencies among Utaybi, his supporters, and other critics of the al-Saud.

Saudi leaders responded by not only scrambling to reestablish their Islamic credentials but also by reempowering religious authority and by transforming the role that religion and religious institutions would play in Saudi Arabia's public sphere. The government greatly expanded the purview and power of the kingdom's Committee to Promote Virtue and Prevent Vice, also known as the *mutawwain,* or religious police, in the 1980s. The *mutawwain,* often supported by armed police escorts, were charged with policing Saudi Arabia's moral order, enforcing separation between the sexes and proper dress, and ensuring that Muslim men attended prayer. Still flush with revenues from the oil booms of the middle and late 1970s, the state also sunk millions of riyals into the endowment of new religious institutions, particularly madrasas and universities. Tens of thousands of students pursued Islamic studies during the 1980s and well into the 1990s. The universities became veritable assembly lines for religious scholars, churning out thousands of graduates.[6]

▨ Rise and Politicization of the *Sahwa*

It was in the context of Islamic renewal and the expansion of religious institutions, and especially universities, that the *al-sahwa al-islamiyya* rose to prominence. Moreover, it was also in this context that the *sahwa* transformed from a mostly marginal network into a full-fledged political phenomenon that challenged Saudi power. The regime's efforts to strengthen religious institutions led directly, albeit unintentionally, to their ascension. Gilles Kepel has argued that "in allowing the ideologues of the 'awakening' to speak out publicly and proselytize openly during the 1980s, the royal family had hoped that this fringe group of radicals, mostly students, would fall in line with the dynasty's interests. The doctrinal foundations on which the *sahwa* rested, however, made such an alliance impossible."[7] Safar al-Hawali, a particularly contentious figurehead, challenged the authority of the al-Saud in his 1986 dissertation when he examined at length the salafi belief that sovereignty belongs to God alone, underscoring that any rule by mankind, including that of the Saudi royal family, was illegitimate in the eyes of Islam.

Members of the *sahwa* had not previously or directly confronted the authority of the al-Saud, preferring to focus on the promotion of a more austere social and cultural worldview. That changed in the 1980s. Inspired by the models of the Muslim Brotherhood in places like Egypt and Syria, and often instructed by former members of those groups in Saudi Arabia's universities, students of the *sahwa* were politically radicalized in the decade following the occupation of the Meccan mosque. Members of the embryonic *sahwa* had previously been critical of the al-Saud, arguing that the regime was a weak theocracy that had abandoned the ulama. The intensified religious climate of the 1980s did not have a placating effect on the *sahwa*. Rather, it energized them. With access to greater funds and with their ranks steadily on the rise, the *sahwa* emerged as the spiritual and political nerve center for the kingdom's restless elements. Their popularity was further reinforced with the widespread mobilization of Saudi religious institutions in support of the anti-Soviet jihad in Afghanistan. Al-Awdah and al-Hawali enthusiastically supported the war, providing impassioned ideological and theological cover and expanding their following as a result.

The US-led Gulf War against Iraq radicalized the leading *sahwa* scholars, whose stand against the presence of US troops on holy Saudi soil won them widespread acclaim. In addition to their criticism of the presence of hundreds of thousands of non-Muslim soldiers in the kingdom, figures such as al-Awdah and al-Hawali also garnered public favor when they warned of the corrosive power of Western liberalism, which appeared to be creeping into Saudi Arabia. In the early 1990s a small group of nonreligious activists championed political reform, calling on the ruling family to loosen its grip on power and open the political system to wider participation. Unlike the *sahwa,* the ruling family's vision of reform did not call for the strengthening of the clergy or the creation of a more perfect theocracy.

In 1994 the Saudi regime, alarmed by the rising popularity of the young scholars and their increasingly emboldened stance against the royal family, imprisoned them. Along with other Islamist and non-Islamist critics of the government, al-Awdah and al-Hawali languished in the Saudi prison system for five years; they were released in 1999 on condition that they desist from criticizing the royal family.

Although chastened by their imprisonment, neither al-Awdah nor al-Hawali surrendered their interest in politics, although the nature of their political sensibilities underwent considerable change. Events shortly after their release prompted the Saudi government to turn to the former *sahwa* figures for political support. In 1999 the most prominent and powerful Saudi cleric, Abdullah Abd al-Aziz ibn Baz, died, creating a vacuum of religious authority. Few others in the official religious establishment—those on the payroll of the state—possessed the moral authority or gravitas of ibn Baz. Because of their independent streak, their willfulness in the face of political pressure and imprisonment, and especially their criticism of royal power, al-Awdah and al-Hawali did. The September 11, 2001, attacks in the United

States and the local terrorism campaign waged by Al-Qaida in Saudi Arabia in 2003 led the Saudi government to encourage the *sahwa* to speak out against extremism and to support the political legitimacy of the royal family, which the two clerics undertook dutifully. The transformation of the *sahwa* from frontline critics of the al-Saud to supporters of the ruling dynasty was profound, although perhaps not surprising given the heavy cost for their earlier dissent.[8]

After their release from prison, al-Awdah and al-Hawali, publicly at least, pursued independent political lines. While al-Awdah rejected and distanced himself from his former radicalism and support for Osama bin Laden, al-Hawali called on his past credentials as a way of situating himself between the state and the new generation of Al-Qaida-inspired radicals. In 2003 and then again in 2004, al-Hawali offered his services to the Saudi government in negotiating the surrender of actual or would-be terrorists. Doing so provided al-Hawali a continuing pretext for relevance. The two clerics disagreed on issues related to Islamic minorities in the kingdom. Whereas al-Awdah expressed and even demonstrated a willingness to sit down with and talk to Shias, Sufis, and Ismailis from around Saudi Arabia, al-Hawali maintained his hard-line intolerance, insisting that the minorities were apostates.

Even though both men avoided direct criticisms of the Saudi regime or royal family, it would be inaccurate to suggest that either al-Awdah or al-Hawali had become puppets of the Saudi state. As they had in the 1990s, both continued to offer sharp and often vicious criticism of the United States and its foreign policy. The US invasion of Iraq in 2003 accelerated the rate of such criticism and fueled increasingly shrill anti-US haranguing, including an open call for the support of an anti-US jihad in Iraq in November 2004.[9] Expressions of outrage against US policy and more important against its presence in the region did not constitute a direct critique of the Saudi government, but were an alarming reminder of the early 1990s, when the line between criticism of the United States and anger at the Saudi regime proved thin. Moreover, given the historically close relationship between the United States and Saudi Arabia, endorsements of violence against the Americans did serve as an indirect criticism of the kingdom, the royal family, and its foreign policy choices. They also served as a stark reminder that both al-Awdah and al-Hawali continued to be savvy and serious political actors in their attempts to shape the Saudi political order.

Although al-Awdah and al-Hawali played very visible roles in the domestic political arena and although government leaders took them very seriously, it is unclear whether the two retain the same influence on the Saudi public today that they possessed in the early 1990s. In addition, the long-term political ambition of the former anti-Saudi clerics remains unclear. It is unlikely that either cleric had set aside their desire to see the creation of an ulama-led theocratic state in Saudi Arabia. Understandably and mostly out of fear future imprisonment, neither presses the case for its realization publicly.

Following their release from prison and through mid-2005, both clerics continued to be politically active in the domestic arena on issues other than terrorism. Beginning in 2003, when an inchoate reform lobby composed of both Islamist and liberal activists pressed the royal family to undertake political reform, both al-Awdah and al-Hawali played an important oppositional role, challenging the reformers and accusing them of being Western lackeys in a smear campaign intended to impugn the credibility of the reformers. In early 2005, both supported candidates for the municipal council elections held that year. Al-Hawali spoke publicly at several campaign events and even lent his backing to victorious candidates. In June 2005, however, al-Hawali's influence suffered a temporary setback when he suffered a debilitating brain hemorrhage. He remained hospitalized through the end of the year and has only recently resumed his activities.

The Spiritual Marketplace and the New Media

Even before al-Hawali's stroke, both he and al-Awdah were confronted with a serious challenge to their influence. New media, most notably the widespread availability of satellite television and the Internet, introduced a vast array of new voices and options for Saudi citizens who were seeking information and guidance, providing choices with regard to news, religion, and politics. A market of competing ideas, ideologies, and personalities has taken shape, crowding the available airwaves, print media, and electronic resources with seemingly limitless alternatives.

The rise of the new marketplace has raised important challenges to the *sahwa* and has reshaped not only religious and political discourse in Saudi Arabia, but also the role that prominent *sahwa* figures such as al-Awdah have sought to play. Although it remains too early to fully determine what kinds of long-term changes the spiritual and political market will generate, competition as well as the expansion of audiences have contributed to redefining the *sahwa*, and perhaps have even helped set in motion the realization of a post-*sahwa* period in the kingdom.

The relegation of the figures such as al-Awdah and al-Hawali from being among the most important voices to solitary voices among many has marked a rapid transformation in its own right. In part, this trend has been the product of internal divisions within the *sahwa* and the pursuit of individual interests since 1999. But it also relates to how the new marketplace functions and the varying responses of different clerics to the new media reality.

For most of its history, the Saudi state enjoyed an almost complete monopoly on the distribution of information in the kingdom. The government closely monitored and censored the print and electronic media, tightly circumscribing access to information and its dissemination. Critics of the government, including Egypt's Gamal Abdul Nasser and a handful of rebellious Saudi dissidents in the middle decades of the twentieth century, had previously used powerful radio signals to broadcast anti-Saudi propaganda into the kingdom. In 1979 and the early 1980s, Iran's Ayatollah Khomeini and his supporters did likewise. But these efforts proved fleeting and mostly originated from outside Saudi Arabia.

In the early 1990s, leading *sahwa* figures disrupted the government's monopoly from inside Saudi Arabia. Both al-Awdah and al-Hawali were early pioneers in the use of technology to achieve political objectives. They gained a widespread following by recording their sermons on audiocassettes, which were then copied, packaged, smuggled across the peninsula, and sold to thousands of eager consumers.[10] The *sahwa*'s technological innovation constituted as important a challenge to Saudi power as their message. For example, the Saudi government, fearing potential fallout with Saddam Hussein's invasion of Kuwait, withheld from the Saudi public information about Iraq's occupation of their northern neighbor for several days. Such tactics would prove unsustainable as a result of the efforts of the *sahwa* clerics. The use of audiocassette recordings undermined the government's ability to control information. The impact of the *sahwa*'s technical abilities and the network that supported them was no less profound. While there is little doubt that the message of dissent held widespread appeal, the *sahwa*'s popularity must be attributed in part to their role as an alternative source of information.

A key element of the *sahwa*'s dissent platform was their effort to make information from both outside and inside the kingdom available, especially with regard to the activities of the US military. But by the end of the 1990s and well into the twenty-first century, the *sahwa* was no longer fulfilling the role of alternative media news outlet. Satellite television, including the nonstop independent Qatar-based news network Al-Jazeera, began broadcasting into the kingdom, providing immediate coverage of regional events in 1996. Satellite television stations and programming expanded dramatically within five years of the appearance of Al-Jazeera, offering dozens of potential sources of information. Even though satellite dishes were and remain illegal inside Saudi Arabia, they are omnipresent, cluttering the rooftops of homes and apartment buildings.

The Internet has also proliferated. Saudi Arabia attempts to closely monitor and restrict Internet access, using a proxy server at the King Abd al-Aziz City for Science and Technology in Riyadh to block material deemed politically or culturally threatening. But this system is only partially successful in deflecting the determined interests of thousands of Saudi citizens, who routinely successfully navigate around the state proxy to access their sites of interest. Thousands of websites that track global and regional events, from news services to jihadist chat rooms, are easily accessible. In 2003 and 2004, Al-Qaida published two monthly online magazines from inside Saudi Arabia, which it made available on a website that regularly shifted its host location in order to evade authorities. Similar pressures exist from outside. Until late 2004, a London-based Saudi dissident, Saad al-Faqih, maintained a popular opposition website for his political network, Harakat al-Islah (the Reform Movement), and even broadcast an anti-Saudi radio program across the very same satellite networks that beamed in Al-Jazeera and the Saudi public television channels.

Both al-Hawali and al-Awdah have recognized the importance of the new media reality and the challenge it has presented to their continued influence.[11] Al-Hawali has approached the new technologies simply as more sophisticated instruments for the spread of his very narrow and personal perspective on politics and faith. He maintains a flashy personal website, in both English and Arabic, that contains links to his scholarly and polemical work, including commentary on social, religious, and political issues.[12] Al-Hawali also heads up a group website, called the Global Campaign to Resist Aggression, that takes direct aim at the United States as well as other states and groups that are characterized as pursuing anti-Islamic policies.

Salman al-Awdah, in contrast, has responded quite differently and in the process has reinvented his image, his ambition, and the role he seeks to play. In a 2005 article examining the development of Islamist discourse in Saudi Arabia, published in al-Awdah's monthly print magazine, 'Abdallah bin Nasser al-Sabih noted that during the US-led Gulf War, clerics "personally undertook the effort to gather news and to offer political analysis or limited translation." Today, however, "the satellite channels do all of this in a more professional manner. . . . In this way, the satellite channels have filled the relationship that used to be between the cleric and his audience."[13] But rather than shrink from the challenge posed by satellite television, the global and regional professional news agencies, and the potential of lost relevance, al-Awdah has responded by cultivating his own multimedia conglomerate and working to carve out space for himself in the congested media market.

In 2001 he established a personal website that, like those of al-Hawali and others, provided access to his scholarship, his rulings (fatwas) on religious matters, political analysis, audio recordings of sermons and lectures, and even discussion forums.[14] But al-Awdah's online presence is more striking in the ways that it differs from those of his *sahwa* colleagues. Five years after he established his personal website, al-Awdah created an online magazine and news agency known as Islam al-Yawm (Islam Today), which serves not only as a repository of his material, but also as a site where readers can access coverage of various global and regional events, and read articles on issues ranging from family matters to jihad, from contributors from across the Arab Middle East. The site is published in four languages: Arabic, English, French, and Chinese.

Since its establishment, Islam Today has become much more than a website. Al-Awdah founded the Islam Today Institute as an umbrella organization for his interests and supporters. Islam Today is rapidly achieving brand status as an organization and small but emerging media empire that is synonymous with its founding cleric. And its ambition has grown in the past few years. In 2005, al-Awdah launched a glossy new print magazine, also named *Islam Today,* that maintains a full-time editorial staff and a team of correspondents and editorialists. The journal's home office is located in Riyadh, although it also has branches in Egypt, Jordan, Yemen, and Kuwait.

The website and magazine allow al-Awdah to continue offering political commentary on Saudi Arabian and regional affairs. But whereas in the 1990s al-Awdah spoke in his own name, today the responsibility for much of the harshest political commentary has been delegated to others—analysts, clerics, and journalists—including many from outside Saudi Arabia. The effect is to provide al-Awdah with political cover. Although he is not completely immune to charges of political troublemaking, by allowing others to articulate criticisms he no doubt shares, al-Awdah is able to distance himself from the most shrill rhetoric, while still enabling it to be distributed from his network.

Occasionally al-Awdah does enter the political fray, although never to challenge the royal family directly on domestic issues. During 2003 and 2004, the Islam Today website served as vehicle for publicizing several petitions, signed by al-Awdah and dozens of others aligned with the 1990s *sahwa* movement, targeting "liberals" in the kingdom—continuing an older mode of action that aimed to undermine domestic rivals for political influence—as well as terrorism. The collaboration of clerics in signing and publicizing petitions keeps alive the appearance of unity when their shared interests are challenged. Al-Awdah also periodically comments on foreign policy matters, including a commentary in the summer of 2006 that was openly supportive of Lebanese Hezbollah and its resistance to Israel. His stand stood in stark contrast to the official Saudi line, which at least at the beginning of hostilities took aim at the Shia group for undertaking an ill-advised "adventure" that threatened regional security.

Despite his challenge to the Saudi foreign policy line and the publication of harsh commentary on the United States by contributors to his website, al-Awdah has worked to cultivate a more moderate political position than in the 1990s. As noted above, he has rejected terrorism as a legitimate political tactic and has even participated in calls for limited political reform in Saudi Arabia, although he has stopped short of publicly endorsing a systematic reform agenda. Part of the reason is clearly self-preservation. Al-Awdah has no desire to return to prison. It is also possible that al-Awdah has moderated over time. But perhaps the most likely explanation is that the urge to be and remain competitive in the regional and domestic media market has compelled him to moderate his tone in order to maintain influence over the largest possible bloc of supporters. Because al-Awdah's tone and politics border on being oppositional but supportive, confrontational but anti-violent, he is able to maximize his appeal.

The Qardawi Effect

While al-Awdah earned relevance for being a preacher in the 1990s who tackled political grievances, in recent years he has taken his role as religious scholar much more seriously, a trend also apparent in and shaped by his expanded media presence. During Ramadan 2005, al-Awdah hosted a live daily call-in show on a major Arabic-language satellite network, the Middle East Broadcasting Center (MBC), called *The Life of the Word,* during which he answered questions about *sharia* and offered counsel to callers inquiring about the religious rules governing their daily lives. The program proved so popular that he continued to appear weekly after the conclusion of the holy month. He participated on a similar daily program during Ramadan 2006 called *The Cornerstone.* Al-Awdah has also appeared regularly as a guest on other satellite networks such as Al-Arabiyya, commenting on Saudi and regional affairs.

Much like Yusuf al-Qardawi, who has long appeared on a weekly Al-Jazeera television program, Salman al-Awdah has enthusiastically embraced the opportunity and exposure provided by MBC, increasing his visibility and his ability to reach a broader non-Saudi audience. The platform has also elevated his stature as both a religious scholar and a political figure. Whereas he was previously considered little more than a preacher, today he commands greater respect as a leading clerical figure. Although al-Awdah still lacks the star power of al-Qardawi, it appears that he is closely following the example set by the Qatar-based senior cleric.

The emulation has paid significant dividends. The heightened visibility and the corresponding rise of his authority over spiritual matters provided by his role on MBC have also served to augment al-Awdah's credibility on matters that are considered simultaneously religious and political by millions of Muslims. In early 2006, al-Awdah and al-Qardawi collaborated in leading the chorus of criticism against Danish newspapers that printed controversial caricatures of the Prophet Muhammad. The two clerics headlined a major international seminar in Manama, Bahrain, criticizing the perceived slight to Islam and calling for sustained efforts to boycott Danish products.

Conclusion

Salman al-Awdah and Safar al-Hawali, the key figures of Saudi Arabia's *al-sahwa al-islamiyya* and once powerful voices of dissent against the Saudi royal family, have undergone profound transformations since the height of their radicalism in the early 1990s. Onetime critics of the al-Saud, the two clerics have recently found themselves acting as visible supporters of the political status quo in the kingdom. Both have also been forced to deal with various challenges to their own relevance and authority. The rise of new media, such as the Internet and satellite television, has introduced an array of alternative sources of information and perspectives on domestic and regional events. Where the leading members of the *sahwa* once rivaled the Saudi state in their ability to control and disseminate information, they have lately become competing voices in a cacophonous spiritual and political marketplace. The new media reality has forced members of the *sahwa* to compete for a share of the market with others from inside and outside the kingdom. One consequence has been the transformation of leading *sahwa* figures as well as of the role of the *sahwa* itself, both inside Saudi Arabia and out. Perhaps the most notable example of this is Salman al-Awdah, who has embraced the new media as a means to expand his profile and his significance.

Notes

1. See Gilles Kepel, *The War for Muslim Minds: Islam and the West,* translated by Pascale Ghazaleh (Cambridge: Harvard University Press, 2004); International Crisis Group, "Saudi Arabia Backgrounder: Who Are the Islamists?" *Middle East Report,* September 21, 2004.

2. Joseph A. Kechichian, "The Role of the Ulama in the Politics of an Islamic State: The Case of Saudi Arabia," *International Journal of Middle East Studies* 18, no. 1 (1986).

3. Toby Craig Jones, "Rebellion on the Saudi Periphery: Modernity, Marginalization, and the Shi'a Uprising of 1979," *International Journal of Middle East Studies* 38, no. 2 (2006).

4. Gwenn Okruhlik, "Empowering Civility Through Nationalism: Reformist Islam and Belonging in Saudi Arabia," in *Remaking Muslim Politics: Pluralism, Contestation, Democratization,* edited by Robert W. Hefner (Princeton: Princeton University Press, 2005), p. 194.

5. Joshua Teitelbaum, *Holier Than Thou: Saudi Arabia's Islamic Opposition* (Washington, DC: Washington Institute for Near East Policy, 2000), pp. 10–12.

6. The universities also became important sites of mobilization for Saudi foreign policy during the 1980s. The government was successfully able to channel the energy of thousands of students as well as their mentors toward the anti-Soviet jihad in Afghanistan, deflecting criticism away from the royal family.

7. Kepel, *War for Muslim Minds,* p. 182.

8. For a more complete discussion of the political transformation of the *sahwa* and their support for the al-Saud, see Toby Craig Jones, "The Clerics, the Sahwa, and the Saudi State," *Strategic Insights* 4, no. 3 (2005).

9. See Jones, "The Clerics, the Sahwa, and the Saudi State." Although the open letter constituted clear support for violence, it was not a signal of support for Iraq's Al-Qaida branch. Nor was it a letter of support for al-Zarqawi and his pursuit of sectarian civil war.

10. See Mamoun Fandy, *Saudi Arabia and the Politics of Dissent* (New York: St. Martin's, 1999).

11. They have responded more quickly and capably to the new media than some of their domestic political rivals. In particular, the 2003 reform lobby maintained no coherent presence on the World Wide Web, reflecting not only their weakness inside the kingdom but also that the movement was only loosely organized and connected. Individual members of the reform lobby do write regularly for various print media, including Saudi Arabia's main traditional newspapers, *Al-Riyadh, Al-Watan,* and *Al-Okaz.* A handful of others write for Gulf regional papers and even for international papers such as the London-based, Saudi-owned *Al-Hayat* and *Al-Sharq al-Awsat.*

12. http://www.alhawali.com.

13. 'Abdallah bin Nasser al-Sabih, *Islam al-Yawm* 1, no. 5 (April 2005): 38.

14. http://www.islamtoday.net.

PART 3

Saudi-US Relations

9

A Most Improbable Alliance: Placing Interests over Ideology

Thomas W. Lippman

It was the opinion of H. St. John Philby, the legendary British adviser to King Abd al-Aziz ibn Saud, that the rules of engagement between Wahhabi Islam and the Christian world were determined by the outcome of the Battle of Sibylla in 1929, four years before the arrival in Saudi Arabia of the first US oil explorers.

Sibylla was the most important engagement of Abd al-Aziz's campaign to crush the Ikhwan, the fanatical and aggressive militias who had been the instrument of his rise to power and his conquest of the Hijaz. Once all of what is now Saudi Arabia was under his rule, he found the Ikhwan troublesome and dangerous because they wished to march on into other countries, putting to the sword those who did not embrace their vision. Consequently, Abd al-Aziz turned on them. By bringing the Ikhwan to heel—with the assistance of the British, who had been offended by Ikhwan raids into Iraq—Abd al-Aziz established that he and only he would rule in the new Kingdom of Najd and the Hijaz; and while he would rule in the name and under the banner of Islam, he would do so in harmony with his neighbors and would use external sources to develop the country he had unified. The Prophet Muhammad had sought the help of infidels when it was needed, Abd al-Aziz declared, and so would he.

Abd al-Aziz did not share the ferocious xenophobia of the desert warriors. On the contrary, early on he had sent clear signals that he would welcome external assistance. Beginning in about 1913—before the Hijazi revolt against the Ottoman Turks and his own power struggle with Sharif Hussein of Mecca—Abd al-Aziz had invited US doctors from the Protestant medical mission in Bahrain to enter Arabia's eastern regions to minister to people there. An English officer, Captain William Shakespeare, fought at his side at Jarrab in 1915, and later that same year Abd al-Aziz entered into a friendship treaty with Britain. He was subsidized by the British during and after the Arab Revolt, and sent his beloved second son, Prince Faisal, on a tour of Europe in 1919. And in 1923, when the Ikhwan were still loyal to him, Abd al-Aziz granted an early, albeit fruitless, oil exploration concession to a New Zealander, Frank Holmes. Abd al-Aziz had met Holmes at the famous Uqayr Conference in 1922, the meeting at which Sir Percy Cox drew the border between Saudi Arabia and Iraq with a red pencil.

The Ikhwan, who opposed any infidel presence in Arabia and disdained all forms of innovation as un-Islamic, denounced Abd al-Aziz's early embrace of outsiders and of the automobile and the telegraph; but Abd al-Aziz found technology interesting as well as useful in consolidating his power. The Ikhwan's backward views could not be allowed to obstruct his vision. Indeed, Abd al-Aziz established a pattern that has prevailed, with minor variations, during the reigns of all his successors, in which the king and senior princes of the House of Saud have propelled their country along the path of technological modernization with outside help, while striving to preserve the rigorous religious orthodoxy and conservative social values prevalent among the population.

"The battle of Sibila marked the end of an epoch," Philby wrote. "Saudi Arabia had virtually assumed its final shape as the result of constant war upon the infidel; and henceforth the infidel would be a valued ally in the common cause of progress. . . . The sting had been taken out of the Ikhwan movement which had played so prominent a part in the creation of the new regime, and could now serve no further useful purpose."[1] More than seven decades later, it can be seen that Philby's assessment was essentially correct, even if his account oversimplified a complicated tale and was less than candid about his own role in bringing about the 1933 concession agreement between Saudi Arabia and the Standard Oil Company of California.

The fact was, Abd al-Aziz, having overpowered all challengers to his authority over Arabia, ruled a prize of dubious value; other than the levies imposed on pilgrims to the Islamic holy sites and the limited taxes the king was able to extract from Hijazi merchants, Saudi Arabia in the early 1930s, when Abd al-Aziz was consolidating his power, had no source of income. As the worldwide Great Depression choked off pilgrimage traffic, even the meager revenue stream from pilgrims' taxes dried up. The king needed money to purchase loyalty among the tribes he had defeated or neutralized. He also needed money to import the food required by his newly acquired subjects. If that need mandated that he turn to outsiders and even non-Muslims for the cash and technology that would sustain his rule and lift up his people, so be it, provided that the outsiders honored the terms he would set down to regulate their work on the kingdom's holy soil.

Those terms were recorded by William A. Eddy, who as chief of the US diplomatic mission in Jidda during World War II became a trusted confidant of the king.

"We will use your iron, but leave our faith alone," the king told Eddy. "The King's position," Eddy recalled, "was that the Koran regulated all matters of faith, family, and property, which were not for unbelievers to get involved with. 'Our patriarchal authority and the veiling of women are none of your business. On the other hand, you have much that we need and will accept: radio, airplanes, pumps, oil-drilling rigs and technical know-how.' This acceptance of technology was far in advance of his people, and the King had to fight many battles with bigots to win support for his suspected friendship with Christian governments and his cordial relationship with the Arabian-American Oil Company."[2]

That was the basis upon which one of the modern world's most improbable bilateral alliances operated for more than half a century. No two countries and no two societies could have been more dissimilar, and yet Saudi Arabia and the United States worked together, to the general satisfaction and benefit of both, through the endless vicissitudes of Middle Eastern politics. If the Saudi worldview sees all humanity as belonging either to *dar al-Islam* (the house of Islam) or *dar al-harb* (the house or land of war), the Saudis were also sufficiently pragmatic to persuade themselves that Americans, as monotheists, need not be consigned to the latter. As diplomat-scholar David Long put it, the Saudi worldview "is a perception, not a blueprint for policy action. Saudi Arabia is no different from any other country in viewing issues in international relations in terms of their national interests, not as part of a rigid formula dictating a set response."[3] After Sibylla, that attitude prevailed, with only sporadic challenge from the absolutists, such as the violent takeover of the Great Mosque in Mecca in 1979.

As for the Americans, they harvested the bounty of Saudi Arabia's oil fields and earned billions of dollars through contracts to develop the country's airports, hospitals, electric power stations, and military bases. The US government, under every president from Harry Truman to George H. W. Bush, valued Saudi Arabia as a redoubt against Soviet penetration of the Gulf region. What made this partnership durable was a commitment by the US government and by major US businesses operating in the kingdom to accept the terms laid down by Abd al-Aziz and to refrain from interference with, challenge to, or even criticism of Saudi Arabia's domestic policies and its social and religious practices.

However abhorrent the Saudi Arabian system may have appeared to them, the Americans who lived and worked in the kingdom and negotiated with Saudi officials generally accepted it as a fact of life, and worked around it. Those Americans who might have been inclined to challenge the system, loosely labeled "Wahhabism," were generally excluded from employment in Saudi Arabia, both by the US government and by the major US corporations doing business there. In return, the Saudi monarchs allowed their American guests to create insulated communities where they could replicate the more comfortable life back home, communities to which ordinary Saudis had little access. In Dhahran, the US oil town in Al-Hasa, and later in other compounds all around the country, Americans and other foreigners conducted Christian religious services, showed movies, drank alcohol, and educated boys and girls in mixed classrooms; men and women socialized together and swam in the same pools. American women drove automobiles and rode bicycles. Such activities were prohibited for Saudi Arabs and indeed for all residents of the kingdom, but they were tolerated in the closed communities because Abd al-Aziz and his successors wished the Westerners there to remain in the country.

As the foreign presence grew over time, there were naturally exceptions and variations to this fundamental arrangement. Some Americans preferred to live among the Arabs, embracing the local culture rather than isolating themselves from it. A few defied the rules, violating pork and alcohol restrictions or committing petty crimes; some of these Americans went to jail, others were quickly deported. Occasionally the non-Muslim religious services became too elaborate or too visible, prompting a crackdown. Quite a few Americans, upon seeing a public display of Wahhabi justice such as a severed hand hanging from a pole, expressed private revulsion, but neither they nor their employers engaged in public criticism, because at all times in this relationship the Saudis held the decisive lever of power, the ability to revoke the oil concession.

The US policy of deference to Saudi customs and tradition was manifest from the earliest days, when the first geologists arrived to look for oil in the autumn of 1933. The Americans wore Arab garb, out of respect for local custom. The emir of the region, as the king's representative, dispatched a squad of soldiers to ensure the safety of the oil team. The easternmost regions of Saudi Arabia were less hostile to outsiders than the Americans might have expected, because a substantial part of the population was not Wahhabi at all but Shia. Nevertheless, the further they ventured inland away from the coast, the more hostility the Americans encountered, and only the strong commitment of the king and the emir ensured their safety.

From those early days through at least the Gulf War of 1991, the archives of the State Department, the US military, and the Arabian American Oil Company were replete with policy statements and exhortations to the effect that Saudi beliefs and practices were to be respected, rather than challenged or ridiculed. However alien the Saudi system might have been to Americans steeped in the values of individual liberty and impartial justice, outsiders were instructed not to concern themselves with it. If the education that the Saudi Arabs acquired under American patronage moderated their views, well and good; but the Americans were constantly reminded that they were in the country for economic and strategic reasons, not to alter Saudi Arabian society. With the exception of modest efforts by Presidents Harry Truman, Dwight Eisenhower, and John Kennedy to persuade the Saudis to abandon their policy of refusing to admit Jews into the country, the US policy of accommodation remained largely in place until the age of terrorism, beginning in the mid-1990s.

This is not to say that the United States and Saudi Arabia always agreed on matters of policy. The Saudis were, and to some extent remain, bitter over US support for the partition of Palestine and the creation of Israel. Deep differences emerged over Saudi participation in the Arab oil embargo of 1973–1974 and over Saudi Arabia's refusal to accept the decision of Egyptian president Anwar Sadat to make peace with Israel. The United States reacted with open fury upon discovering in 1988 that Saudi Arabia had secretly acquired nuclear-capable ballistic missiles from China. But these arguments were never about internal conditions in Saudi Arabia, and it can be argued that one reason the bilateral strategic and economic relationship survived these confrontations was that the Saudis appreciated the US policy of noninterference in their domestic affairs—a policy that gave them incalculable benefits at little political cost.

Washington not only accepted Saudi Arabia's domestic system but sometimes even endorsed it, to the point of obsequiousness. For example, the terms under which the Saudis agreed to let the United States build and operate a military airfield at Dhahran specified that the US team that was dispatched there to train Saudi personnel "may not include anyone whose presence is considered undesirable by the Saudi Arabia government and the United States Government will submit a list of the names and identity of the staff and employees."[4] In practice, this meant that no Jews and no women were to be deployed, and that anyone who offended the Saudis in any way was to be promptly sent home. When members of Congress protested this policy, the State Department took the position that "it is fundamental that sovereign states have the right to control the internal order of their affairs in such a manner as they deem to be in their best interests."[5]

The behavioral guidance given to new American employees by US government agencies, the US military, and private US corporations was unequivocal and consistent. This is the Saudis' country and they can run it as they wish, Americans were told. If you respect their ways and behave appropriately in public, you can prosper here; if you insult the Arabs or violate their rules, you will be in trouble. "Never ridicule the appearance, customs or religious practices of the people. Theirs is an old culture and U.S. military personnel are guests of their government," airmen assigned to Dhahran were advised. "The Arab is not about to discard age-old habit and custom without reason, and is in no hurry."[6]

In its extreme form, the willingness of US corporations to comply with Saudi customs obliged workers hired for jobs in the kingdom to convert to Islam. This practice was even upheld by the US federal court system in the case of Wade Kern, a helicopter pilot. Kern was hired in 1978 by Dynalectron

Corporation, a defense contractor that was engaged to provide security services in Saudi Arabia, including helicopter flights over Mecca and Medina
during pilgrimage season to watch for possible trouble among the hajjiis and
to spot fires that might break out. Because non-Muslims are not permitted in
the holy cities, Dynalectron required pilots assigned to this duty to convert
to Islam. Kern, a Baptist, did so, but then changed his mind, whereupon the
company canceled his assignment. Dynalectron offered him another job, but
he sued in federal court in Texas, alleging religious discrimination. The
court found that because of the unique circumstances of the holy cities, the
conversion rule was a "bona fide occupational requirement," not discrimina-
tory in intent, and thus permissible under US law.[7]

For the first decade after Standard Oil geologists began to look for oil,
the US government and the State Department paid scant attention to Saudi
Arabia. What bilateral business needed to be done was in effect conducted
through the oil company. Washington recognized Abd al-Aziz's government
and maintained nominal diplomatic relations with the kingdom, but no US
officials lived in the kingdom and there was no US diplomatic presence in
Jidda until the later years of World War II, when President Franklin Roose-
velt and his advisers began to recognize the strategic potential of Saudi Arabia and its oil.

All that had changed by 1951, when the United States was fully engaged in the Cold War. Radical pro-Moscow Arab nationalism was not yet
the threat Washington later perceived it to be, but Saudi Arabia was already
regarded as a redoubt of pro-US stability in a volatile and sometimes hostile region. In February of that year, the State Department distributed to its
posts throughout the Middle East an extensive, secret document titled "Comprehensive Statement of US Policy Toward the Kingdom," which recognized
the importance of Saudi Arabia and set out a detailed plan for maintaining
stability and ensuring that the country remained friendly to the United States.
With that document, deference to the social and religious customs of Saudi
Arabia was enshrined as official US policy—a policy that went essentially
unchallenged for the next forty years.

Noting that the United States had been the target of extensive criticism
from the Arabs because of its support for the partition of Palestine and the
creation of Israel, the document said that "Saudi Arabia has remained firm
in its friendship to the United States. It has served as our spokesman and
interpreter to less friendly Arab states and has, through the prestige and conservative nature of its King, exerted a stabilizing influence on the Near East
generally." In fact, Abd al-Aziz had bitterly opposed US policy in Palestine,
but he refrained from an open rupture with Washington because he had economic and security interests that overrode his sentiments about Zionism.

In addition to supporting the king and providing military and technological assistance, the policy statement said that the United States should "observe

the utmost respect for Saudi Arabia's sovereignty, sanctity of the holy places, and local customs. . . . In all our efforts to carry out our policies in Saudi Arabia, we should take care to serve as guide or partner and avoid giving the impression of wishing to dominate the country." Rather than criticizing Saudi Arabia's harsh laws and retributive justice, the State Department advised Americans that they should recognize that the kingdom "is trying very hard to improve itself and it has done well, considering that its sustained efforts have been only a post-war development. It has also had a serious internal obstacle in the fanatical opposition to change and the growth of western influences. It behooves us, therefore, to applaud what Saudi Arabia has done and is doing, and not criticize it for what it has not yet been able to do."[8] At least this document acknowledged that there was a "fanatical" element in Saudi Arabia. Most of the time, in negotiations and policy discussions, US officials and business executives avoided the topic; how the rulers of Saudi Arabia dealt with this problem was up to them, not up to anybody from the United States.

After King Faisal visited the United States in December 1964, for example, President Johnson wrote him a letter expressing satisfaction with their discussions. "It is with great interest that we in this country have been following the progress in your program of economic development and social reform for Saudi Arabia. The efforts to broaden educational opportunities for your people and better enable women to contribute to the general productiveness of the country are ones of which I am especially aware. These problems also occupy much of my time in America. Your success in preserving the fundamental guiding religious principles, while at the same time modernizing social relationships, draws our respect and admiration."[9] To judge from official records, Johnson—like his predecessors and successors—refrained from raising such subjects as religious intolerance, plural marriage, amputation of body parts, sequestration of women, the absence of democratic institutions, or any of the other Saudi Arabian practices so unpalatable to Americans.

In 1976, Congress overrode a veto by President Gerald Ford to add a human rights policy to the International Security and Arms Export Control Act. In the annual country reports on human rights that the State Department issued in compliance with that legislation, it routinely criticized Saudi Arabia for its religious intolerance, disenfranchisement of women, and arbitrary justice. Yet those same reports from a stepchild unit of the State Department, the Bureau of Democracy, Human Rights, and Labor, had hardly any policy impact on the bilateral relationship with Riyadh.

Even Ford's successor, Jimmy Carter, who made human rights a cornerstone of his foreign policy, praised the Saudi rulers effusively and refrained from pressing them about internal affairs. Arriving in Riyadh in January 1978, Carter said at an airport ceremony, "Seeing the generosity of this welcome, I feel that I am among my own people and know that my steps will not be hindered, because I walk the same path as Your Majesty, King Khalid, toward a common goal of even greater friendship among our people, between our two countries, and of peace for all the people of the world."[10] Later that year, when King Khaled visited Washington, D.C., he was Carter's guest at a White House luncheon. A White House statement afterward listed the topics that were discussed—mostly relating to the Camp David peace agreement between Israel and Egypt—and noted that "these discussions were carried out in an atmosphere of longstanding friendship, deep mutuality of interest, and well-tested sprit of cooperation."[11] Never mind that the Saudis opposed that agreement and eventually cut off aid to Egypt because of it. Nothing in the public record about Khaled's visit indicates that Carter even raised the subject of Saudi domestic policies.

This bilateral "don't ask, don't tell" arrangement began to unravel with Iraq's invasion of Kuwait in 1990. Convinced by the United States that Saudi Arabia was next on the target list of Iraqi president Saddam Hussein, King Fahd ibn Abd al-Aziz took the fateful decision to allow half a million US and other foreign troops into his country, first to protect the kingdom from possible invasion, then to wage the 1991 campaign to liberate Kuwait known as Operation Desert Storm.

General Norman Schwarzkopf, the US commander of that campaign, recalled in his memoir that he and US diplomats spent many hours trying to minimize the impact of this mammoth inflow of foreigners upon the social, cultural, and religious life of the host country. "To my consternation," Schwarzkopf wrote of the Saudi leadership, "their most pressing concern was neither the threat from Saddam nor the enormous joint military enterprise on which we were embarked. What loomed largest for them was the cultural crisis triggered by this sudden flood of Americans into their kingdom."[12] The Saudis' apprehension was well-founded. Schwarzkopf and other US commanders went to considerable lengths to ensure that the troops' behavior did not clash with Saudi sensibilities—no alcohol, no female entertainers, no bare heads on female soldiers—but the sheer magnitude and ubiquity of the foreign presence nonetheless created a backlash.

In retrospect, it can be seen that the Desert Storm deployment was the catalyst for the difficulties that have beset the bilateral relationship ever since. It overpowered the consensus among Saudis that foreigners could be tolerated in the kingdom if they were there to improve conditions for the populace; these foreigners in uniform were in the country for reasons that had little to do with developing the infrastructure or educating the people. The deployment incited antigovernment sentiment among critics who questioned why Saudi Arabia could not defend itself despite its massive expenditures on military equipment and training.[13] It angered the devout, who asked why Saudi Arabia would ally itself with infidels in a war against fellow

Muslims. And it inflamed Osama bin Laden, who—having participated in the successful jihad against the Soviet Union in Afghanistan—offered himself as the Sword of Islam to defend the holy soil of Arabia, only to be rebuffed by a king who joined forces with the United States. These passions, coupled with the Wahhabi extremism that had been permitted, even encouraged, in the country's schools and mosques for the previous decade as a counterweight to the Shia revolution spreading from Iran, led to the age of terror, in which the Washington-Riyadh alliance has been so sorely tested.

At the same time, the breakup of the Soviet Union and the end of the Cold War quelled the threat of global communism, resistance to which had been a strong common interest of Saudi Arabia and the United States for decades. No longer threatened by this atheistic ideology, the Saudis were liberated to expand their economic and political interests into previously closed corners of the world, notably China. Thus within a year or so of the Desert Storm campaign, relations between the United States and Saudi Arabia entered a whole new era, in which the basic "oil for security" bargain forged in the 1940s would have to be renegotiated, a process that is still ongoing.

Before the onset of domestic terrorism in Saudi Arabia with the 1995 bomb attack against the National Guard Training Center in Riyadh, in which five Americans died, Americans and other Westerners in the kingdom generally lived privileged lives of safety and prosperity. Ordinary street crime was unknown, and terrorism was a phenomenon of other places, not Saudi Arabia. The tranquillity of the kingdom was part of its attraction for the hundreds of thousands of Americans who lived and worked there in the fifty years after World War II.

Other than the relative few who actually went there, however, Americans knew little about Saudi Arabia beyond the broadest generalities absorbed from the news media. Most Americans, after all, were of European stock. Their religion, literature, cuisine, music, and ideas about the organization of society were traceable to Europe, not the Arabian Peninsula, and Americans had no emotional ties to the Saudi kingdom. In general, so long as the oil flowed, Saudi Arabia was not a country of great interest. The curriculum of Saudi schools was of no concern to people in Cleveland or Albuquerque.

The age of terror has changed this over the past decade. As the attacks on the USS *Cole* and the embassies in eastern Africa made clear that Americans were targets, Americans naturally began to examine the source of this threat, and to a great extent they did not like what they saw. And after the attacks of September 11, 2001, in New York and Washington, D.C., it was suddenly open season on Saudi Arabia in American newspapers and books, on television, and in Congress. In many forums, "Wahhabism" became a synonym for violent, xenophobic extremism. This atmospheric shift left the State Department little choice but to declare Saudi Arabia in 2004 a "country of particular concern" under the International Religious Freedom Act, which requires the US government to take action against countries deemed responsible for especially severe violations of religious freedom.

In designating its "concern" over Saudi Arabia on this issue, the State Department was only stating the obvious. Saudi Arabia does not have and does not advocate freedom of religion. All Saudi citizens must be Muslims, and no other faith may be practiced in public. Apostasy is punishable by death. In fact, under Saudi law, the entire purpose of the state is the protection and propagation of Islam, not the protection or liberty of the individual. But this has been true since Americans first started venturing there in the 1920s, and Americans have in the past chosen to accept Saudi Arabia as it is, not as they would like it to be.

It might seem, then, that in the changed environment since September 11, Saudi Arabia would have been a logical target of the George W. Bush administration's campaign to promote democracy and freedom of expression in the Middle East, but such was not the case. The administration appeared to have recognized the uniqueness of Saudi Arabia as a society and its value as an economic partner, and that alienating the country would be counterproductive. The "Final Report of the National Commission on Terrorist Attacks in the United States," known as the "9/11 Commission Report," which "found no evidence that the Saudi government as an institution or senior Saudi official individually funded" the Al-Qaida network,[14] gave the Bush administration political cover to continue to treat Saudi Arabia as a valuable if troubled ally rather than as an enemy—which is the course the administration chose to follow.

The administration mostly accepted the declarations by King Abdullah and other senior princes that the Saudi regime, itself the target of a domestic terror campaign inspired by followers of bin Laden, would ally itself with the United States in the "war on terror" and commit itself to expunging extremism from its mosques and classrooms. This policy was reflected in repeated congressional testimony by administration officials about Saudi Arabia's helpfulness on this front, even if the country still has a long way to go. It was reasserted in the decision by Secretary of State Condoleezza Rice to refrain from imposing the economic sanctions nominally required by the religious freedom finding.

When Rice went to Saudi Arabia in November 2005, it was not to scold or criticize the Saudis but to advance the bilateral "strategic dialogue" initiated by President Bush and by Abdullah, still crown prince at that time, when they met at the president's ranch in April of that year. Rice and her Saudi counterpart, Prince Saud al-Faisal, announced in Jidda the creation of six "working groups" on subjects of mutual interest: counterterrorism, military affairs, energy, economic and financial affairs, consular affairs and partnership, and education exchange and human development in the United

States and Saudi Arabia. Democracy and political reform were conspicuously not among the subjects of the working groups. Clearly these groups' discussions of terrorism and "human development" could have included tough conversations about Saudi Arabia's domestic human rights policies, but the Bush administration chose to avoid a public argument with the Saudis on these subjects.

That choice was stated explicitly in the joint declaration issued by Bush and Abdullah after their April 2005 meeting in Texas: "Today we renewed our personal friendship and that between our nations," the two leaders said. The word "Wahhabism" did not appear in the text. It said that "the United States respects Saudi Arabia as the birthplace of Islam, one of the world's great religions, and as the symbolic center of the Islamic faith as custodian of Islam's two holy places in Mecca and Medina. Saudi Arabia reiterates its call on all those who teach and propagate the Islamic faith to adhere strictly to the Islamic message of peace, moderation, and tolerance and reject that which deviates from these principles."

Democratization was given short shrift in the declaration: "While the United States considers that nations will create institutions that reflect the history, culture, and traditions of their societies, it does not seek to impose its own style of government on the government and people of Saudi Arabia. The United States applauds the recently held elections in the Kingdom for representatives for municipal councils"—in which women were banned from voting, let alone running—"and looks for even wider participation in the accordance with the Kingdom's reform program."[15]

In the language of diplomacy, this amounted to a promise by the United States to let the Saudis manage their internal affairs without interference, even if it is no longer possible for Americans to turn a blind eye to what the Saudis do. After all, Saudi Arabia is the largest trading partner of the United States in the Middle East, a multibillion-dollar market for US business, and a crucial supplier of oil. Those economic considerations continue to trump human rights and religious freedom, as they have for more than half a century.

The bilateral relationship between Washington and Riyadh will never again be as it was from the 1940s through the 1980s. Saudi Arabia is no longer an undeveloped country and the Saudis no longer need Americans to show them how to fly aircraft, lay pipelines, or perform surgery. The kingdom has new economic partners, especially China. The US-Saudi alliance has a different rationale now; the common enemy is violent religious extremism, not communism. In this new phase, Saudi Arabia is still a country where the form of Islam known to outsiders as Wahhabism prevails and influences all decisionmaking, but this fact does not exclude the kingdom from the American embrace any more than it ever did.

▨ Notes

1. H. St. John Philby, *Saudi Arabia* (Beirut: Librarie du Liban, 1955), p. 313.

2. William A. Eddy, "Our Faith and Your Iron," *Middle East Journal* 17, no. 3 (1963): 257.

3. David Long, *The Kingdom of Saudi Arabia* (Gainesville: University of Florida Press, 1997), p. 109.

4. This wording was recorded in an internal State Department memorandum on July 31, 1951, by Raymond A. Hare, US ambassador to Saudi Arabia at that time. A copy is available in *Mulligan Papers* (Washington, DC: Georgetown University Library), box 7, folder 23.

5. The State Department paper on this subject is in the records of the Senate Foreign Relations Committee hearing of July 20, 1956.

6. US Military Training Mission to Saudi Arabia, "Handbook for Newcomers" (Dhahran, 1961), pp. 14–15.

7. *Kern v. Dynalectron Corporation,* US District Court, Northern District of Texas, October 19, 1983, reported in 577 Fed Supplement 1196.

8. US Department of State, *Foreign Relations of the United States, 1951,* vol. 5, p. 1027.

9. US Department of State, *Foreign Relations of the United States, 1964–1968,* vol. 21, pp. 458–459.

10. *Public Papers of the Presidents, 1978* (Washington, DC: US Government Printing Office), pp. 118–119.

11. Ibid., p. 1876.

12. H. Norman Schwarzkopf, *It Doesn't Take a Hero* (New York: Bantam, 1992), p. 386.

13. See especially the August 1996 "Declaration of War" against the United States by Osama bin Laden, which cites "the inability of the regime to protect the country" despite "unjustified heavy spending" on military equipment. An English text is available in Barry Rubin and Judith Colp Rubin, *Anti-American Terrorism and the Middle East* (New York: Oxford University Press, 2002), pp. 137–142.

14. *Final Report of the National Commission on Terrorist Attacks Upon the United States* (New York: Norton, n.d.), p. 171.

15. The text can be read online at http://www.state.gov/p/nea/rls/rm/5327.htm.

10

Official Wahhabism and the Sanctioning of Saudi-US Relations

F. Gregory Gause III

There is no doubt that Wahhabism's intolerant and xenophobic view of non-Muslims has complicated Saudi Arabia's relationship with its foreign patrons, Great Britain and the United States. Salafi opponents have castigated the al-Saud for their close relations with unbelievers and the moral pollution those relations have brought to Arabia. Despite this formidable ideological constraint, however, the Saudi rulers have successfully maintained the closest of relations with their great power foreign allies. Paradoxically, Wahhabism has had very little influence on Saudi Arabia's relations with the United States, understood as bilateral state-to-state relations.

The al-Saud have been able to finesse this contradiction because of the ideological and institutional development of the Wahhabi ulama in the twentieth century. The ulama have become agents of the state; their fortunes and religious project are directly linked to the continuation of al-Saud rule in Arabia. They have developed the original Wahhabi insights, which were politically revolutionary (particularly in the religious sanction they gave to acts of war against fellow Muslims) into a status quo doctrine that gives the Saudi rulers maximum discretion in the realm of foreign policy, while maintaining for themselves control (or substantial influence) over the interpretation and implementation of Islam at home. When salafi opponents attack the regime for its relations with the United States (and Great Britain earlier), the ulama provide the rulers with a religious sanction of their right to rule. That sanction has helped the al-Saud prevent the salafi opposition from being able to mobilize widespread support in Saudi society.[1]

▨ Wahhabism and Saudi Policy Toward the Great Powers

It is hard to imagine that an interpretation of Islam that justified attacks on fellow Muslims in Arabia and that found the sultan-caliph of the Ottoman

Empire an unfit Muslim ruler would look kindly on close strategic relations with infidel powers. Indeed, challengers to al-Saud rule from within the Wahhabi tradition have consistently made Riyadh's relations with Western powers a major part of their case against the rulers. However, in the four most serious challenges, analyzed below, the Wahhabi ulama came to the defense of the rulers. It is interesting to note that they only occasionally offered a religious justification for the policy choices of the al-Saud. Rather, they asserted that there is no religious justification for opposition to a ruler who implements Islamic law. It is not that the ulama necessarily supported Saudi policy. However, they accorded the rulers wide discretion in foreign policy, because the stability of the Saudi state was necessary for them to retain their position in that state—both in terms of their personal interests and in terms of their corporate interest, the continuation of a Wahhabi Islamic state in Arabia.

The Ikhwan Revolt of the Late 1920s

As long as King Abd al-Aziz's strategic interests in bringing the Arabian Peninsula under his rule were in accord with the Ikhwan's interests in spreading the true faith, the latter did not publicly object to the former's protectorate treaty of 1915 with Great Britain. However, by the mid-1920s, tensions arose between a number of Ikhwan leaders and Abd al-Aziz over the continuation of the jihad. The king accepted the borders between Iraq, Kuwait, and Saudi Arabia drawn at the Uqayr Conference in 1922, and thought it prudent not to challenge the British-imposed border with Transjordan. Elements of the Ikhwan thought otherwise. They objected to Abd al-Aziz's effort to limit their ability to take the jihad across these borders (along with a number of his other policies, regarding taxes, technological innovations, administration of the Hijaz, and treatment of Shias). In late 1926 a group of restive Ikhwan leaders met in Al-Artawiyya and charged the king with a number of offenses. One of these was the fact that he had sent his son Faisal to London in August 1926 to negotiate with the British, an act of collaboration with an infidel power.

In February 1927 the ulama of Riyadh found merit in several of the charges and recommended that the king reverse his policy. However, they were silent on the charge that consorting with the British was an offense against Islam, and they emphasized that only the imam, Abd al-Aziz, had the right to proclaim jihad—in effect, to conduct foreign policy.[2] Shortly thereafter the king signed a new treaty with Great Britain, the May 1927 Treaty of Jidda, which ended the protectorate relationship established in the 1915 treaty. London recognized the complete independence of Abd al-Aziz's realm, and the king accepted the territorial status quo with Britain's mandates and protectorates surrounding his kingdom. The sources indicate no objection from the Wahhabi ulama to the new treaty, though the king's Ikhwan opponents accused him of selling himself to the English.[3]

Tensions mounted as the rebellious Ikhwan continued their raids into Kuwait, Iraq, and Transjordan. Their leaders even drew up plans for dividing Abd al-Aziz's realm among them, when the time came. The king convened a large assembly of Najdi notables, tribal shaikhs, and ulama in December 1928 to reassert his authority. He consolidated support with a dramatic offer to abdicate, which was met with reaffirmations of loyalty from the assembled group. He justified his relations with Great Britain and technological innovations such as the telegraph, which he allowed in his realm on the grounds that these were necessary for establishing and maintaining the state. While no formal fatwa from the ulama in attendance is recorded, one of their number followed Abd al-Aziz's presentation with a speech that emphasized his right to rule and the religious obligation to obey him.[4] Abd al-Aziz sent members of the ulama to dissuade the rebellious Ikhwan shaikhs from continuing their disobedience. On one occasion, Ikhwan leader Faisal al-Dawish accused a prominent alim sent to him by the king of sacrificing his religious principles to be on the al-Saud payroll.[5] The conflict eventually ended in the violent clash between Abd al-Aziz's forces—levies from the towns of Najd along with loyal tribes—and the tribal Ikhwan forces, at Sibylla in March 1929. The king routed his opponents, and followed up that victory with subsequent attacks on his enemies through 1929. By the end of the year, the revolt had been crushed.

No one can argue that the rebellious Ikhwan were not good Wahhabis. On the contrary, they seemed to represent much more faithfully the commitment to *dawa* and jihad that characterized the first Saudi realm than the more cautious and diplomatic Abd al-Aziz. Many of their complaints against the king were accepted by the Riyadh ulama in their February 1927 fatwa. However, in the end the ulama stood foursquare behind the monarch, who was building a state that privileged their role and was imposing a social peace that allowed them to implement their interpretation of Islamic law. Joseph Kostiner speculates: "The fear of anarchy and civil war must have had a decisive impact on the *ulama* in Najd, who have usually adhered to law and order and supported organized government, under which their profession thrived. They therefore opted for obedience and the maintenance of Ibn Saud's power."[6] It is hard to disagree with his analysis.

The Takeover of Mecca's Grand Mosque in 1979

On November 20, 1979, the first day of the Muslim calendar year 1400, Juhayman al-Utaybi and a group of followers, who might have numbered as many as a thousand, seized the Grand Mosque in Mecca, the most important shrine in the Muslim world.[7] Juhayman sought the overthrow of al-Saud rule and its replacement by one of his compatriots, Muhammad al-Qahtani, who was proclaimed the Mahdi, the leader long expected by certain millenarian interpretations of Islam. Juhayman condemned the al-Saud for straying from the path of true Islam. His critique, developed in a number of "letters" circulated before his attack on the Grand Mosque, was self-consciously in the tradition of the Ikhwan objections of the 1920s. He condemned the al-Saud for their treatment of the Ikhwan forces, for their current alliances with Christian powers, and for their tolerance, even encouragement, of deviations from the model of Muslim life presented by the early Muslim communities, as interpreted by the Wahhabi tradition. His emphasis on rule by the Mahdi was a doctrinal innovation in Wahhabism, but the bulk of his theological and political ideas were firmly in the tradition of salafi opponents of the al-Saud.[8]

While Juhayman's theological formulations were explicated at length in his writings before the takeover, the core of his political message was broadcast over the public address system after he had taken control of the Grand Mosque. Along with the overthrow of the al-Saud, he called for the end of emulation of Western social norms, the breaking of diplomatic relations with Western states, the end of petroleum exports to the United States, and the expulsion of all foreign civilian and military advisers in the country.[9] Like his Ikhwan forebears, Juhayman saw the Western influence allowed in Saudi Arabia by the al-Saud as central to their lack of religious legitimacy.

After the takeover of the Grand Mosque, the Saudi rulers immediately turned to the leading ulama for support and for a religious justification to combat the rebels. They were not disappointed. On November 24, 1979, twenty-nine leading figures in the religious institutions of the country issued a fatwa and a lengthier commentary sanctioning the government's use of force against those who had captured the mosque. The religious scholars relied upon quranic verses condemning those who profane holy places, and a specific verse that permitted the fighting of infidels in the holy mosque, if the infidels initiated the conflict. The scholars were careful to note that those holding the mosque were Muslims, but that the verse applied to them as well. They also cited a saying (hadith) of the Prophet Muhammad sanctioning the use of force against "who[m]ever comes to you while you are unanimous in your opinion and wants to divide you and disperse you." The commentary asked God to save the Muslims from "sedition."[10]

It is interesting to note that the ulama chose not to refute any of Juhayman's charges against the regime, nor to defend the regime's links to the West, which were such a central part of Juhayman's indictment. They limited their justification of the use of force against the rebels to the general prohibition against profaning holy places like the Grand Mosque, and to the specific obligation of Muslims not to revolt against their leaders and thus divide the community. Whether the scholars thought that any of the charges raised by Juhayman were legitimate is impossible to know, but there is indirect evidence that one important scholar found at least some of his ideas, as opposed to his actions, to be tolerable in the Wahhabi tradition. Shaikh Abdullah Abd al-Aziz ibn Baz was one of the senior clerics in the country, the chairman of the Council of Senior Ulama who would, in 1991, be named Grand Mufti (chief issuer of religious judgments) of Saudi Arabia. He was one of the twenty-nine signers of the November 24 fatwa. In 1978, Juhayman and a number of others had been arrested in Riyadh following the publication of one of his letters, "Rules of Allegiance and Obedience: The Misconduct of Rulers." Shaikh ibn Baz interrogated them, and they were subsequently released.[11]

If the shaikh had any sympathy for Juhayman's ideas, it is clear that the sympathy was not returned. Juhayman was caustic in his criticism of the official ulama of Saudi Arabia, directly accusing ibn Baz of being "little better than a tool for the family's manipulation of the people."[12] He saw the ulama as having traded their religious ideals for the comforts of state positions. One of Juhayman's letters was subtitled: "Revealing the Duping by the Rulers of the Seekers of Knowledge and the People." In that letter he asked a hypothetical religious official: "Where did you get this money? Was it from conquest and expelling the unbelievers from the Arabian Peninsula? Or, on the contrary, was it from bringing the unbelievers among the Muslims and raising their flags in the Arabian Peninsula?"[13] Like the Ikhwan earlier, Juhayman saw the ulama as nothing more than creatures of the Saudi state. Whether or not they were, in this instance they acted in that capacity, delegitimating the rebellion and urging support for the state's leaders, while staying silent on the substantive charges brought by the rebels against the leaders.

The Gulf War of 1990–1991 and Its Aftermath

The Saudi decision to open the country to hundreds of thousands of US and other foreign troops in the wake of Saddam Hussein's occupation of Kuwait in August 1990 elicited sharp criticism from salafi activists. That criticism gathered momentum over the course of the crisis and helped spawn a most unusual phenomenon in modern Saudi history: a public campaign by Islamists to rally grassroots support and pressure the government to change its domestic and foreign policies. The government once again turned to the ulama, who not only provided religious sanction to its foreign policy decisions in the Gulf War but also supported its subsequent crackdown on the salafi critics.

During the Gulf crisis, Safar al-Hawali and Salman al-Awdah emerged as significant salafi critics of Saudi policy, spreading their criticism of the decision to allow US forces into the kingdom through taped cassettes of their lectures.[14] Both focused on the greater threat to Islam in general and Saudi Arabia in particular from the prospect of US domination of the region than from the Iraqi occupation of Kuwait.[15] Their criticism of the regime's foreign policy continued after the Gulf War, with al-Hawali publishing a collection of his sermons under the title *Truths About the Gulf Crisis* in 1991. The popularity of his critique can be indirectly discerned from the fact that, though it was harshly critical of the Saudi government, it was published in Saudi Arabia itself. Unlike past critics of the regime from the religious trend, al-Hawali concentrated not on Islamic texts to make his case but on an analysis of international relations, citing Henry Kissinger more often than the Quran. But his message was clear: the United States sought the domination of the Muslim world, and the result of such domination would be the triumph of secularism, Christianity, and Judaism over Islam.[16]

If al-Hawali and al-Awdah had limited themselves to the occasional sermon and public broadside against the regime, the al-Saud might have tolerated their activities. They were unable to organize any significant public expression of opposition to the state during the Gulf crisis. However, they made a concerted effort to widen the scope of their opposition movement in the wake of the crisis. They were driving forces in the composition of the "memorandum of advice" *(mudhakkarat al-nasiha)* in the summer of 1992, a detailed, forty-six-page critique of the full range of Saudi government policy signed by 107 members of the ulama and salafi activists. On defense issues, the memorandum called for a stronger Saudi army so the state could defend itself "without reliance on anyone," an implicit criticism of policy during the Gulf War, and for diversification of Saudi arms purchases, to avoid reliance "on one specific country, which gives us what it wants, denies us what it does not want us to have, exploits us in times of trouble and bargains with us during times of calamity." In foreign policy, the memorandum criticized the "intense desire" of the regime to avoid conflict with the Western regimes, "which lead the assault against Islam," manifested by Saudi Arabia "following the United States in almost every area." The signers warned the government to "avoid any form of alliance or cooperation which serves imperialist goals."[17] Unlike the Ikhwan in the 1920s or Juhayman in 1979, the salafi activists who composed the memorandum did not call for revolt against the al-Saud. However, there was no mistaking their unhappiness about the relationship between the government and the United States.

The Saudi rulers turned to the official ulama for support during the Gulf crisis, and the ulama, in responding to their salafi critics afterward, did not disappoint. Shaikh Abd al-Aziz ibn Baz issued fatwas giving religious sanction both to the government's invitation to US and other foreign forces to enter Saudi Arabia, and to the war to drive Iraqi forces out of Kuwait.[18] In December 1991 he publicly criticized the salafi activists who were pressuring the government, terming their assertions "lies" and "conspiracies against Islam and Muslims."[19] The Council of Senior Ulama condemned the advisory memorandum after its contents had been publicized in the international media, accusing the authors of "planting rancor" in Saudi society and judging it "at variance with the forms of legitimate advice and the justice in word and deed it requires."[20] King Fahd shortly thereafter removed seven members of the council who had not joined the condemnation of the memorandum, replacing them with more loyal clerics in an assertion of the state's control of the religious establishment.[21] The official ulama continued to stand by the regime in its crackdown on the salafi opposition in 1994, with the arrest of al-Hawali, al-Awdah, and over 150 other activists, and in the face of attacks in 1995 and 1996 on US military personnel and military trainers in Riyadh and Dhahran. The opposition subsequently went abroad (most notably Osama bin Laden, who was stripped of his Saudi citizenship in 1994) or went underground, to resurface in Saudi Arabia in 2003.[22]

Once again, the official religious establishment supported the rulers' foreign policy decisions, particularly the alliance with the United States, in the face of salafi criticism. Given the severity of the threat posed by the Iraqi invasion of Kuwait and the unprecedented nature of the Saudi decision to invite US forces into the country, the senior cleric, Shaikh ibn Baz, went beyond the past practice of the ulama and gave explicit religious sanction to the government's wartime decisions. After that, the religious establishment followed its previous pattern of keeping silent on foreign policy issues, but criticizing those who raised objections to the state's foreign policy and calling upon them to cease such criticism and give their loyalty to the al-Saud. Despite the active opposition by the salafi activists to Riyadh's de facto alliance with the United States, Saudi-US relations became even closer after the Gulf War, with the stationing of a US air wing in the country and with open Saudi support for controversial US initiatives on Iraq and on Arab-Israeli peace issues. The official ulama once again gave the regime the religious cover it needed to pursue a foreign policy based explicitly on state and regime interest, not Wahhabi Islam.

September 11, 2001, and Its Aftermath

Al-Qaida's attacks on New York and Washington, D.C., on September 11, 2001, placed Saudi Arabia squarely in the center of a worldwide crisis; Osama bin Laden's Saudi origins and the fact that fifteen of the nineteen hijackers that day were Saudis ensured this result. Instantly, the Saudis' core security alliance had been put at risk, as Americans looked to Riyadh for both explanations of what had happened and decisive action against the jihadist strain of salafi Islam that the Saudis had helped to foster since the fight against the Soviet Union in Afghanistan. Bin Laden and his sympathizers brought the crisis home to the Saudi rulers in May 2003, with an attack on foreign housing compounds in Riyadh itself, followed by other violent assaults on symbols of Western power in Saudi Arabia (the US consulate in Jidda, foreign oil service companies, and housing compounds in various parts of the country) and on symbols of the Saudi state (the Ministry of Interior, a police station, security personnel). The Saudis faced a concerted assault on their right to rule at home and on the centerpiece of their foreign and security policy.

Bin Laden's critique of the al-Saud was not simply a restatement of that of the Ikhwan in the 1920s or of Juhayman in 1979. His thinking was more influenced by Qutbist currents of Islamist thought, emanating from the mid-twentieth-century writings of Egyptian Islamist Sayyid Qutb, than by Muhammad ibn Abd al-Wahhab. However, his core complaints about the al-Saud were familiar to those earlier opponents of Saudi policy: the regime had drifted away from true Islam and was consorting too closely with infidels. Bin Laden had as early as 1994 declared his opposition to the al-Saud rulers, accusing them of "waging war on Islam" after the arrest of Salman al-Awdah and Safar al-Hawali.[23] His declaration of war on the United States, issued from Afghanistan in August 1996, called the US "occupation" of Saudi Arabia "the greatest disaster to befall the Muslims since the death of the Prophet Muhammad."[24] The Saudi branch of Al-Qaida, which emerged with the May 2003 bombing, echoed bin Laden's line of criticism. A communiqué issued shortly before that bombing told the Saudi rulers: "We will not hesitate to kill you as long as you are in the line of the Jews and the Christians."[25]

In the face of outside pressure—from both bin Laden and the United States—and the violent challenge to their rule at home, the al-Saud once again turned to the religious establishment for support. The ulama denounced bin Laden and the attacks of September 11 in unambiguous terms from the outset. The Grand Mufti of Saudi Arabia, Shaikh Abd al-Aziz Al al-Shaikh, on September 15, 2001, said that the attacks were "counter to the teachings of Islam," characterizing them as "gross crimes and sinful acts."[26] After the May 2003 bombings, the ulama conducted a public campaign against what they termed "excessiveness" *(al-ghulu)* in religion and against "deviant" understandings of Islamic teachings concerning jihad. The Grand Mufti at that time reminded Saudis that it was their religious obligation to obey their rulers, "even if they are oppressive. . . . He who rebels against the prince rebels against God."[27] Shortly after the May bombings, 343 religious officials were removed from their positions in mosques around the country, and 1,347 were required to undergo retraining.[28] As in the past, the official ulama did not comment on the state's foreign policy, and thus did not explicitly endorse the Saudi-US relationship, but they left no doubt as to the right of the rulers to rule and the duty of the ruled to obey.

The willingness of the religious establishment to rally to the defense of the al-Saud in crisis was not surprising. The more interesting post–September 11 phenomenon was the ability of the Saudi rulers to elicit the support of many of their salafi critics, some of whom had led the opposition movement in the early 1990s and had spent time in Saudi jails. With the Saudi state under international pressure and domestic assault, these critics put aside their differences with the rulers and came to their defense.[29] Shaikh Salman al-Awdah is a good example. After September 11, he condemned extremism in the Muslim world, calling it a "deviant understanding" of Islam or a "deviant application of legitimate teachings."[30] After the May 2003 bombings, a number of prominent salafi activists, including al-Awdah and al-Hawali, issued a statement condemning violence against the state. Unlike the official ulama, however, these activists continued to be vocal in their criticism of US policy in the region, and, indirectly, of Saudi-US relations. The May 2003 statement condemning the Riyadh bombings called US foreign policy "arbitrary, expansionist and unilateral" and said that the Muslim world was the "first target" of US hostility.[31] As much as they continued to oppose the United States, however, they clearly saw the stability of the Saudi state as central to their long-term political agenda, and were willing to back it despite their distaste for its US connection.

For their part, the Saudi rulers have worked assiduously in the post–September 11 period to repair their relations with the United States, despite the strong anti-US feelings in Saudi public opinion occasioned by the wars in Afghanistan and Iraq and by Israeli-Palestinian tensions. They have made no efforts to appease either their bin Ladenist opponents or their salafi critics by drawing away from the special relationship with the United States. On the contrary, they have cooperated (though quietly) with US military planners during the wars in both Afghanistan and Iraq, and have openly allied themselves with Washington in the "war on terror." The US air campaigns at the outset of both the Afghan and the Iraq conflicts were coordinated from the Prince Sultan Airbase, south of Riyadh.[32] Particularly since the May 2003 bombing of housing complexes in Riyadh by Saudis aligned with Al-Qaida, the Saudi government has both conducted a strong security campaign against local Al-Qaida sympathizers and used its official religious institutions to delegitimate bin Laden's message. It has also manifested more willingness than previously to cooperate with the United States in the "war on terror" concerning issues such as limiting the financing of Islamist extremist organizations by Saudi citizens.[33] In all, while September 11 has undoubtedly changed Saudi-US relations, it has not done what its masterminds intended it to do—rupture forever the relationship.

Conclusion

It is hard to avoid the conclusion that Wahhabism places no substantial barriers against Saudi Arabia's relationships with outside powers. The official Wahhabi religious establishment has given the al-Saud wide latitude to conduct foreign policy, and has defended it from the 1920s to September 11, 2001, and since, against domestic opponents who contend that Saudi foreign policy contradicts the requirements of Islam. Even contemporary salafi critics of the regime will not justify revolt against al-Saud rule on the basis of the family's connection to the United States. Wahhabism is undoubtedly one element of Saudi public opinion that can lead to anti-US sentiment, and this sentiment can act as a constraint on Saudi policy toward the United States. But Saudi public opinion in general is a weak constraint on Saudi foreign policy, and the sources of anti-US feeling among the Saudi public go well beyond Wahhabism. While the Saudi rulers always monitor the pulse of their public, they have demonstrated on numerous occasions that public opinion does not guide their policy toward the United States.

It is also important to note that the exceptions to the overall pattern of close Saudi-US relations in the past seven decades have had nothing to do with Wahhabism: differences in the early and middle 1950s over Saudi support for Egypt's Gamal Abdul Nasser, the oil embargo of 1973, and Saudi opposition to the Camp David Accords of 1978. In each case, Saudi-US tensions stemmed from Saudi maneuverings in Middle Eastern regional politics that ran against US preferences. There is no evidence in any of these cases that Wahhabi ideological strictures or pressure from the religious establishment or from Wahhabi-influenced public opinion drove Saudi policy.

On the other side of the bilateral relationship, Wahhabism has discomfited US leaders from time to time, who have had to justify to the American public close relations with a country that unapologetically implements domestic policies that are at extreme variance from American liberal ideals. In the past, when US administrations valued the relationship for reasons of oil, regional security, and Cold War politics, this public relations problem was simply a minor irritant. For decades, Washington tended to view Saudi Arabia's promotion of its interpretation of Islam outside its borders as a complementary part of the global US strategy against communism, and, after 1979, against the revolutionary Shia Islam propagated by Iran.[34] But since September 11, 2001, Wahhabism has for the first time become a major issue on the US side of the bilateral relationship. The George W. Bush administration worked assiduously to protect the relationship from those who saw Saudi Arabia as the wellspring of salafi jihadism. Whether subsequent administrations will work so hard to protect the Saudi connection remains to be seen. On its part, the Saudi regime has also begun to feel the need to distance itself somewhat from US policy in the Middle East; King Abdullah went so far as to characterize the US occupation of Iraq as "illegal" in his speech at the Arab summit in Riyadh in March 2007.[35] The confluence of circumstances both in the United States and in the Middle East has the potential to further muddy the waters of Saudi-US relations in the near future.

Notes

1. This interpretation of the relationship between the rulers and the official religious establishment has been put forward by a number of scholars. See, in particular, Abdulaziz H. al-Fahad, "From Exclusivism to Accommodation: Doctrinal and Legal Evolution of Wahhabism," *New York University Law Review* 79, no. 2 (2004); Ayman al-Yassini, *Religion and State in the Kingdom of Saudi Arabia* (Boulder: Westview, 1985); Alexander Bligh, "The Saudi Religious Elite (Ulama) as Participant in the Political System of the Kingdom," *International Journal of Middle East Studies* 17, no. 1 (1985).

2. Alexei Vassiliev, *The History of Saudi Arabia* (London: Saqi, 1998), pp. 273–274; Joseph Kostiner, *The Making of Saudi Arabia, 1916–1936: From Chieftancy to Monarchical State* (New York: Oxford University Press, 1993), p. 116.

3. Kostiner, *Making of Saudi Arabia,* p. 113.

4. Ibid., p. 131. See also Vassiliev, *History of Saudi Arabia,* p. 277.

5. Abdulaziz H. al-Fahad, "The Imama vs. the Iqal: Hadari-Bedouin Conflict and the Formation of the Saudi State," in *Counter-Narratives: History, Contemporary Society, and Politics in Saudi Arabia and Yemen,* edited by Madawi al-Rasheed and Robert Vitalis (New York: Palgrave Macmillan, 2004), p. 113.

6. Kostiner, *Making of Saudi Arabia,* p. 131.

7. Vassiliev, *History of Saudi Arabia,* p. 396, cites the thousand figure. At the end of the sixteen-day siege and series of battles that finally restored government control over the mosque, Juhayman surrendered alongside 170 of his followers. James Buchan, "The Return of the Ikhwan, 1979," in *The House of Saud,* edited by David Holden and Richard Johns (New York: Holt, Rinehart, and Winston, 1981), p. 526.

8. For an analysis of Juhayman's thought, see Joseph A. Kechichian, "Islamic Revivalism and Change in Saudi Arabia: Juhayman al-'Utaybi's 'Letters' to the Saudi People," *Muslim World* 80, no. 1 (1980).

9. Kechichian, "Islamic Revivalism and Change in Saudi Arabia," p. 12. Kechichian cites as his source for Juhayman's announcements in the Grand Mosque a 1981 pamphlet published by a Saudi opposition group.

10. Text of the fatwa and the commentary in Joseph A. Kechichian, "The Role of the Ulama in the Politics of an Islamic State: The Case of Saudi Arabia," *International Journal of Middle East Studies* 18, no. 1 (1986); text on pp. 66–68. In this article, Kechichian attributes more institutional independence to the Saudi ulama than I do here.

11. Buchan, "Return of the Ikhwan," p. 518.

12. Ibid., p. 515.

13. Rifat Sayyid Ahmad, *Rasa'il Juhayman al-'Utaybi* (Cairo: Maktabat Madbuli, 1988), p. 61; title of the letter is on p. 55.

14. Joshua Teitelbaum, *Holier Than Thou: Saudi Arabia's Islamic Opposition* (Washington, DC: Washington Institute for Near East Policy, 2000), pp. 28–32.

15. The best analysis of their political views can be found in Mamoun Fandy, *Saudi Arabia and the Politics of Dissent* (New York: St. Martin's, 1999), chaps. 2–3.

16. Safar al-Hawali, *Haqa'iq Hawl 'Azmat al-Khalij* (Mecca: Dar Makka al-Mukarrama, 1991).

17. Quotes taken from a copy of the memorandum that I obtained in Saudi Arabia in 1992. For a general discussion of the memorandum in the context of Saudi politics, see F. Gregory Gause III, *Oil Monarchies: Domestic and Security Challenges in the Arab Gulf States* (New York: Council on Foreign Relations, 1994), pp. 35–36.

18. Text of the former fatwa can be found in *Al-Sharq al-Awsat,* August 21, 1990. On January 20, 1991, the *New York Times* reported a fatwa from Shaikh ibn Baz sanctioning the offensive against Iraq as a legitimate jihad.

19. *New York Times,* December 31, 1991.

20. *Al-Hayat,* September 18, 1992.

21. Teitelbaum, *Holier Than Thou,* pp. 39–40.

22. For discussions of the Saudi salafi opposition in the 1990s, see ibid., pp. 4–7; Fandy, *Saudi Arabia and the Politics of Dissent,* chaps. 4–6.

23. After the arrests, bin Laden issued a statement through his office in London in which he accused King Fahd of waging war against Islam, and called upon those working for the Saudi state not to obey its orders. Advice and Reform Committee, Communiqué no. 6, "Al-Sa'udiyya Tusfir 'an Muharibatha lil-Islam wa 'Ulamahu" [Saudi Arabia Displays Its Attack on Islam and the Ulama], September 13, 1994 (copy in author's possession).

24. A translation can be found in Bruce Lawrence, ed., *Messages to the World: The Statements of Osama bin Laden* (London: Verso, 2005), doc. 3, p. 25.

25. The quote is from the website of the Movement of Islamic Reform in Arabia, headed by Saad al-Faqih, a Saudi salafi opposition figure in London: "Nashrat al-Islah" [Reform Communiqué] no. 366, May 12, 2003, http://www.miraserve.com. The most thorough account of the conflict between Al-Qaida of the Arabian Peninsula and the Saudi government is Roel Meijer, "The Cycle of Contention and the Limits of Terrorism in Saudi Arabia," in *Saudi Arabia in the Balance: Political Economy, Society, and Foreign Affairs,* edited by Paul Aarts and Gerd Nonneman (London: Hurst, 2005).

26. "Saudi Grand Mufti Condemns Terrorist Acts in U.S.," http://www.saudi embassy.net/press_release/press_release00.htm, September 15, 2001.

27. See, for example, the statement by the Grand Mufti in *Al-Hayat,* August 22, 2003.

28. This announcement from the Saudi Ministry of Islamic Affairs can be found in *Al-Hayat,* May 28, 2003.

29. For a fuller discussion of this trend, see F. Gregory Gause III, "Saudi Perceptions of the United States Since 9/11," in *With Us or Against Us: Studies in Global Anti-Americanism,* edited by Tony Judt and Denis Lacorne (New York: Palgrave Macmillan, 2005).

30. See, in particular, his article "Al-Tatarruf wa al-Tatarruf al-Mudad" [Extremism and Counter-Extremism], http://www.islamtoday.net, December 12, 2001.

31. *Al-Hayat,* May 20, 2003.

32. On Saudi cooperation in the war in Iraq, see Michael R. Gordon and Bernard E. Trainor, *Cobra II: The Inside Story of the Invasion and Occupation of Iraq* (New York: Pantheon, 2006), pp. 164, 174, 327–328. On Saudi cooperation in the war in Afghanistan, see David B. Ottaway and Robert G. Kaiser, "After September 11, Severe Tests Loom for Relationship," *Washington Post,* February 11, 2002.

33. For a discussion of the Saudi security campaign since 2003, see Meijer, "'Cycle of Contention.'"

34. Rachel Bronson, *Thicker Than Oil: America's Uneasy Partnership with Saudi Arabia* (New York: Oxford University Press, 2006), pp. 7–9.

35. Hassan M. Fattah, "U.S. Iraq Role Is Called Illegal by Saudi King," *New York Times,* March 29, 2007.

PART 4

Conclusion

11

The Impact of the Wahhabi Tradition

John O. Voll

What is the long-term impact of the Wahhabi tradition? A look at the head-lines at the beginning of the twenty-first century gives the impression that the Wahhabi tradition is having a major global impact. During the summer of 2006 alone, claims were made that "Wahhabi groups" were to blame for or were a part of serious events of political opposition, militant extremism, and terrorism in many different parts of the world. Reports of such activities came from many places, as widely different as Kyrgyzstan, North Caucasus, Serbia and Bosnia, Somalia, Indonesia, the United Kingdom, and the United States.[1] However, it is not clear what is meant when people attach the label of "Wahhabi" to an individual or group. Instead, it is clear that in the first decade of the twenty-first century, many people mean different things when they speak about "Wahhabis" and "Wahhabism."

An assessment of the impact of the Wahhabi tradition on movements of renewal and reform in the Muslim world requires examination of a wide range of issues. Three questions are particularly important in such an exam-ination: What are the characteristics of renewal movements in Islam, espe-cially in the origins of the Wahhabi movement?[2] What type of a reformer-teacher was Muhammad ibn Abd al-Wahhab? What are the narratives that define the role of Wahhabism in the Muslim world?

Muslim Movements of Renewal

From the early days of the Islamic community, movements of reform and renewal arose to meet the challenges of changing historical conditions while maintaining adherence to the fundamentals of the Islamic message.[3] These movements took many different forms, depending on the particular contexts of era and location. The period from the sixteenth through the eighteenth centuries was a time of major transformations in societies across the globe. In this era "before modernity," intellectuals and activists in many societies were working to reshape their societies in a time of increasing globalization but not yet of industrial modernization.

Current scholarship often labels this period as being "early modern," and the developments in global societies are viewed through presentist lenses. As a result, movements in this era are often discussed in relationship to modern developments. While there are important continuities, it is also useful to remember that this era was a distinctive time in all of the major world societies. However, many of the interpretive questions start with modern and contemporary premises.

One such contemporary question relating to Islamic history and experience starts with the conclusion that somehow things have gone wrong in modern history for Muslims and Islamic societies. If one starts with that assumption, the obvious question is the one posed in the title of Bernard Lewis's best-selling book *What Went Wrong?*[4] Analysis of this question must look to the immediately "premodern" era, because up until the sixteenth century, Muslim societies were among the strongest and most powerful in the world. The contrasts between the Muslim world of the sixteenth and the nineteenth centuries are dramatic. As Marshall G. S. Hodgson clearly put it, "In the sixteenth century of our era, a visitor from Mars might well have supposed that the human world was on the verge of becoming Muslim. He would have based his judgment partly on the strategic and political advantages of the Muslims, but partly also on the vitality of their general culture."[5] By the nineteenth century, the global situation was dramatically different, and the Muslim world was falling under the control of non-Muslim powers. This historical context set the framework for renewal and reform in the modern Muslim world, thus focusing attention on movements of renewal in the eighteenth century.

Examinations of these movements of renewal and reform often begin with the question: Does Islam need a reformation? For more than a century, the Western European experience of the Protestant Reformation has been a part of the discussions about needed Islamic reform. Early activist Islamic reformers like Jamal al-Din al-Afghani viewed Martin Luther as a "hero" and "seem[ed] to have hoped to play the role of a Muslim Luther."[6] Similarly, influential modernist Muhammad Rashid Rida "found consolation in and drew inspiration from the [Protestant] reformation movement, which he considered to be one of the major factors contributing to the West's progress."[7] This continues at the beginning of the twenty-first century, with a wide range of Muslim and non-Muslim scholars discussing the prospects for an "Islamic reformation."

While many of the discussions of Islamic reformation deal with contemporary issues and developments, there is usually also a broader sense of historical contexts and issues. In discussions that present reform programs as well as analyses of reform movements in the modern era, the starting point is frequently at least some discussion of the movement of Muhammad ibn Abd al-Wahhab. South Asian reformist intellectual Muhammad Iqbal called the movement of ibn Abd al-Wahhab "the first throb of life in modern Islam."[8] However, most discussions of Islamic reformations and Muslim Luthers deal with twentieth- and twenty-first-century issues. Highly visible advocacy for the development of "Islamic Protestantism," like that of Iranian intellectual Hashem Aghjari, or of intellectuals in many parts of sub-Saharan Africa, is significant but tends to be defined more by contemporary concerns than by the specific nature of the Lutheran reformation.[9]

The basic terminology tends to be used generically, thus creating a degree of confusion. The historical contexts relevant to thinking in terms of an Islamic reformation were clearly defined by Marhsall Hodgson:

> I would suggest that the common Muslim thought that Islam requires a Luther or a Reformation of its own is likely to be misleading unless it is taken only in the most rarefied allusive sense. Luther does not yet represent the Christian confrontation with Modernity in its essential features. The fifteenth- and sixteenth-century Protestant movements can well be compared, for example, for the extent of their historical impact in their own time, to the fifteenth- and sixteenth-century Shi'i movements, which transformed the religious configuration of Iran.[10]

Following Hodgson's reminder, it is important to identify the Wahhabi movement, in its origins, as an eighteenth-century movement. The question "What went wrong?" in terms of Muslims' confrontation with modernity does not apply to that time and place. Muhammad ibn Abd al-Wahhab, like Luther, did not represent the Islamic "confrontation with modernity" in its essential features. It was only in the subsequent centuries that Wahhabism began to participate in the broader dynamics of the global transformations of modernity.

The Eighteenth-Century Context of Religious Reform

Before one can describe the Wahhabi movement's role in the context of the twentieth and twenty-first centuries, it needs to be identified in the context of the historical developments of that time.[11] This identification should take into account the more global developments of the time; too narrow a definition of developments within the Muslim world might distort the understanding of movements like the one launched by ibn Abd al-Wahhab. The heated debate over the question of whether or not Islam had an "enlightenment" provides a good case study to begin analyzing some of the issues involved.[12] Reinhard Schulze argued that "Islamic history did, as early as the 16th century, and on the strength of an independent tradition, participate in elaborating a modern culture, which in many respects shows distinct parallels with European cultural history."[13] Whether or not one agrees with Schulze's conclusions about an "Islamic enlightenment," it is important to view the Muslim world in the eighteenth century as a part of the broader global context. To insist that it is not possible for terms applicable to European experience to be relevant for analysis of Islamic experiences continues an unfruitful, old-style exceptionalism from the days of classical Orientalism.

The study of the Islamic world in the eighteenth century is frequently treated as a peripheral part of some other history. Often, "this era is regarded either as a decrepit extension of the flourishing Islamic civilization, studied only to give the heyday of Islam more relief, or as the background to 'modernization,' studied in order to provide a starting point to measure the effects of the impact of the West. . . . The 18th century was therefore not deemed worthy of being studied for its own sake."[14] However, this era, conceptually located between "the medieval" and "the modern" in the minds of many intellectuals and scholars, was a distinctive era, both in the Muslim world and in the broader world of global interactions of which the Muslim world was part.

In the emerging more cosmopolitan approaches to world history, the eighteenth century has received greater attention. Developments in the era from 1500 to 1800 are examined in their own contexts and seen as significantly shaping global and local histories. However, little of this new attention is given to the religious dimension of human life during that time. Once coverage of the European reformation and religious wars of the seventeenth century is completed, the center of most analytical attention shifts to the analysis of economic, social, and scientific developments.

In fact, during the eighteenth century, especially if considering the major monotheistic traditions of Middle Eastern origin, significant developments in religious thought, practice, and organization were taking place. In a number of areas, movements calling for a return to the original articulation of the faith arose, rejecting institutions and structures that had developed over the centuries. Preachers charged that the intellectual and doctrinal structures that had developed were lifeless and were harmful innovations. They often advocated a renewal based on more careful and literal attention to the basic texts of the faith.

This spirit of activist renewal has a call that sounds salafi to those familiar with Muslim movements, and is manifest in many different monotheistic traditions. In central Europe, for example, reformers in the tradition of German pietism "emphasized a return to primitive Christianity."[15] There was also an emphasis on scripture rather than tradition: "Pietism during its classical

period centered its concept of religious authority on a biblicism set originally against the formidable but lifeless theological systems of Protestant
orthodoxy."[16] Similar calls for renewal can be seen in the Great Awakening
in the British colonies in North America. Among Roman Catholics, some of
this renewalist spirit can be seen in the conflict between the Jesuits, who
"had come to a theological position that accommodated itself to the more
secular spirit of the times," and the Jansenists, who "wanted a return to the
primitive church."[17] Hasidism can be seen as the emergence of a religiously
enthusiastic reformism in Judaism at this same time.

While all of these movements are significantly different, their existence
emphasizes that the eighteenth century was not simply a time of developing
enlightenment rationalism and politics in Western Europe and decline in non-
Western parts of the world. The world was being transformed in terms of new
globalizing exchanges of goods and technologies. In this context of what has
been called "the first globalization,"[18] in addition to the changes in social,
political, and cultural lifestyles, there were important movements of religious
revival and renewal. It was in this world that the Wahhabi movement developed, in a time of more "pietist" and salafi perspectives relating to religious
reform. The Wahhabis were not alone globally in their efforts, and they were
not alone specifically within the Muslim world.

Ibn Abd al-Wahhab: What Kind of Reformer?

Muhammad ibn Abd al-Wahhab was at the center of one of the modes of
articulating this broad salafi-pietistic spirit of renewal and reform. Leaders in
such movements operate in many different ways, and it is useful to identify
what type of reformer ibn Abd al-Wahhab actually was. In this definition, it
is important to remember that "reform" means purification or rectification
of something, rather than its rejection.[19] Clearly, Muhammad ibn Abd al-
Wahhab was a "reformer" and not someone initiating a "new religion."

Reform implies two different elements interacting with each other. One
is an unchanging foundational truth and the other is the product of what
humans do with that unchanging truth. This human dimension involves creating institutions and intellectual-theological constructs. Most Muslim
reformers argue that they are not changing Islam, but are only changing what
humans constructed on the foundations provided by Islam. Reform in this
sense is "fundamentalist"—involving a return to the "fundamentals" or, as in
Christian pietism, a return to the "primitive" faith community.

This salafi-pietist mode of advocating change differs from messianic
advocacy for change. The messianic style affirms the coming of a new age
in which "old" truths are transformed or transcended. In Muslim tradition,
the new age is the era that is initiated by a divinely guided person, usually

given the title of "Mahdi." However, the concept of the person engaged in salafi-pietist reform involves a leader or movement engaged in *re*newal, not in creating something "new." The historical Muslim title for such a reformer is *mujaddid* ("renewer"). According to a tradition from the Prophet Muhammad, God will send to His community, "at the head of each century," someone who will "renew" the community's faith. Discussions of the role of these *mujaddid*s emphasize that there is a major difference between "renewal" and "innovation."[20] It is important to recognize that *mahdi* and *mujaddid* are two different modes of advocacy for changing current conditions that are judged to be bad.[21]

Muhammad ibn Abd al-Wahhab was of the *mujaddid* tradition, not of the *mahdi* tradition. Muhammad ibn Abd al-Wahhab was not attempting to challenge or change the basic fundamentals of the faith. He was not announcing the coming of a "new age." He has received recognition in this role of a renewer, especially in the discussions of Islamic renewal that were written before the current portrayals of Wahhabis as advocates of violence and perpetrators of terrorism. Muhammad Rashid Rida mentioned Muhammad ibn Abd al-Wahhab as a *mujaddid,* although noting that he was among those renewers whose message was somewhat regionally restricted,[22] and Abd al-Mutaal al-Saidi devoted a section to ibn Abd al-Wahhab in his relatively comprehensive older study of *mujaddid*s.[23]

One aspect of the differences between *mahdi*s and *mujaddid*s is their role in the political systems with which they interact. The idea of "the Mahdi" contains strong expectations of direct political leadership. In ibn Khaldun's description, the Mahdi "will confirm the faith *[din],* and will make justice victorious. Muslims will follow him, and he will become master over the Islamic kingdoms *[al-mamalik al-islamiyyah].*"[24] However, the hadith on which the concept of *mujaddid* is based says simply, "God will send to this Ummah, at the head of each century, one who will renew for it its *din* ['religion']." However broadly one might define *din,* it is different from "state" or "mastery over the Islamic kingdoms." Older descriptions like al-Saidi's note that the person with the title *mujaddid* "does not seek to attain rule over the people."[25]

This difference does not mean that the *mujaddid* is somehow a "secular" figure. One of the common generalizations about "Islam" is that it does not separate church and state. Since it is frequently affirmed by scholars and believers alike that Islam is a "total way of life," one might question the distinction between *mahdi* and *mujaddid* in terms of their political roles. However, especially in Islamic contexts, it is very important to distinguish between "separation of church and state" (i.e., separation of formal religious institutions from formal governmental ones) and "separation of religion and politics." The institutional separation of political and "religious" institutions in

Islam by the tenth and eleventh centuries was clear. "Though the modalities of 'state' and 'religion' in the Islamic world are quite different from those of 'state' and 'church' in the west, Islamic society, in fact, if not in its own theory, is one of those societies in which religious and political institutions are separate."[26]

Muhammad ibn Abd al-Wahhab's position with regard to the state can be best understood within this context of institutional separation. He was not a ruler or a governor, and in this he was not unique or distinctively different from many renewalist teachers within the Islamic tradition. The important interaction between activist-reformist ulama in Saudi Arabia and the state in the late twentieth century, as examined by Toby Craig Jones in Chapter 8 of this volume, reflects the continuing strength of the *mujaddid* style within the Wahhabi tradition. As Jones notes, scholars like Salman al-Awdah and Safar al-Hawali had a complex relationship of both opposition and support for the Saudi state.

In the caliphate state as it developed in the first centuries of Islamic history, the ruler had important limitations. During the lifetime of the Prophet Muhammad, the synthesis of politics and religion was complete, but very rapidly in the years after his death, functional diversification developed in the increasingly complex and emerging community of believers. As the political community evolved, the limitations on the power of the caliph were institutionalized in Sunni Islam. The caliph could not determine doctrine, was not involved in the development of Islamic law, and was not involved in interpreting scripture. The caliph's primary role was executive. He had the obligation to defend the faithful and the community, and to maintain law and order. In the words of an older Orientalist formulation of this issue, the caliph was not a pope.[27]

A special social grouping emerged that did have the responsibility for interpreting revelation and determining the Islamic rules and understanding of how people and society should operate. These people were those who possessed "knowledge" *(ilm)* and were simply identified as the people of *ilm*, known as ulama. The prestige and authority of the ulama was separate from that of the state and the caliph. The people who are now identified as the "founders of the schools of Islamic Law" were not rulers or even government officials. There emerged separate religious institutions that handled legal affairs—that were separate from the administrative power authority of the caliph. This particular functional division of power continued through the sultanate system, in which the state was in the hands primarily of the military. The concept of an alliance between a nongovernmental scholar and the person who controls military force, with the ability to enforce obedience—the alliance between the emir and the teacher—has been a long-standing style of operation within Islamic history.

This set of structures does not mean that the classical caliphate was a secular structure. It does not mean that the sultanates were secular. This was not a separation of religion and politics. This was a functional division of labor within a faith community, and the caliphate and later the sultanates were "Islamic" in their source of authority, even though their "religious" functions were limited. The alliance between commander and scholar has been an important format for effective movements in Islamic history, and has reflections in modern times as well. Jamal al-Din al-Afghani, the famous advocate of Pan-Islam, was not trying to establish a state to be ruled by himself as a sultan; he was trying to find some ruler with whom he could make an arrangement—similar to that made by Muhammad ibn Abd al-Wahhab with Muhammad ibn Saud. He came closest to this model in his work with the Ottoman sultan, Abdulhamid II, but the result was ineffective, at least from al-Afghani's perspective.

This type of arrangement is reflected even in that most contemporary of political Islamists, Ayatollah Khomeini. In the constitutional structure that essentially he alone created for the Islamic Republic of Iran, Khomeini was not the president, nor the prime minister, nor the head of government, no matter how much his political science was based on *vilayat al-faqih* (the rule by the scholar). He was the supreme guide. He did not have to do anything for governmental operation. He participated as a teacher and corrector of governmental actions but not as a governmental actor himself.

Muhammad ibn Abd al-Wahhab, then, was a reformer in this style of *mujaddid*. He worked closely with the rulers but was not a ruler himself, maintaining the distance necessary to be able to give guidance. This situation is illustrated by his discussion of the initiation and carrying out of a jihad. The imam (teacher) "is responsible for issuing the call to jihad and for ensuring that its conduct is in keeping with the appropriate parameters," but the emir (commander) is "the political leader of the jihad expedition, responsible for directing military action and leading the troops. . . . The *amir*'s actions are always subject to the spiritual guidance of the *imam*."[28]

Khalid al-Dakhil argues in Chapter 3 of this volume that ibn Abd al-Wahhab and the Wahhabiyya represent an important stage in state formation in the Arabian Peninsula, as an urban movement within the framework of long-term sociopolitical developments. However, the state formed by the alliance of ibn Saud and ibn Abd al-Wahhab had a distinctive character and was within the traditions of *mujaddid* political actions. By the late twentieth century, as Gwenn Okruhlik argues in Chapter 7, tension between the exclusivity of *mujaddid* Wahhabism and the imperatives of inclusionary nation making created important difficulties for Saudi political life. Ibn Abd al-Wahhab's role as a prototypical renewalist who set the parameters for political action but did not conduct such action himself was significant in shaping the nature of the state that was being formed.

Narratives Defining the Role of Wahhabism

There are two narrative traditions that are important in defining Wahhabism and its place in the Muslim world since the mid-eighteenth century. These are alternative and competing narratives and reflect committed rather than dispassionate history. One is the narrative account of the actual historical movement, with versions written by both supporters and opponents of the movement as well as nonadvocate scholars, and the second is the narrative associated with a broader sense of the aura or influence of the movement, often in a conspiracy mode of presentation.

The first narrative mode deals with the basics of regular historical research and analysis. In simple terms, this is the effort to find out and present what actually happened. Basic questions can be raised in this context. For example, Ottoman historians like Cevdet Pasa provide important narratives of relations between Wahhabis and Ottomans, but it becomes important to distinguish between Ottoman policy perspectives and historical narrative in deciding the actual nature of the course of events.

The issues in the first narrative mode are part of the debates that have shaped the historical discipline for two centuries. One problem is the disagreement regarding how close narratives by historians are to a presentation that shows "what actually happened," to use the often-quoted phrase of nineteenth-century German historian Leopold von Ranke. Even most of those contemporary scholars who emphasize the subjective character of the efforts involved in constructing a historical narrative still recognize that the efforts of historians as scholars involve attempts to understand what actually happened in historical times and places. A distinction is made between fiction and fictional dramatizations on the one hand, and portrayals that avoid fictional reconstructions for interpretive (or polemical) purposes on the other.

Although scholars engaged in historical analysis and narrative construction for the life of Muhammad ibn Abd al-Wahhab and the history of the "Wahhabi" movement can have strong and vigorous disagreements, the effort to construct a history of Wahhabism is not dissimilar to what von Ranke was actually attempting to accomplish. The general context of his often-quoted phrase is usually ignored. Von Ranke had noted that "history" was often "assigned the office of judging the past, of instructing the present for the benefit of future ages," and then stated: "To such high offices this work does not aspire: It wants only to show what actually happened."[29] Even in this task, von Ranke stated that the "purpose of a historian depends upon his point of view."[30] His goal is an important one in the study of subjects like the history of the Wahhabi movement: it is to avoid, as much as possible, the use of historical narrative as a tool for making value judgments about movements and people rather than understanding what historically happened.

The concrete history of the Wahhabi movement is the first basic narrative. Determining this narrative is not simple and is itself a controversial subject. Twenty-first-century assumptions and concerns sometimes shape interpretations of eighteenth-century realities. Natana DeLong-Bas's analysis in Chapter 2 of this volume illustrates the importance of dealing directly with the writings of ibn Abd al-Wahhab in determining the foundational views of the Wahhabi tradition. Even in this basic effort there is controversy, but the debates regarding the concrete narrative remain in the realm of historical analysis rather than in the realm of mythically constructed generic narratives.

Readers of the concrete historical narrative, in its many forms, come to see the movement as an interesting and somewhat important part of the modern history of Muslims and the Islamic world. However, until the final decade of the twentieth century, this narrative was not viewed as being an especially important part of current modern Islamic history. General surveys of modern Islamic thinkers and movements written before the 1990s tend to discuss the concrete historical experiences of the Wahhabi movement, but do not see it as central to the Muslim experience. Albert Hourani's major work on Arabic thought makes only passing references to the Wahhabi movement, noting, for example, that "the Wahhabi ideal of Islam, still uncorroded by wealth, aroused much sympathy among reformers of the school of Rida."[31] The major movements discussed by Hourani were more closely associated with the development of more secular nationalism. One interesting reflection of the marginal impact of Wahhabism is noted by Thomas Lippman in Chapter 9 of this volume. Lippman notes that the content of Wahhabism has had remarkably little impact on the nature of relations between the United States and Saudi Arabia, despite the apparent contrasts between American and Saudi-Wahhabi worldviews.

It is clear that both Muslim and non-Muslim scholars dealing with the broader subject of modern Islamic history were aware of the histories of the Wahhabi movement and the Saudi state, but these standard historical narratives do not indicate any major role for Wahhabism. However, there is a second narrative, in which Wahhabism, defined in a more mythic manner, has a significant role. This second historical narrative is the history of how the label "Wahhabi" has been used in the past two centuries as a negative identification for Muslim extremists.

In many accounts of Muslim activism, especially those covering the late eighteenth and early nineteenth centuries, Wahhabism is seen as the core of a network of movements engaged in renewalist activities. T. W. Arnold's classic description of the spread of Islam, written before World War I and the effective establishment of the twentieth-century Saudi state, provides a good example of this image. Arnold wrote of "the revival of religious life [in the Muslim world] which dates from the Wahhabi reformation at the end of the eighteenth century; though this new departure has long lost all political significance outside the confines of Najd, as a religious revival its influence is felt throughout Africa, India and the Malay Archipelago even to the present day, and has given birth to numerous movements which take rank among the most powerful influences in the Islamic world."[32]

Although Arnold's image is relatively positive, most descriptions of this influence identify "Wahhabism" as a source for militant and extremist movements. The process is usually described as involving a pilgrimage to Mecca, where organizers of jihads in their homelands, like Ahmad Barelvi in India, were thought to have "absorbed Wahhabi elements in Hijaz."[33] British officials in India during the nineteenth century came to label most Muslim activist movements in South Asia as "Wahhabi," using the term as a useful negative label for opposition to British rule.[34] However, later scholarship came to recognize that the "Wahhabi" protests were "spontaneous and indigenous, though the leaders soon came in touch with the Arabian parallel of that name, and appreciated the similarities."[35]

In this way, "Wahhabi" entered the lexicon of generic terms utilized as labels for troublemakers and "bad people." One of the most important and widely used terms for murderous villains, "assassin," is an important example of this transformation, over the centuries, of a specific identification into a generic label. Although "assassin" originally applied to a small movement in medieval Islam, the Nizari Ismailis, the term is now applied generically to any person who engages in murder for political purposes.

Application of the term "Wahhabi" to groups other than those directly involved in the movement has an interesting difference from the current usage of "assassin." At the beginning of the twenty-first century, the label "Wahhabi" has not become fully generic. In all accounts of "Wahhabi" activities during the summer of 2006, for example, there was some presumption that "real" Wahhabis were in some way involved in all the activities, and that people called "Wahhabis" in the various places around the world had some direct connections to Saudi and Saudi-Wahhabi activities.

The second narrative of the impact of Wahhabism is related to this broader sense of the term "Wahhabi" as a useful label for something that may or may not have direct connections with the Wahhabi movement whose history is presented in the first narrative. The usage has changed and evolved over time. Initially, there were local arguments in the Fertile Crescent area and "Wahhabi" became a label for theological extremists. For example, some of the debates surrounding the activities and teachings of a major renewalist teacher early in the nineteenth century, Khalid al-Naqshbandi (d. 1827), involved charges that he was "Wahhabi" in his opinions.[36]

Two simple generalizations can be made as a result of examining the two narrative modes relating to Wahhabism. First, the actual movement of Wahhabism probably was not and is not as important as the imagined importance of the movements given the generic "Wahhabi" label. In the very first years of the movement, Muhammad ibn Abd al-Wahhab was clearly a scholar who circulated in some interesting intellectual networks. There were itinerant scholars and teachers coming from throughout the Muslim world of that time, interacting in the great centers in the core areas. In these networks, ibn Abd al-Wahhab was a participant, primarily as a student. However, as David Commins shows in Chapter 4 of this volume, the Najd was always somewhat marginal in the networks of scholars, and ibn Abd al-Wahhab created a "new" scholastic culture there that was not a major center for scholars from outside the region. The biographical dictionaries of the time do not record many of the itinerant scholars making their way to ibn Abd al-Wahhab's center, and few of his students appear to have gone on "missionary" teaching missions, in contrast to, for example, the students of Ahmad ibn Idris, who taught on the Arabian Peninsula and whose students ultimately spread out from Southeast Asia to North Africa.

The Najd of the Wahhabis in the eighteenth and early nineteenth centuries was not a special training ground for militant jihadists. Ibn Abd al-Wahhab and his descendants were not the Osama bin Ladens of that era. Ibn Abd al-Wahhab was a relatively strict scholar living at the center of his own little circle. There was no interregional Wahhabi network. Instead, there were broader networks of scholars, often interested in encouraging renewal, with whom he at one point or another interacted.

The second generalization in comparing the two narratives is to note that Wahhabism was a relatively doctrinaire and dogmatic movement. However, in its actual history, at times it exhibited a degree of flexible pragmatism, as shown in Chapter 6 in William Ochsenwald's analysis of Saudi-Wahhabi rule in the Hijaz in 1926–1939. This is in contrast to the rigid fundamentalism that would be predicted by the narrative that uses "Wahhabi" as a label for religious extremists.

During the nineteenth century, the Wahhabi reputation for "fundamentalism" continued, but by the end of the century the generic usage of the term "Wahhabi" had shifted to the more benign definitions, as seen in the works of Orientalists like T. W. Arnold or in the somewhat later discussions of Rida. By the 1920s, Wahhabism was viewed as more a curiosity than a threat. The development of the Saudi state at that time, as described by John Habib in Chapter 5 of this volume, was praised by Rida, but the actual state experience had little impact on Rida's political thought.

The forces viewed as dangerous by Western observers shifted. A good example of this shift appeared in the analysis of Muslim movements by Lothrop Stoddard, which was widely read in the 1920s. At the end of World War I, Stoddard viewed "Pan-Islamism" as a major force in the world. Stoddard spoke of the Wahhabi movement as "the first stage" of "modern Pan-Islamism,"[37] but he saw this first simple, puritanical phase as having been transcended by the early twentieth century. During the nineteenth century, Pan-Islamic militancy had been uncoordinated, but the "beginnings of self-conscious, systematic Pan-Islamism date from about the middle of the nineteenth century," when the movement began to crystallize around the effective organization of major Sufi brotherhoods, especially the Sanusiyya ("Sennussiya," in Stoddard's terminology).[38]

C. A. Willis, director of intelligence in the Anglo-Egyptian Sudan, provided a similar picture in 1922. He wrote a "speculative" report, which was to provide a "general résumé" of political propaganda and movements. The report provided a wide-ranging summary of Islamic movements that might have been security risks, ranging from the very local (like a teacher in Nyala in western Sudan) to grand Pan-Islamic schemes in which Willis portrayed Mustafa Kemal (Ataturk), the Sansusis, Saad Zaghloul's Egyptian nationalists, and others as part of a large pattern of resistance to the West.[39] The interesting aspect of this report from the perspective of assessing the impact of Wahhabism is that Willis made absolutely no mention of the Wahhabis. Clearly, at least as reflected in the contents of this report, the Wahhabis were no longer a significant security concern, even in Sudan, directly across the Red Sea from Arabia.

During the final quarter of the twentieth century, much attention was given to the Islamic resurgence (and the Islamic threat). However, in the early narratives of the Islamic resurgence, little attention was given to the Wahhabis or to possible Wahhabi inspiration. The older twentieth-century narrative is still the core. "Wahhabism" is recognized as the ancestor of contemporary militant resurgence but is no longer the primary focus of attention. By the 1980s, some mention was made of Saudi financial support for theologically conservative groups, but this was not viewed as important. A good example of this is one of the early popular books, *Militant Islam,* written by G. H. Jansen in 1979. In his chapter on militant Muslim responses to the West, Jansen wrote, "Before we describe militant Islam's counter-attacks it is right and proper that we should give precedence to the very first organized manifestation of militant Islam in modern times. This was the movement started by Muhammad ibn Abdel-Wahhab (1703–87), because of which the word 'Wahhabism' has become synonymous with militant puritanical Islam."[40] Jansen then quickly moved on to discuss movements of the day and made virtually no mention of the historical Wahhabis.

By the 1990s, the distinction between the two narratives—the historical account of the actual movement and the development of "Wahhabism" as a generic term for Muslim extremism—became visible. In the history of the actual movement, it became clear that the old "puritanical brotherhoods," so feared by Stoddard, had been "invariably defeated by either urban political forces . . . or by European military might."[41] Earlier activist revivalist movements were seen as having experienced "profound structural changes and were consequently transformed into reformist or fairly modernistic entities. . . . Even Wahhabism became after the foundation of the Kingdom of Saudi Arabia in the 1920s and 1930s a subordinate ingredient in the evolving institutions of the new state."[42]

At the beginning of the twenty-first century, in an assessment of the historical movement, Gilles Kepel argued: "Left to its own devices, Wahhabism probably would not have prospered worldwide in the last quarter of the twentieth century, even with the assistance of oil revenues. Adapted to an arid tribal ecosystem, it lacked the intellectual tools necessary to take on the challenges of the modern world. . . . By the early 1950s, Wahhabite Islam had triumphed over 'heresies' within Saudi Arabia but it seemed politically maladapted to reach beyond this closed society."[43]

The global impact is not so much the result of actions and influence of the core historical movement as it is the product of offshoots from that historical movement. These new groupings are influenced and shaped by other movements, beyond the Wahhabi "tradition." Many of these new groupings, like Al-Qaida, are in fact militantly opposed to the institutions and leaders of the historical Wahhabi movement.

In a remarkable terminological development, this extremist style of renewalism (sometimes representing opposition to historical Wahhabism) has frequently come to be identified with the generic label "Wahhabi." By the beginning of the twenty-first century, many analysts were combining the label "Wahhabi" with another, "Salafi" (i.e., those who seek to restore the practice of the pious ancestors, or Salaf, in a fundamentalist manner), as a term for "extremist." Either by itself or in combination as "Salafi-Wahhabism," the generic term "Wahhabi" came to be the label for extremist Muslim groups. In this way, the position of Hizb al-Tahrir in "radical Sunni Islamism's ideological vanguard" is described by Zeyno Baran as "combining fascist rhetoric, Leninist strategy, and Western sloganeering with Wahhabi theology."[44] Similarly, a discussion of Tablighi Jamaat that views that organization as part of "Jihad's stealthy legions," speaks of the Tablighi creed as being "hardly distinguishable from the radical Wahhabi-Salafi jihadist ideology that so many terrorists share."[45] Similarly, an analysis of the evolution of Chechen resistance ideology notes that "radical Islamists convert Chechens from their indigenous Sufi practices toward extremist Salafi or Wahhabi doctrine."[46]

This terminology is interesting in terms of what it ignores. While the meaning of the term "Wahhabi" is quite clear in the contexts in which it is used in the twenty-first-century literature about terrorism and counterterrorism, it tends to ignore the relationships (or lack of relationships) to the historical movement. The term has become, as Jansen noted, "synonymous with militant puritanical Islam,"[47] even when applied to anti-Saudi and anti-Wahhabi groups. The contemporary "Wahhabi-Salafi" movements have a number of important basic texts that define and present this position. To a remarkable extent, these key texts make little reference to explicitly historical Wahhabi texts. Specifically, there is surprisingly little citation of the works of Muhammad ibn Abd al-Wahhab. One of the early expressions of this militant puritanism is the booklet *Al-Faridah al-Gha'ibah,* by Abd al-Salam Faraj. Remarkably, although Faraj quotes extensively from the writings of many important Muslim scholars, especially Ahmad ibn Taymiyya,[48] Muhammad ibn Abd al-Wahhab is not among the authorities cited. Similarly, in the later polemics of the "Wahhabi-Salafis" associated with the Al-Qaida tradition, there is a notable absence of reference to or citation of the works of ibn Abd al-Wahhab. Abdullah Yusuf Azzam, one of the early teachers and associates of Osama bin Laden, wrote a major tract titled "Defence of the Muslim Lands: The First Obligation After Iman." In this there is frequent citation of ibn Taymiyya but no citation of ibn Abd al-Wahhab.[49] In the many proclamations and messages from bin Laden, one can note references to ibn Taymiyya and some to Ahmad ibn Hanbal, but ibn Abd al-Wahhab is absent.[50]

The texts of late-twentieth-century and early-twenty-first century Muslim militancy reflect the dual heritage of narratives about Wahhabism. Generic militancy that is labeled as "Wahhabi" is not the same as historical Wahhabism.

◼ Conclusion

Assessing the impact of the Wahhabi tradition on renewal and reform in the modern Muslim world is a complex task. The tradition begins as a part of the eighteenth-century world of movements of religious renewal. In the Muslim world, the early Wahhabi movement both was shaped by other movements and teachers who defined Islamic renewal, and also helped to shape those movements by example. Later scholars began to identify the eighteenth-century movement as a pioneer in the movements of *tajdid* in the modern era. In the words of Muhammad Iqbal, it was "the first throb of life in modern Islam."[51] For Hamilton A. R. Gibb, it was "the extreme expression of a tendency which can be traced in many parts of Islam in the course of the eighteenth century [of] the movement for the return to the pure monotheism" of the early Muslim community, and became an important "religious force within the Muslim community."[52] Analysts at the beginning of the twenty-first century, like Gilles Kepel,[53] have continued to recognize the Wahhabi tradition as the pioneer movement of renewal in the modern era. One dimension of the impact of the Wahhabi tradition is the heritage of its origins as a visible eighteenth-century movement of renewal.

A second dimension of the impact of the Wahhabi tradition is the nature of the leadership style, as set initially by Muhammad ibn Abd al-Wahhab. In the repertoire of leadership modes in the Islamic tradition, the

Mahdist-messianic and the puritanical teacher are the most common and powerful. The relatively nonpolitical reformist teacher was common among salafi-pietist movements of religious renewal in the eighteenth century, among both Muslims and non-Muslims. The Wahhabi tradition firmly set the renewer-teacher, or *mujaddid*, model as a visible and powerful style of leadership for movements of Islamic resurgence, and this continued throughout the modern era. In the contemporary world, the relations between the Saudi state and the ulama religious establishment, as analyzed by F. Gregory Gause in Chapter 10 of this volume, reflect both the strengths and the potential risks of a separate scholarly establishment that provides statements of religious support for government policies and is also a possible source for critiques of those policies.

Finally, a third aspect of the influence of the Wahhabi tradition is that it provided the basis for an additional narrative of activist Muslim movements. In addition to the narrative of the experience of the historical movement, the term "Wahhabi" itself came to have a historical narrative. This second narrative describes the evolution of the label from applying specifically to the historical movement to being one of the identifying terms for militant and often violent activism in the name of puritanical renewal in the Muslim world. At the beginning of the twenty-first century, this second narrative complicates the task of assessing the impact of the Wahhabi tradition, since many (if not most) of the groups that are called "Wahhabi" have little or no direct connection to the historical movement.

Whatever might be the specific assessment of the impact of the Wahhabi tradition, it is clear that the Wahhabi movement and its terminological echoes are a significant part of the modern history of the Muslim world.

Notes

1. Such reports can be found in many sources. A sampling from the US Department of Commerce NTIS translations for summer 2006 includes: "Official Says Wahhabi Group Possibly Involved in 12 May Incidents in Kyrgyzstan," *Interfax*, May 15, 2006, Dialog File no. 985, Accession no. 225900283. Other examples are "Somali Premier Equates Islamist Leader Aweys to Bin-Ladin," *HornAfrik Online*, July 10, 2006, Dialog File no. 985, Accession no. 228700913; "Former Wahhabi Urges Bosnian Authorities to Take Action Against Radical Islam," *ONASA*, June 16, 2006, Dialog File no. 985, Accession no. 227500581; "Wahhabi Numbers 'Increase Greatly' in Serbia's Sandzak Region," *Radio B92*, June 6, 2006, Dialog File no. 985, Accession no. 227000319.

2. It is frequently noted that people within the movement have reservations about the label "Wahhabi," and prefer their self-identification as *muwahhidin*. However, for convenience of presentation, this chapter will simply use the term "Wahhabi," as was the case in most of the conference discussions.

3. For a general discussion of this, see John O. Voll, "Renewal and Reform in Islamic History: Tajdid and Islah," in *Voices of Resurgent Islam*, edited by John L. Esposito (New York: Oxford University Press, 1983).

4. Bernard Lewis, *What Went Wrong? Western Impact and Middle Eastern Response* (New York: Oxford University Press, 2002).

5. Marshall G. S. Hodgson, "Modernity and the Islamic Heritage," in *Rethinking World History,* edited by Edmund Burke III (Cambridge: Cambridge University Press, 1993), p. 97.

6. Nikki R. Keddie, *An Islamic Response to Imperialism* (Berkeley: University of California Press, 1983), pp. 45, 82.

7. Emad Eldin Shahin, *Through Muslim Eyes: M. Rashid Rida and the West* (Herndon, VA: International Institute of Islamic Thought, 1993), p. 45.

8. Muhammad Iqbal, *The Reconstruction of Religious Thought in Islam* (Lahore: Sh. Muhammad Ashraf, 1968), p. 152. Examples of other discussions by reform-minded Muslims are Malek Bennabi, *Islam in History and Society,* translated by Asma Rashid (Islamabad: Islamic Research Institute, 1988), p. 21; Fazlur Rahman, *Islam,* 2nd ed. (Chicago: University of Chicago Press, 1979), pp. 196–201.

9. For discussions of the specific examples mentioned, see Ayelet Savyon, "Call for Islamic Protestantism: Dr. Hashem Aghjari's Speech and Subsequent Death Sentence," *MEMRI* [Middle East Media Research Institute] *Special Dispatch Series,* December 2, 2002; Roman Loimeier, "Is There Something Like 'Protestant Islam'?" *Die Welt des Islams* 45, no. 2 (2005).

10. Hodgson, "Modernity and the Islamic Heritage," p. 218. For discussions of many different dimensions of this subject, see Michaelle Browers and Charles Kurzman, eds., *An Islamic Reformation?* (Lanham: Lexington, 2004).

11. For an important and more extended analysis of Wahhabism in the eighteenth-century context, see Natana J. DeLong-Bas, *Wahhabi Islam: From Revival and Reform to Global Jihad* (New York: Oxford University Press, 2004), chap. 1.

12. For basic presentations of the positions, see Reinhard Schulze, "Das Islamische Achtzehnte Jahrhundert: Versuch Einer Historiographischen Kritik," *Die Welt des Islams* 30, nos. 1–4 (1990); and the response in Bernd Radtke, "Erleuchtung und Aufklärung: Islamische Mystik und Europäischer Rationalismus," *Die Welt des Islams* 34, no. 1 (1994).

13. Reinhard Schulze, *A Modern History of the Islamic World* (New York: New York University Press, 2000), p. 2.

14. Rudolph Peters, "Reinhard Schulze's Quest for an Islamic Enlightenment," *Die Welt des Islams* 30, nos. 1–4 (1990): 160.

15. Frank Lambert, *Inventing the "Great Awakening"* (Princeton: Princeton University Press, 1999), p. 129.

16. F. Ernest Stoeffler, "Pietism," in *The Encyclopedia of Religion,* edited by Mircea Eliade (New York: Macmillan, 1987), p. 324.

17. Robert Wuthnow, *Communities of Discourse* (Cambridge: Harvard University Press, 1989), pp. 169–170.

18. Geoffrey C. Gunn, *First Globalization: The Eurasian Exchange, 1500–1800* (Lanham: Rowman and Littlefield, 2003).

19. This statement reflects comments made by Andrew March in the April 2006 conference discussions.

20. See, for example, the discussion in S. Abul A'la Maududi, *A Short History of the Revivalist Movement in Islam,* translated by Al-Ash'ari (Lahore: Islamic Publications, 1979), p. 35.

21. For a discussion of these two styles of reform, see John O. Voll, "Wahhabism and Mahdism: Alternative Styles of Islamic Renewals," *Arab Studies Quarterly* 4, nos. 1–2 (1982).

22. Muhammad Rashid Rida, *Ta'rikh al-Ustadh al-Imam al-Shaykh Muhammad Abduh (1266–1323 H./1849–1905 M.)* (Cairo: Dar al-Fasilah, 2003), p. 1. Part 1; page *j*.

23. Abd al-Mutaal al-Saidi, *Al-Mujaddidun Fi al-Islam Min al-Qarn al-Awwal Ila al-Rabi Ashar* (Cairo: Maktabah al-Adab, 1962), pp. 437–441. Al-Saidi cites Rida's views on p. 14.

24. Abd al-Rahman ibn Khaldun, *Muqaddimah ibn Khaldun,* edited by Darwish al-Juwaydi (Beirut: Al-Maktabah al-Asariyyah, 1995), p. 287. The English translation of this passage, according to Franz Rosenthal, is: The Mahdi "will strengthen the religion and make justice triumph. The Muslims will follow him, and he will gain domination over the Muslim realm." Abd al-Rahman ibn Khaldun, *The Muqaddimah: An Introduction to History,* translated by Franz Rosenthal (New York: Pantheon, 1958), pp. 2, 156.

25. al-Saidi, *Al-Mujaddidun Fi al-Islam Min al-Qarn al-Awwal Ila al-Rabi Ashar,* p. 589.

26. Ira M. Lapidus, "The Separation of State and Religion in the Development of Early Islamic Society," *International Journal of Middle East Studies* 6, no. 4 (1975): 385.

27. See the article, written originally in 1931, by George Stewart, "Is the Caliph a Pope?" in *The Traditional Near East,* edited by J. Stewart-Robinson (Englewood Cliffs, NJ: Prentice-Hall, 1966).

28. DeLong-Bas, *Wahhabi Islam,* pp. 211–212.

29. This is from the preface to von Ranke's *Histories of the Latin and Germanic Nations from 1494–1514,* as reprinted in Fritz Stern, ed., *Varieties of History* (Cleveland, OH: World Publishing, 1956), p. 57.

30. Stern, *Varieties of History,* p. 55.

31. Albert Hourani, *Arabic Thought in the Liberal Age, 1798–1939* (London: Oxford University Press, 1962), p. 295.

32. T. W. Arnold, *The Preaching of Islam: A History of the Propagation of the Muslim Faith,* reprint ed. (Lahore: Sh. Muhammad Ashraf, 1965), p. 431.

33. Aziz Ahmad, *Studies in Islamic Culture in the Indian Environment* (Oxford: Clarendon, 1964), p. 216.

34. Good examples of the more generic usage of the term "Wahhabi" can be found in W. W. Hunter, *The Indian Musalmans,* reprint ed. (Delhi: Indological Book House, 1969).

35. Wilfred Cantwell Smith, *Modern Islam in India: A Social Analysis* (Lahore: Minerva, 1943), p. 1.

36. See, for example, the discussion in Sean Ezra Foley, "Shaykh Khalid and the Naqshbandiyya-Khalidiyya, 1776–2005," PhD diss., Washington, DC, Georgetown University, 2005.

37. Lothrop Stoddard, *The New World of Islam* (New York: Scribner, 1921), p. 48.

38. Ibid., p. 52.

39. *Sudan Monthly Intelligence Report* no. 328 (November 1921), enclosing memorandum by C. A. Willis, January 11, 1922.

40. G. H. Jansen, *Militant Islam* (New York: Harper and Row, 1979), p. 87.

41. Youssef M. Choueiri, *Islamic Fundamentalism* (Boston: Twayne, 1990), p. 29.

42. Ibid., pp. 29–30.

43. Gilles Kepel, *The War for Muslim Minds: Islam and the West,* translated by Pascale Ghazaleh (Cambridge: Harvard University Press, 2004), pp. 170–171.

44. Zeyno Baran, "Fighting the War of Ideas," *Foreign Affairs* 84, no. 6 (2005): 68.

45. Alex Alexiev, "Tablighi Jamaat: Jihad's Stealthy Legions," *Middle East Quarterly* 12, no. 1 (2005): 4.

46. Lorenzo Vidino, "How Chechnya Became a Breeding Ground for Terror," *Middle East Quarterly* 12, no. 3 (2005): 59.

47. Jansen, *Militant Islam,* p. 87.

48. See, for example, the translation of this booklet in Johannes J. G. Jansen, *The Neglected Duty: The Creed of Sadat's Assassins and Islamic Resurgence in the Middle East* (New York: Macmillan, 1986), pp. 175–182.

49. See the translated text as it appears on the Religioscope website, beginning at http://www.religioscope.com/info/doc/jihad/azzam_defence_2_intro.htm.

50. See, for example, the relatively comprehensive collection in Bruce Lawrence, ed., *Messages to the World: The Statements of Osama bin Laden* (London: Verso, 2005). For ibn Hanbal references, see pp. 5, 199; for ibn Taymiyya references, see pp. 5, 9, 11, 26, 60, 80, 118, 229, 249.

51. Iqbal, *Reconstruction of Religious Thought in Islam,* p. 152.

52. H. A. R. Gibb, *Mohammedanism: An Historical Survey,* 2nd ed. (London: Oxford University Press, 1953), pp. 168–169.

53. Kepel, *War for Muslim Minds.*

Bibliography

ibn Abd al-Wahhab, Muhammad. *Ar-Rasaeil Ash-Shakhsiyah.* In the series Mualafat Ash-Sheikh al-Imam Muhammad ibn Abd al-Wahhab. Vol. 5. Riyadh: Islamic University of Imam Muhammad ibn Saud, n.d.

———. "Fatawa wa-Masa'il al-Imam al-Shaykh Muhammad ibn Abd al-Wahhab." In *Mu'allafat al-Shaykh al-Imam Muhammad ibn Abd al-Wahhab.* Riyadh: Islamic University of Imam Muhammad ibn Saud, 1977.

———. *Kashf Ashubuhat.* Translated by Mualafat Ash-Sheikh al-Imam Muhammad ibn Abd al-Wahhab. Vol. 1. Riyadh: Islamic University of Imam Muhammad ibn Saud, n.d.

———. "Kitab al-Jihad." In *Mu'allafat al-Shaykh al-Imam Muhammad ibn Abd al-Wahhab.* Riyadh: Islamic University of Imam Muhammad ibn Saud, 1977.

———. "Kitab al-Tawhid." In *Mu'allafat al-Shaykh al-Imam Muhammad ibn Abd al-Wahhab.* Riyadh: Islamic University of Imam Muhammad ibn Saud, 1977.

———. "Kitab al-Tawhid." In *Majmu'at al-Tawhid al-Najdiyya*, edited by Rashid Rida. Riyadh: Al-Amana al-Amma li'l-Ihtifal bi-Murur Miat Am ala Tasis al-Mamlaka, 1999.

ibn Abd al-Wahhab, Suleiman. *Al-Sawaiq al-Ilahiyyah Fi al-Radd Ala al-Wahhabiyyah.* Istanbul: Library of Ishiq, 1975.

Abu Khalil, Asad. *The Battle for Saudi Arabia: Royalty, Fundamentalism, and Global Power.* New York: Seven Stories, 2004.

Ahmad, Aziz. *Studies in Islamic Culture in the Indian Environment.* Oxford: Clarendon, 1964.

Ahmad, Rifat Sayyid. *Rasail Juhayman al-Utaybi.* Cairo: Maktabat Madbuli, 1988.

Alexiev, Alex. "Tablighi Jamaat: Jihad's Stealthy Legions." *Middle East Quarterly* 12, no. 1 (2005).

Algar, Hamid. *Wahhabism: A Critical Essay.* Oneonta, NY: Islamic International, 2002.

Arebi, Saddeka. *Women and Words in Saudi Arabia.* New York: Columbia University Press, 1994.

Arnold, T. W. *The Preaching of Islam: A History of the Propagation of the Muslim Faith.* Reprint ed. Lahore: Sh. Muhammad Ashraf, 1965.

Ayalon, Ami. "The Hashemites, T. E. Lawrence, and the Postage Stamps of the Hijaz." In *The Hashemites in the Modern Arab World,* edited by Asher Susser and Aryeh Shmuelevitz. London: Cass, 1995.

169

al-Azmeh, Aziz. *Islams and Modernities.* London: Verso, 1966.
——. "Wahhabite Polity." In *Arabia and the Gulf: From Traditional Society to Modern States,* edited by Ian R. Netton. London: Croom Helm, 1986.
Baran, Zeyno. "Fighting the War of Ideas." *Foreign Affairs* 84, no. 6 (2005): 68–78.
al-Bassam, Abd Allah ibn Abd al-Rahman. *Ulama Najd Khilal Thamaniyat Qurun.* 6 vols. Riyadh: Dar al-Asima, 1998.
Bennabi, Malek. *Islam in History and Society.* Translated by Asma Rashid. Islamabad: Islamic Research Institute, 1988.
ibn Bishr, Uthman. *Anwan Al al-Majd Fi Tarikh al-Najd.* Riyadh: Dar Bann all Taba'ah Wal Tajlid, 1953.
——. *Unwan Almajd Fi Tarikh Najd.* 2 vols. Riyadh: Darat Almalik Abdul-Aziz, 1982.
Bligh, Alexander. "The Saudi Religious Elite (Ulama) as Participant in the Political System of the Kingdom." *International Journal of Middle East Studies* 17, no. 1 (1985): 37–50.
Bronson, Rachel. *Thicker Than Oil: America's Uneasy Partnership with Saudi Arabia.* New York: Oxford University Press, 2006.
Browers, Michaelle, and Charles Kurzman, eds. *An Islamic Reformation?* Lanham: Lexington, 2004.
Buchan, James. "The Return of the Ikhwan 1979." In *The House of Saud,* edited by David Holden and Richard Johns. New York: Holt, Rinehart, and Winston, 1981.
al-Bulayhi, Ibrahim Abd al-Rahman. *Letter to the West: A View from Saudi Arabia.* Riyadh: Ghainaa, 2004.
Burdett, Anita L. P. *King Abdul Aziz: Diplomacy and Statecraft.* Chippenham: Archive Editions, 1998.
Butenschon, Nils, Uri Davis, and Manuel Hassassian, eds. *Citizenship and the State in the Middle East.* New York: Syracuse University Press, 2000.
Chaudhry, Kiren Aziz. *The Price of Wealth: Economies and Institutions in the Middle East.* Ithaca: Cornell University Press, 1997.
Choueiri, Youssef M. *Islamic Fundamentalism.* Boston: Twayne, 1990.
Cobbold, Evelyn. *Pilgrimage to Mecca.* London: Murray, 1934.
Commins, David. "Reinterpreting Wahhabism: The Formation of a Regional Religious Tradition." Paper presented at the annual meeting of the Middle East Studies Association, Anchorage, AK, November 2003.
——. "Traditional Anti-Wahhabi Hanbalism in Nineteenth Century Arabia." In *Ottoman Reform and Muslim Regeneration,* edited by Itzchak Weismann and Fruma Zachs. London: Tauris, 2005.
——. *The Wahhabi Mission and Saudi Arabia.* London: Tauris, 2006.
Cook, Michael. *Commanding Right and Forbidding Wrong in Islamic Thought.* Cambridge: Cambridge University Press, 2000.
——. "The Expansion of the First Saudi State: The Case of Washm." In *The Islamic World: From Classical to Modern Times,* edited by C. F. Bosworth, C. Issawi, R. Savory, and A. Udovitch. Princeton: Darwin, 1989.
Croucher, Sheila. "Perpetual Imagining: Nationhood in a Global Era." *International Studies Review* no. 5 (2003): 1–24.
DeGaury, Gerald. *Faisal: King of Saudi Arabia.* New York: Praeger, 1966.
Dahir, Mas'ud. *Al-Mashriq al-Arabi al-Muasir: Min al-Badawah Ila al-Dawlah al-Hadithah.* Beirut: Mahad al-Inma al-Arabi, 1986.
al-Dakhil, Khalid. *Social Origins of the Wahhabi Movement.* Los Angeles: University of California Press, 1998.

DeLong-Bas, Natana J. *Jihad for Islam: The Struggle for the Future of Saudi Arabia.* New York: Oxford University Press, 2009.

————. *Wahhabi Islam: From Revival and Reform to Global Jihad.* New York: Oxford University Press, 2004.

Doumato, Eleanor Abdella. *Getting God's Ear: Women, Islam, and Healing in Saudi Arabia and the Gulf.* New York: Columbia University Press, 2000.

Doumato, Eleanor Abdella, and Gregory Starrett, eds. *Teaching Islam: Textbooks and Religion in the Middle East.* Boulder: Lynne Rienner, 2006.

Eddy, William A. "Our Faith and Your Iron." *Middle East Journal* 17, no. 3 (1963): 257–263.

Eickelman, Dale F., and James Piscatori. *Muslim Politics.* Princeton: Princeton University Press, 1996.

el-Fadl, Khaled Abou. *The Great Theft: Wrestling Islam from the Extremists.* San Francisco: Harper, 2005.

Ende, Werner. "The Nakhawila: A Shiite Community in Medina Past and Present." *Die Welt des Islams* 37 (1997): 263–348.

Fabietti, Ugo. "State Policies and Bedouin Adaptations in Saudi Arabia, 1900–1980." In *The Transformation of Nomad Society in the Arab East,* edited by Martha Mundy and Basim Musallam. Cambridge: Cambridge University Press, 2000.

al-Fahad, Abdulaziz H. "From Exclusivism to Accommodation: Doctrinal and Legal Evolution of Wahhabism." *New York University Law Review* 79, no. 2 (2004): 485–519.

————. "The Imama vs. the Iqal: Hadari-Bedouin Conflict and the Formation of the Saudi State." In *Counter-Narratives: History, Contemporary Society, and Politics in Saudi Arabia and Yemen,* edited by Madawi al-Rasheed and Robert Vitalis. New York: Palgrave Macmillan, 2004.

al-Fakhri, Muhammad O. *Tarikh al-Fakhri.* Edited by Abdullah al-Shible. Riyadh: General Secretariat for Celebrating the Centennial of the Kingdom of Saudi Arabia, 1999.

Fandy, Mamoun. *Saudi Arabia and the Politics of Dissent.* New York: St. Martin's, 1999.

Foley, Sean Ezra. "Shaykh Khalid and the Naqshbandiyya-Khalidiyya, 1776–2005." PhD diss., Washington, DC, Georgetown University, 2005.

Forest, James J. F. "Training Camps and Other Centers of Learning." In *Teaching Terror: Strategic and Tactical Learning in the Terrorist World,* edited by James J. F. Forest. Lanham: Rowman and Littlefield, 2006.

Gause, F. Gregory, III. *Oil Monarchies: Domestic and Security Challenges in the Arab Gulf States.* New York: Council on Foreign Relations, 1994.

————. "Saudi Perceptions of the United States Since 9/11." In *With Us or Against Us: Studies in Global Anti-Americanism,* edited by Tony Judt and Denis Lacorne. New York: Palgrave Macmillan, 2005.

Ghannam, Hussein ibn. *Tarikh Najd.* Edited by Nassir Addin Al-Asad. Beirut: Shorouq International, 1985.

Gibb, H. A. R. *Mohammedanism: An Historical Survey.* 2nd ed. London: Oxford University Press, 1953.

Glubb, John Bagot. *War in the Desert.* London: Hodden and Stoughton, 1960.

Gordon, Michael R., and Bernard E. Trainor. *Cobra II: The Inside Story of the Invasion and Occupation of Iraq.* New York: Pantheon, 2006.

Gunn, Geoffrey C. *First Globalization: The Eurasian Exchange, 1500–1800.* Lanham: Rowman and Littlefield, 2003.

Habib, John. *Ibn Saud's Warriors of Islam: An Interpretive Study of a Special Relationship.* Leiden: Brill, 1973.

———. *Saudi Arabia and the American National Interests.* Boca Raton, FL: Universal, 2003.

al-Hawali, Safar. *Haqaiq Hawl Azmat al-Khalij.* Mecca: Dar Makka al-Mukarrama, 1991.

Herb, Michael. *All in the Family: Absolutism, Revolution, and Democracy in the Middle Eastern Monarchies.* Albany: State University of New York Press, 1999.

Hodgson, Marshall G. S. "Modernity and the Islamic Heritage." In *Rethinking World History,* edited by Edmund Burke III. Cambridge: Cambridge University Press, 1993.

———. "The Role of Islam in World History." In *Rethinking World History,* edited by Edmund Burke III. Cambridge: Cambridge University Press, 1993.

Hourani, Albert. *Arabic Thought in the Liberal Age, 1798–1939.* London: Oxford University Press, 1962.

ibn Humayd, Muhammad ibn Abd Allah. *Al-Suhub al-Wabila Ala Daraih al-Hanabila.* 3 vols. Edited by Bakr Abd Allah Abu Zayd and Abd al-Rahman ibn Sulayman al-Uthaymin. Beirut: Muasassat al-Risala, 1996.

Hunter, W. W. *The Indian Musalmans.* Reprint ed. Delhi: Indological Book House, 1969.

International Crisis Group. "Saudi Arabia Backgrounder: Who Are the Islamists?" *Middle East Report,* September 21, 2004.

Iqbal, Muhammad. *The Reconstruction of Religious Thought in Islam.* Lahore: Sh. Muhammad Ashraf, 1968.

al-Isa, Mayy bint Abd al-Aziz. *Al-Haya al-Ilmiyya Fi Najd Mundhu Qiyam Dawat al-Shaykh Muhammad ibn Abd al-Wahhab wa Hatta Nihayat al-Dawla al-Saudiyya al-Ula.* Riyadh: Darat al-Malak Abd al-Aziz, 1997.

ibn Issa, Ibrahim. *Tarikh Badhul Hawadith Alwaqiah Fi Najd.* Riyadh: Dar al-Yamamah, 1966.

Jansen, G. H. *Militant Islam.* New York: Harper and Row, 1979.

Jansen, Johannes J. G. *The Neglected Duty: The Creed of Sadat's Assassins and Islamic Resurgence in the Middle East.* New York: Macmillan, 1986.

Jarman, Robert L., ed. *The Jedda Diaries, 1919–1940.* 4 vols. Melksham: Archive Editions, 1990.

Jones, Toby Craig. "The Clerics, the Sahwa, and the Saudi State." *Strategic Insights* 4, no. 3 (2005).

———. "Rebellion on the Saudi Periphery: Modernity, Marginalization, and the Shi'a Uprising of 1979." *International Journal of Middle East Studies* 38, no. 2 (2006): 213–233.

Joseph, Suad, ed. *Gender and Citizenship in the Middle East.* Syracuse: Syracuse University Press, 2000.

———. "Introduction: Gender and Citizenship in Muslim Communities." *Citizenship Studies* 3, no. 3 (1999): 293–294.

al-Juhany, Uwaidah M. *Najd Before the Salafi Reform Movement: Social, Religious, and Political Conditions During the Three Centuries Preceding the Rise of the Saudi State.* Reading, UK: Ithaca, 2002.

Kayali, Hasan. *Arabs and Young Turks: Ottomanism, Arabism, and Islamism in the Ottoman Empire.* Berkeley: University of California Press, 1997.

Kechichian, Joseph A. "Islamic Revivalism and Change in Saudi Arabia: Juhayman al-'Utaybi's 'Letters' to the Saudi People." *Muslim World* 80, no. 1 (1980): 1–16.

———. "The Role of the Ulama in the Politics of an Islamic State: The Case of Saudi Arabia." *International Journal of Middle East Studies* 18, no. 1 (1986): 53–71.

Keddie, Nikki R. *An Islamic Response to Imperialism.* Berkeley: University of California Press, 1983.

Kepel, Gilles. *The War for Muslim Minds: Islam and the West.* Translated by Pascale Ghazaleh. Cambridge: Harvard University Press, 2004.

ibn Khaldun, Abd al-Rahman. *The Muqaddimah: An Introduction to History.* Translated by Franz Rosenthal. New York: Pantheon, 1958.

———. *Muqaddimah ibn Khaldun.* Edited by Darwish al-Juwaydi. Beirut: Al-Maktabah al-Asariyyah, 1995.

Kishk, Muhammad Jalal. *Al-Saudiyah Wal Hal al Islami.* London: Moody Graphics and Trans. Centre, 1961.

Knysh, Alexander. "A Clear and Present Danger: 'Wahhabism' as a Rhetorical Foil." *Saudi-American Forum* no. 24 (2003).

Kostiner, Joseph. *The Making of Saudi Arabia, 1916–1936: From Chieftaincy to Monarchical State.* New York: Oxford University Press, 1993.

Krimly, Rayed Khalid. "The Political Economy of Rentier States: A Case Study of Saudi Arabia in the Oil Era, 1950–1990." PhD diss., Washington, DC, George Washington University, 1993.

Lambert, Frank. *Inventing the "Great Awakening."* Princeton: Princeton University Press, 1999.

Lapidus, Ira M. "The Separation of State and Religion in the Development of Early Islamic Society." *International Journal of Middle East Studies* 6, no. 4 (1975): 363–385.

Lawrence, Bruce, ed. *Messages to the World: The Statements of Osama bin Laden.* London: Verso, 2005.

Lewis, Bernard. *The Crisis of Islam.* New York: Modern Library, 2003.

———. *What Went Wrong? Western Impact and Middle Eastern Response.* New York: Oxford University Press, 2002.

Loimeier, Roman. "Is There Something Like 'Protestant Islam'?" *Die Welt des Islams* 45, no. 2 (2005): 216–254.

Long, David. *The Kingdom of Saudi Arabia.* Gainesville: University of Florida Press, 1997.

Makdisi, George. "The Hanbali School and Sufism." In *Actas iv Congresso de Estudos Arabes e Islamicos.* Leiden: Brill, 1971.

———. "Hanbalite Islam." In *Studies on Islam,* edited by Merlin L. Swartz. New York: Oxford University Press, 1981.

al-Manna, Muhammad. *Arabia Unified.* London: Hutchinson Benham, 1980.

al-Manqour, Ahmad. *Tarikh al-Manqour.* Edited by Abdulaziz al-Khuwaiter. Riyadh: General Secretariat for Celebrating the Centennial of the Kingdom of Saudia Arabia, 1999.

Maududi, S. Abul A'la. *A Short History of the Revivalist Movement in Islam.* Translated by Al-Ash'ari. Lahore: Islamic Publications, 1979.

Meijer, Roel. "The 'Cycle of Contention' and the Limits of Terrorism in Saudi Arabia." In *Saudi Arabia in the Balance: Political Economy, Society, and Foreign Affairs,* edited by Paul Aarts and Gerd Nonneman. London: Hurst, 2005.

Mohammed, Abdalla M., and A. Al al-Sheikh Mohammed. *Has Usama bin Laden Sprung from the Womb of Wahhabism?* Merrifield, VA: Saudi Studies Center, 2002.

al-Mukhtar, Salah al-Din. *Tarikh al-Mamalakat Al-Arabiya al-Sa'udiyah fi Madiha wa Hadirha.* Beirut: Dar al-Hayat, 1958.

Mutawa, Abdullah M. "The Ulama of Najd from the Sixteenth Century to the Mid-Eighteenth Century." PhD diss., Los Angeles, University of California, 1989.

Nallino, C. A. *Raccolta di Scritti Editi e Inediti.* Rome: Istuto per l'Oriente, 1938.
Ochsenwald, William. "Islam and Loyalty in the Saudi Hijaz, 1926–1939." *Die Welt des Islams* 47, no. 1 (2007): 1–32.
———. *Religion, Society, and the State in Arabia: The Hijaz Under Ottoman Control, 1840–1908.* Columbus: Ohio State University Press, 1984.
———. "Saudi Arabia." In *The Politics of Islamic Revivalism,* edited by Shireen T. Hunter. Bloomington: University of Indiana Press, 1988.
———. "Saudi Arabia and the Islamic Revival." *International Journal of Middle East Studies* 13, no. 3 (1981): 271–286.
O'Kinealy, J. "Translation of an Arabic Pamphlet on the History and Doctrines of the Wahhabis, Written by Abdullah, Grandson [*sic*] of Abdul Wahhab, the Founder of Wahhabism." *Journal of the Asiatic Society of Bengal* 43 (1874): 68–82.
Okruhlik, Gwenn. "Empowering Civility Through Nationalism: Reformist Islam and Belonging in Saudi Arabia." In *Remaking Muslim Politics: Pluralism, Contestation, Democratization,* edited by Robert W. Hefner. Princeton: Princeton University Press, 2005.
———. "The Irony of Islah (Reform)." *Washington Quarterly* 28, no. 4 (2005): 153–170.
———. "Making Conversation Permissible: Islamism in Saudi Arabia." In *Islamic Activism: A Social Movement Theory Approach,* edited by Quintan Wiktorowicz. Bloomington: University of Indiana Press, 2004.
Peters, Rudolph. "Reinhard Schulze's Quest for an Islamic Enlightenment." *Die Welt des Islams* 30, nos. 1–4 (1990): 160–162.
Philby, H. St John. *Saudi Arabia.* Beirut: Librarie du Liban, 1955.
Piscatori, James. "Managing God's Guests: The Pilgrimage, Saudi Arabia, and the Politics of Legitimacy." In *Monarchies and Nations: Globalisation and Identity in the Arab States of the Gulf,* edited by Paul Dresch and James Piscatori. London: Tauris, 2005.
al-Qabesi, Mohyiddin, ed. *The Holy Qur'an & the Sword.* Modified 4th ed. Riyadh: Saudi Desert House, 1998.
al-Qadi, Muhammad ibn Uthman ibn Salih. *Rawdat al-Nazirin an Maathir Ulama Najd wa Hawadith al-Sinin.* 3rd ed., vol. 2. Riyadh: Matbaat al-Halabi, 1989–1990.
al-Qassim, Abdulrahman, ed. *Addurar Al-Saniya fi Alajwibati Annajdiya,* 16 volumes. Riyadh: no publisher, 2004.
ibn Rabiah, Muhammad. *Tarikh ibn Rabiah.* Edited by Abdullah Ashible. Riyadh: Annadi al-Adabi, 1986.
Radcliffe, Sarah, and Sallie Westwood. *Remaking the Nation: Place, Identity, and Politics in Latin America.* New York: Routledge and Kegan Paul, 1996.
Radtke, Bernd. "Erleuchtung und Aufklärung: Islamische Mystik und Europäischer Rationalismus." *Die Welt des Islams* 34, no. 1 (1994): 48–66.
Rahman, Fazlur. *Islam.* 2nd ed. Chicago: University of Chicago Press, 1979.
al-Rasheed, Madawi. "God, the King, and the Nation: The Rhetoric of Politics in Saudi Arabia in the 1990s." *Middle East Journal* 50, no. 4 (1996): 359–371.
———. *A History of Saudi Arabia.* New York: Cambridge University Press, 2002.
Rida, Muhammad Rashid. *Tarikh al-Ustadh al-Imam al-Shaykh Muhammad Abduh (1266–1323 H./1849–1905 M.).* Cairo: Dar al-Fasilah, 2003.
al-Rihani, Amin. *Ibn Saoud of Arabia: His People and Land.* London: Constable, 1928.
———. *Muluk al Arab.* Beirut: Dar al-Rihani Lil Tabaa Wal Nashr, 1960.
———. *Najd Wal Mulhaqatihu.* Beirut: Dar al-Rihani Lil Tabaa Wal Nashr, 1964.

Rubin, Barry, and Judith Colp Rubin. *Anti-American Terrorism and the Middle East.* New York: Oxford University Press, 2002.

al-Saidi, Abd al-Mutaal. *Al-Mujaddidun Fi al-Islam Min al-Qarn al-Awwal Ila al-Rabi Ashar.* Cairo: Maktabah al-Adab, 1962.

Salame, Ghassan. "Strong States and Weak States: A Qualified Return to the Muqaddimah." In *The Arab State,* edited by Giacomo Luciani. Berkeley: University of California Press, 1990.

Savyon, Ayelet. "Call for Islamic Protestantism: Dr. Hashem Aghjari's Speech and Subsequent Death Sentence." *MEMRI* [The Middle East Media Research Institute] *Special Dispatch Series,* December 2, 2002.

Schulze, Reinhard. "Das Islamische Achtzehnte Jahrhundert: Versuch Einer Historiographischen Kritik." *Die Welt des Islams* 30, nos. 1–4 (1990): 140–159.

———. *A Modern History of the Islamic World.* New York: New York University Press, 2000.

Schwarzkopf, H. Norman. *It Doesn't Take a Hero.* New York: Bantam, 1992.

Sedgwick, Mark. "Saudi Sufis: Compromise in the Hijaz, 1925–40." *Die Welt des Islams* 37, no. 3 (1997): 349–368.

Shahin, Emad Eldin. *Through Muslim Eyes: M. Rashid Rida and the West.* Herndon, VA: International Institute of Islamic Thought, 1993.

al-Shaikh, Abd al-Rahman ibn Hasan. "Qurrat Uyyun al-Muwahhidin Fi Tahqiq Dawat al-Anbiya wa al-Mursalin." In *Majmuat al-Tawhid al-Najdiyya,* edited by Rashid Rida. Riyadh: Al-Amana al-Amma li'l-Ihtifal bi-Murur Miat Am ala Tasis al-Mamlaka, 1999.

al-Shaykh, Abd al-Rahman ibn Abd al-Latif Al. *Mashahir Ulama Najd wa Ghayrihim.* Riyadh: Dar al-Yamama, 1972.

al-Shaykh, Abd al-Rahman ibn Hasan Al. *Al-Maqamat.* Riyadh, n.d.

al-Sinani, Isam ibn Abd Allah, ed. *Baraat Ulama al-Umma Min Tazkiyat Ahl al-Bida wa al-Madhamma.* Ajman: Maktabat al-Furqan, 2000.

Smith, Rogers. "Citizenship and the Politics of People Building." *Citizenship Studies* 5, no. 1 (2001): 73–96.

Smith, Wilfred Cantwell. *Modern Islam in India: A Social Analysis.* Lahore: Minerva, 1943.

Steinberg, Guido. *Religion und Staat in Saudi-Arabien: Die Wahhabitischen Gelehrten, 1902–1953.* Wurzburg: Ergon, 2002.

———. "The Wahhabi Ulama and the Saudi State: 1745 to the Present." In *Saudi Arabia in the Balance: Political Economy, Society, and Foreign Affairs,* edited by Paul Aarts and Gerd Nonneman. New York: New York University Press, 2005.

Stewart, George. "Is the Caliph a Pope?" In *The Traditional Near East,* edited by J. Stewart-Robinson. Englewood Cliffs, NJ: Prentice-Hall, 1966.

Stoddard, Lothrop. *The New World of Islam.* New York: Scribner, 1921.

Stoeffler, F. Ernest. "Pietism." In *The Encyclopedia of Religion,* edited by Mircea Eliade. New York: Macmillan, 1987.

Teitelbaum, Joshua. *Holier Than Thou: Saudi Arabia's Islamic Opposition.* Washington, DC: Washington Institute for Near East Policy, 2000.

———. *The Rise and Fall of the Hashemite Kingdom of Arabia.* New York: New York University Press, 2001.

al-Uthaymin, Abdullah. *Tarikh al-Mamlaka al-Arabiyya al-Saudiyya.* 4th ed. Riyadh: Maktaba al-Ubaykan, 1998.

Tibi, Bassam. *Arab Nationalism.* 3rd ed. New York: Macmillan, 1997.

Vassiliev, Alexei. *The History of Saudi Arabia.* London: Saqi, 1998.

Vidino, Lorenzo. "How Chechnya Became a Breeding Ground for Terror." *Middle East Quarterly* 12, no. 3 (2005).

Viorst, Milton. "The Storm and the Citadel." *Foreign Affairs* 75, no. 1 (1996): 93–107.

Voll, John. "The Non-Wahhabi Hanbalis of Eighteenth Century Syria." *Der Islam* 49 (1972): 277–291.

———. "Renewal and Reform in Islamic History: Tajdid and Islah." In *Voices of Resurgent Islam,* edited by John L. Esposito. New York: Oxford University Press, 1983.

———. "Wahhabism and Mahdism: Alternative Styles of Islamic Renewals." *Arab Studies Quarterly* 4, nos. 1–2 (1982): 110–126.

von Ranke, Leopold. "Histories of the Latin and Germanic Nations from 1494–1514." In *Varieties of History,* edited by Fritz Stern. Cleveland, OH: World Publishing, 1956.

Wahba, Hafiz. "Wahhabism in Arabia: Past and Present." *Journal of the Central Asian Society* 26, no. 4 (1929): 456–467.

Wahhab, Hafiz. *Al-Jazirat al-Arabiyah Fil Qarn al-Ashrin.* Cairo: Matbaat al-Nahdat al-Misriyah, 1961.

Williams, Rhys, and Timothy Kubal. "Movement Frames and the Cultural Environment: Resonance, Failure, and the Boundaries of the Legitimate." In *Research in Social Movements, Conflict, and Change,* edited by Michael Dobkowski and Isidor Wallimann. Stamford: JAI, 1999.

Wolf, Eric. "The Social Organization of Mecca and the Origins of Islam." *Southwestern Journal of Anthropology* 7, no. 4 (1951): 329–356.

Wuthnow, Robert. *Communities of Discourse.* Cambridge: Harvard University Press, 1989.

Yamani, Mai. "Changing the Habits of a Lifetime: The Adaptation of Hejazi Dress to the New Social Order." In *Languages of Dress in the Middle East,* edited by Nancy Lindisfarne-Tapper and Bruce Ingham. Richmond: Curzon, 1991.

———. *Cradle of Islam: The Hijaz and the Quest for an Arabian Identity.* London: Tauris, 2004.

———. "You Are What You Cook: Cuisine and Class in Mecca." In *A Taste of Thyme: Culinary Cultures of the Middle East,* edited by Sami Zubaida and Richard Tapper. London: Tauris Parke, 2000.

al-Yassini, Ayman. *Religion and State in the Kingdom of Saudi Arabia.* Boulder: Westview, 1985.

Zaman, Muhammad Qasim. *The Ulama in Contemporary Islam: Custodians of Change* Princeton: Princeton University Press, 2002.

The Contributors

Mohammed Ayoob is University Distinguished Professor of international relations and coordinator of the Muslim studies program at Michigan State University. He has written on security issues relating to South Asia, the Middle East, and Southeast Asia; conceptual and theoretical issues relating to security and conflict in the international system; and the intersection of religion and politics in the Muslim world. His books include *The Politics of Islamic Reassertion* (1981), *The Third World Security Predicament: State Making, Regional Conflict, and the International System* (1995), and *The Many Faces of Political Islam* (2008).

David Commins is professor of history at Dickinson College, Carlisle, Pennsylvania. He has received Fulbright grants to fund Arabic study at Damascus University (1981–1982), to research Islamic modernism in Ottoman Syria (1982–1983), and to study Wahhabism in Saudi Arabia (2001–2002). His books include *Islamic Reform: Politics and Social Change in Late Ottoman Syria* (1990), the *Historical Dictionary of Syria* (1996), and *The Wahhabi Mission and Saudi Arabia* (2006).

Khalid S. al-Dakhil is a Saudi writer and academic. He has been assistant professor of sociology at King Saud University, Riyadh, since 1998. He was a regular columnist for the London-based newspaper *Al-Hayat* from 1999 to 2003. He has been a regular columnist for *Al-Ittihad* in Abu Dhabi since 2000, and regularly contributes to several Arabic journals.

Natana J. DeLong-Bas is lecturer in theology at Boston College and visiting lecturer in Islamic studies at Brandeis University, Massachusetts. Her books include *Women in Muslim Family Law* (with John L. Esposito, 2001), *Wahhabi Islam: From Revival and Reform to Global Jihad* (2004), *Notable*

177

Muslims: Muslim Builders of World Civilization and Culture (2006), and *The Clash Within Civilization: The Jihad for the Soul of Islam in Contemporary Saudi Arabia* (2007).

F. Gregory Gause III is associate professor of political science at the University of Vermont and director of its Middle East studies program. His books include *Saudi-Yemeni Relations: Domestic Structures and Foreign Influence* (1990), and *Oil Monarchies: Domestic and Security Challenges in the Arab Gulf States* (1994).

John S. Habib is professor of history and government at the University of Maryland's European division in Heidelberg, Germany, and an international management and security consultant. He has served in US embassies and missions in Cairo, Doha, Kuwait, Paris, Rabat, and Riyadh, and on special assignments in Europe, the Middle East, and North Africa. He is author of *Ibn Sa'ud's Warriors of Islam: The Role of the Ikhwan Movement in the Creation of the Modern Sa'udi State* (1973).

Toby Craig Jones is a postdoctoral fellow at Dartmouth College. He was formerly a Gulf analyst for the International Crisis Group, and has written previously on Saudi Arabia for the *Middle East Report* and the *Daily Star.* His publications include "Rebellion on the Saudi Periphery: Modernity, Marginalization, and the Shi'a Uprising of 1979" (*International Journal of Middle East Studies,* May 2006).

Hasan Kosebalaban is assistant professor of political science at Lake Forest College, Illinois. He has published numerous articles on Turkish and Middle East politics in journals such as *Middle East Policy, Critique, World Affairs,* and *Mediterranean Quarterly.*

Thomas W. Lippman is a Washington, D.C.–based author and journalist who has specialized in Middle Eastern affairs and US foreign policy for more than three decades, including as Middle East bureau chief for the *Washington Post* during the 1990s. His books include *Understanding Islam* (1982; 3rd rev. ed., 2002), *Egypt After Nasser* (1989), *Madeleine Albright and the New American Diplomacy* (2000), and *Inside the Mirage: America's Fragile Partnership with Saudi Arabia* (2004).

William Ochsenwald is professor of history at Virginia Tech. He has published widely on Middle Eastern politics and is currently researching the development of national unity in Saudi Arabia from 1926 to 1945. His books include *Religion, Economy, and State in Ottoman-Arab History* (1998) and *The Middle East: A History* (6th ed., 2004).

Gwenn Okruhlik is a visiting scholar at Trinity University, Department of Political Science. She specializes in the politics of the Arabian Peninsula with a focus on Saudi Arabia, where she has conducted extensive fieldwork and has had two Fulbright Awards. She is author of many articles, which have appeared in academic journals such as *Middle East Journal, Comparative Politics,* and *Middle East Report.*

John O. Voll is professor of Islamic history and associate director of the Prince Alwaleed bin Talal Center for Muslim-Christian Understanding at Georgetown University. He has lived in Cairo, Beirut, and Sudan, and has traveled widely in the Muslim world. In 1991 he received a Presidential Medal in recognition for scholarship on Islam from President Husni Mubarak of Egypt. His books include *Islam: Continuity and Change in the Modern World* (2nd ed., 1994) and *Makers of Contemporary Islam* (with John L. Esposito, 2001).

Index

181

imposition of Najdi patterns in, 81; opposition to Saudi rule in, 76, 80–82; Ottoman control of, 61, 75; religious basis of Saudi rule in, 76; religious zeal in, 77–79; resistance to annexation in, 75; royalties from oil operations in, 86; rules for women in, 84; secular institutions in, 83–84; *sharia* in, 77; Shias in, 78; suppression of internal public criticism in, 80; ulama support in, 76; use of military and police in, 82–83; use of religious police in, 77

Hijazi Liberation Party, 81

Hizb al-Tahrir al-Hijazi, 8, 81

Holmes, Frank, 124

Hourani, Albert, 158

House of Saud, 38*n31;* challenges to legitimacy of, 7; need to reasses commitment to, 8; state-making project in Najd and, 6; tensions with radical Wahhabis, 7. *See also* al-Saud family

ibn Humayd, Muhammad ibn Abdullah, 47, 50

bin Hussein, Faisal, 70*n3*

Ibadah: inclusion of social obligations in, 28; as ultimate expression of obedience, 28

ibn Ibrahim, Shaikh Muhammad, 51*n9*

Ideologies: controversial, 36*n3;* modern Islamist, 3; negative, 8; politicalization of, 19*n2,* 69; radical, 3; reactionary, 8; religious, 57; secular, 11; state, 36*n3;* of state formation, 23–35; statist, 2; *takfiri,* 12, 19*n7;* Wahhabi, 19*n2*

Idolatry, 13, 39, 41, 43, 46, 49

Ijtihad, 44, 47

Ikhwan, 49, 72*n21,* 72*n26;* assistance in consolidation of Saudi empire, 110–111; campaign by ibn Saud against, 123; creation of, 65; dedication to Wahhabism, 65; denunciation of ibn Saud's embrace of outsiders by, 124; fanaticism of, 62, 66; fundamentalism of, 6; indispensability of, 65, 66; narrow worldview of, 67; raiding by, 62, 136, 137; relations with ibn Saud, 7; religious zealotry of, 65, 66; revolt by, 136–137; ruptured relations with ibn Saud, 66, 67; settlement of, 65

Infidels, 12–16

International Religious Freedom Act (2004), 131, 132

International Security and Arms Export Control Act (1976), 129

Internet, 49, 109, 115–118, 120*n11*

Iqbal, Muhammad, 151

Iran, 156; invades Kuwait, 4; revolution in, 3

Iraq, 39, 41; invasion of Kuwait by, 129; occupation of, 144; raided by Ikhwan, 62; Saudi raids on, 58; study tours to, 42; US invasion of, 113

Islah, 97–100

Islam: conversion to, 12; as "correct" religion, 19*n7;* death penalty in, 13; division of labor in, 156; hatred for polytheism in, 19*n7;* historical perspective, 149–153; importance of the hajj in, 76; law in, 155; legal principles in, 13; militant, 161; nomadism and, 33; obligation to obey ruler in, 36*n17;* pillars of, 26, 44; pluralism in, 41; political, 36*n3,* 49; proper observance of, 12; radical, 6; reform movements in, 149–151; respect for Christianity and Judaism, 17; retreat of, 30; *sharia* in, 33, 67, 68, 77, 78, 82; Shia, 7, 11, 18, 20*n24,* 66, 68, 78, 98, 110, 126, 131; Sufi, 11, 40, 47, 78, 161; Sunni, 20*n24,* 41, 66, 78, 155, 162; as total way of life, 154; urban roots of, 38*n32*

Islamic: fundamentalism, 2; radicalism, 1

Islamic Liberation Party, 49

"Islamic Protestantism," 151

Islam Today Institute, 117

Islam Today (magazine), 117

Islam Today (website), 116, 117

Israel, 127, 128; United States support for, 2

Jacobites, 15

Jansenism, 153

Jesus Christ, 15, 17

Jihadism, 12, 13, 156; transnational, 1, 2

Jizya, 18, 20*n12*

Johnson, Lyndon, 129

Judaism, 127, 140, 153; *jizya* payment and, 14; recognition of, 17; special status of, 14

Jurisprudence, 42, 57, 70*n1,* 92, 155

Kafir: defining, 13; deliberate act after proper instruction, 13

Kashf al-Shubuhat (ibn Abd a-Wahhab), 49

Kennedy, John F., 126

ibn Khaldun, Abd al-Rahman, 31

characteristic of, 33; variants of, 3; writings on, 8

Wahhabiyya: alteration of of Najdi society by, 24; cleansing objective of, 25, 26; defining, 23; endorsement of political alliance with Muslim Brotherhood, 40; as *hadari* movement, 24; historical shift of, 27; Khaldunian model and, 30, 31, 32, 33; modernization thesis in, 30–33; nomadic character of, 23, 24, 25; nomadic environment effects on, 30–33; origination in Najd, 23; origin in eighteenth century, 23; polemics, 39–50; as political force, 24; religious thesis in, 25–30; resistance from ulama to, 39; as state ideology, 36*n3;* as subject of ideological controversy, 36*n3;* tribal characteristic of social structure of, 23;

as tribal movement, 30; unreligious roots of, 25

White Army, 67, 69

Willis, C. A., 161

Women: compulsory marriage for, 84; disenfranchisement of, 129; dress codes for, 125; and elections, 98; inheritance rights of, 33; participation in religious rituals, 78; protection of honor of, 96; rights of, 103–104; rules in Hijaz for, 77, 78; social conservatism and, 91; status of, 4; strict views on moral conduct of, 77, 78

World War I, 61

World War II, 69, 70, 86, 124

Zabayr: anti-Wahhabism in, 42

Zaghloul, Saad, 161

About the Book

What is Wahhabism? What is its relationship with the Saudi state? Does it play a part in Islamist terrorist threats? These are among the complex questions tackled in *Religion and Politics in Saudi Arabia.* Moving from the historical, social, and political contexts in which Wahhabism originated and flourished, to its current internal divisions and its impact on Saudi-US relations, the authors offer thought-provoking, cutting-edge research that helps to unravel the mystery that has long surrounded the subject.

Mohammed Ayoob is University Distinguished Professor of international relations and coordinator of the Muslim studies program at Michigan State University. **Hasan Kosebalaban** is assistant professor of political science at Lake Forest College.